To Professor
Sir Michael
Rawlins with
respect and
kindest regards,

[signature]

London, 2006.

THE AGE
OF VILLAGES

The small village vs. the global village

Alfredo Toro-Hardy

THE AGE OF VILLAGES

The small village vs. the global village

Foreword

VICTOR BULMER THOMAS
Director
Royal Institute for International Affairs
Chatham House, London

Villegas
editores

This book has been published
in Colombia by
VILLEGAS EDITORES S.A.
Avenida 82 No. 11-50, Interior 3
Bogotá, D.C., Colombia
Telephone (57-1) 616 1788
Fax (57-1) 616 0020 / 616 0073
e-mail: informacion@VillegasEditores.com

Publisher
BENJAMÍN VILLEGAS

English Translation
JIMMY WEISKOPF

Art Departament
OLGA LUCÍA NOVOA

First edition, July, 2002

ISBN
958-8160-15-4

Pre-press, ZETTA COMUNICADORES
Printed in Colombia by QUEBECOR WORLD BOGOTÁ

VillegasEditores.com

*To Gaby, companion of the route
and the illusions,
with all thanks*

*To Alfredo, my great pride,
for his unshakeable
spirit of struggle
and improvement*

TABLE OF CONTENTS

II. THE ECONOMIC VIEWPOINT

III. LATIN AMERICA:
WHO ARE WE AND WHERE ARE WE GOING?

Many thanks to Benjamín Villegas,
for stamping this work
with the seal of his distinguished
publishing house

I would also like to express my thanks to
Isabel Torre de Beiboer
and Cristina Villasmil
for their invaluable support
outside of working hours.

INTRODUCTION

BENJAMÍN VILLEGAS
Publisher

There are few dates in history that stand out so clearly as a turning point for mankind as September 11, 2001. Few times has an event like the terrorist attack that occurred on that date produced such an earthshaking impact on the entire world. It has affected every dimension of world affairs and caused a radical disruption of the international order.

What happens next? Will the world order rearrange itself in accordance with the rules the West played by for such a long time? Is it still possible for this to happen? Will the pieces that were swept into disorder be arranged into new patterns, following a different, more heterodox view that welcomes the striking diversity of the new voices on the international scene? Has the world changed so much? Are we in the midst of a conflict that is really dividing humanity into irreconcilable positions? These and other critical questions of our times have become major concerns for the leading thinkers and analysts of contemporary society and answers to them are now beginning to emerge.

Some of the clearest come from Alfredo Toro Hardy, the eminent Venezuelan specialist in economic affairs and international relations. In this admirable book, he offers us a profound analysis of the nature of the great confrontation that grips the world today and its curious and often alarming ramifications.

As the publisher of this book, I add that the opportunity to present this timely, original and deeply serious study of current affairs to the reading public is a motive of enormous pleasure and satisfaction.

FOREWORD

VICTOR BULMER THOMAS
Director
Royal Institute for International Affairs
Chatham House, London

History rarely marches in a straight line. The era of globalisation, in which we all – for better or for worse – live, is no exception. The forces that lead us inexorably towards the erosion of national sovereignty and the blurring of national boundaries are matched by a growing attachment to the local community, the revival of ancient loyalties and a reverence for traditional cultures.

This contradiction at the heart of globalisation is the theme of this thoughtful and provocative book by the well-known Venezuelan intellectual Alfredo Toro-Hardy. The author provides ample evidence of the transfer of national sovereignty upwards to regional or supra-national bodies; of the growth of giant companies whose operations straddle the globe and whose senior management are citizens of the world; of the migrations from state to state and continent to continent that are leading to the globalisation of the labour market for certain kinds of skilled workers such as software engineers and the clamour for greater freedom of movement for the less skilled.

However, the author is also sensitive to the reaction in different parts of the world to this process of globalisation. He draws our attention to the appeal of right-wing politicians in Europe whose support is based in part on a nostalgia for the past and a fear of the future; to the rise of Islamic fundamentalism whose popularity is achieved in part through a rejection of the values that underpin globalisation; and to the psychological need of so many for a local identity that will give meaning and value to their lives.

In drawing this contrast, so skilfully captured by the title of the book itself, Alfredo Toro Hardy shows great sensitivity to the different levels at which the analysis must be carried out: global, regional, national and sub-national. It is this broad understanding of the forces that are shaping our world, which makes this book so worthwhile to read.

At the global level, the author devotes a great deal of space to the economic forces that have led to trade and investment being concentrated in the hands of a relatively small number of giant companies. These companies, whose leaders are unelected, exercise a huge influence over the daily lives of all of us whether we work for them or not. No international negotiations are meaningful without taking their views into account.

At the regional level, such as in the European Union, the author shows how states have tried to pool sovereignty to provide a counterbalance both to the concentration of private capital and to the need to transfer decision-making to supra-national bodies.

At the national level, the author demonstrates how durable is the idea of sovereignty and how – even in the most globalised societies – there is a reluctance to abandon traditional instruments of diplomacy. Toro Hardy warns us against assuming that the loss of national sovereignty will be a smooth process as globalisation proceeds and reminds us of the strong loyalties that exist at the national level in many countries.

At the sub-national level, we learn in this book of the bonds that citizens form with their communities – ties that help to explain the explosion in the number of Non-Governmental Organisations (NGOs) in the last 20 years and the popularity they have achieved despite their unelected status.

In combining these different levels of analysis (global, regional, national and sub-national), the Americas are of particular interest. Alfredo Toro Hardy gives us a series of insights into the dynamics of both the United States and Latin America that make this book especially readable.

The United States is the most powerful nation in the world and yet it is not well understood. It is too often assumed, by those of us who speak English, that a shared language makes for shared values. The author demonstrates the dangers in this assumption through a series of insightful chapters that show us the numerous ways in which the United States differs from other countries and how these differences are unlikely to disappear.

A significant part of the book is also devoted to Latin America, where the author tackles difficult questions about identity, cultural history and the influence of colonialism. What emerges is a rich and complex picture of a Latin America that is heterogeneous in almost every respect while still sharing certain common values.

Alfredo Toro Hardy is well-qualified to write this excellent book. Educated in his native Venezuela as well as France and the United States, he has served his country with distinction as ambassador to Brazil, Chile, the United States and the United Kingdom. These postings have provided the opportunity to reflect on the nature of the societies in which he was living as well as giving him access to the motives and interests of key decision-makers.

The result is an excellent book that will help readers to make sense of the contradictions at the heart of globalisation. *The Age of Villages: the small village vs. the global village* is a reminder that we are all citizens of the world despite our local loyalties and that the march of civilisation is never smooth.

PREFACE

If there is one thing that characterizes the era in which we live it is the conflict between the global village and the small villages. That is, the clash between the forces of uniformity and of diversity. Between the homogenizing tendencies that seek to subdue all that lies in their way and the currents of identity, particularity and tradition.

Thanks to fiber optic cables, satellites and digitalization, distances have shrunk and the world has grown smaller. By the year 2005, the Internet superhighways will unite a billion human beings and by 2010, 3.5 billion people will be interconnected. Symbols like McDonald's, Microsoft, Adidas or Coca-Cola are familiar in every corner of the planet. 1.5 billion people have a command of English, which has been transformed into the universal language, and it is impossible to land in any international airport in the world without having to use it. Everywhere in the world, the multi-media conglomerates and the international financial markets fashion trends of behavior that are impossible to overturn. Mergers between the great multinationals make states seem small by comparison: of the 100 biggest economic entities of the world, 51 are corporations and only 49 are countries. Supra-nationality is being strongly imposed on a political and economic level, subjecting states to norms and dictums established beyond their frontiers. In short, we live in a genuine global village, interdependent and homogenous.

At the same time, however, the value of identities and particularities, of the local, projects itself with an unusual strength. Islamic fundamentalism seeks to immerse the believer in the omnipresent and totalitarian rules of its tradition. Macedonians and Albanians reproduce the rituals of violence practiced by Kosovars and Serbs or Serbs and Bosnians. Tutsis and Hutus massacre each other by the hundreds of thousands as each band seeks to assert its own tribal superiority. The ancestral practice of female circumcision and mutilation continues to affect 2 million women in Africa every year. It is the small villages which are trying to draw precise borders around their preserves of cultural identity.

But it is not only in the Southern hemisphere or in the former communist world where you feel the agitation of the small villages. In the industrial world as well they are expressing themselves with a renewed energy. Leaders of the European ultra-right - like Le Pen, Heider, Bossi or Schonhuber – appeal to the purifying value of tradition and the nostalgia for "serene and peaceful" societies that have now been transformed and upset by modernity and immigration. In the United States, the neo-populists call for the restoration of the lost values of a White and Protestant society, with its "simple and predictable" norms, as opposed to the disorder brought by globalization and masses of immigrants. In the same country, Afro-Americans and Hispanics entrench themselves within their own frameworks of cultural reference, turning them into barriers against outsiders. In Canada, Belgium, Italy, France and Spain, regional identities are taking on a new vigor, in some cases threatening the very integrity of the state.

The twenty-first century will be the scenario for an inevitable collision course between those who aim at a uniformity of values and rules of behavior and those who demand respect for their identities and the weight of their customs. At bottom, those who advocate uniformity try to impose it within the terms defined by those who move fastest, by those who are in the vanguard of changes and innovations. It would seem, however, that the stragglers do not have a last resort. For the hundreds of millions of human beings who cannot or do not want to move at the speed which the global village demands of them, there is no compromise solution. It is not strange, therefore, that in the face of the limitless anxieties which the rapidity of change brings with it, there are so many who wish to cling to the protective shelter of identities, who assert the right to live at the rhythm of their small villages, who react with violence to the homogenizing impact of the global village.

The terrorist attacks of September 11, 2001 and the subsequent U.S. reaction were an expression of the destruction that this clash of villages may cause.

A few years before, the United States, the maximum expression of the global village, had got its first taste of the intensity of the hatred towards the forces of uniformity which has accumulated in the small villages, with the Oklahoma City bombing for which Timothy McVeigh was convicted and executed.

This book seeks to review not only the dynamics of the clash between the two kinds of villages and the changes which it has brought, but also the particular characteristics of each one through an examination of their diverse variables and multiple identities. At the same time, it tries in a broader way to reflect on the process of great changes which the world is going through at the present time. Instead of giving answers, this work tries to create concerns. Instead of offering certainties, it seeks to move the reader to undertake his own reflections on a set of highly important current issues. We will approach these issues from both a political and economic angle. Within this context special attention is given to the analysis of issues that specifically concern Latin America and of the risks and challenges presented by its insertion into the global village.

I

THE POLITICAL VIEWPOINT

FROM AFGHANISTAN TO AFGHANISTAN: FROM ONE COLD WAR TO ANOTHER

Between 1979 and 1989 the Soviet Union fought an agonizing and interminable war in Afghanistan. The death of fifteen thousand soldiers and the spending of five billion dollars annually was the cost of this conflict for Moscow. But aside from the numbers, Afghanistan represented the Soviets' Waterloo – a decisive episode that wore out their will to fight and exposed their gigantic vulnerabilities. The role played in this defeat by the United States was a key one. As Ahmed Rashid points out: "With the active support of the CIA and the intelligence services of Pakistan, an effort was made to turn the Afghani *jihad* into a global war of the Muslim states against the Soviet Union, in which around 35,000 Muslim radicals from forty Islamic countries joined in the war in Afghanistan."[1] Nadia Yacine, for her part, states: "For the United States, Islam became the ideal barrier against communism: the U.S. saw

1. "The Taliban: Exporting Extremism", Foreign Affairs, November/December 1999.

in it a perfect identity for holding back the Red menace".[2]

By concentrating on a short-term view and visualizing the Afghan conflict within the East-West frame of reference, the United States ignored fourteen centuries of history and helped to open a Pandora's box whose contents are now turning into its worst nightmare. It forgot, in fact, that forty years of bipolar confrontation were no more than a passing incident in the 1,400 year-long clash between the Western world and the Islamic one. It forgot about the destabilizing impact of Islamism, a phenomenon which has been gaining strength since 1928 and whose most recent great expression had been the Khomeini revolution in Iran in 1979. It forgot that the enemy which Islamism seeks to defeat is secular materialism and that it is of little concern to it whether this takes the form of the historical materialism preached by the Soviets or the hedonist materialism of the West, symbolized, above all, by the United States. It forgot that, for the Muslim world, Afghanistan represented the first great contemporary victory of the Muslim world based on the *jihad*, the Muslim religious war. It forgot that, as soon as one of the world's two super-powers had been defeated, the renewed self-esteem and sense of strength felt by a triumphant Islamism would inevitably be turned against the remaining power. In short, as Samuel Huntington remarks: "The war (of Aghanistan) left behind it a

2. *Le Nouvel Observateur*, October 4-10, 2001

coalition of Islamic organizations which seek to advance Islam against all non-Muslim powers. It also left a legacy of combat experience and experienced soldiers, training camps and logistical facilities, an extensive network of trans-Islamic organizational and personal relations, a substantial amount of military equipment, including 300-500 Stinger missiles, and most important of all, a reckless sense of power and self-confidence, together with a thirst for new military victories".[3]

Afghanistan, the final cruel chapter of the old Cold War, became the first cruel chapter of the new Cold War. Just as the former represented a systematic and long-term effort to hold back communism, the latter will force the United States to mobilize its fundamental energies in a long-term fight against Islamism. In the final reckoning, the term "Cold War" was a Spanish invention of the thirteenth century to describe an ideological clash with the Muslim world. We may even wind up looking back with nostalgia on the nuclear terror, always rational, which governed the bipolar era.

WHY THE UNITED STATES?

Why has the United States managed to gain the enmity of the radical Islamic movements? Consider-

3. *The Clash of Civilizations and the Remaking of the World Order*, New York, Simon and Schuster, 1996, p. 247

ing that it was not a colonial power in the Middle East and, on the contrary, held back the hegemonic return of the English and the French during the Suez Canal crisis in 1956, history should have taken a different turn. Why, then, the United States?

In the first place, because of its traditional support for Israel. A curious equation has prevailed here for many years. The U.S. Executive trying to protect the interests and positions of the moderate Arabs, the U.S. Jewish community determining Congress's position on the Middle East, Congress prevailing over the White House with regard to U.S. policy on the region and the State of Israel maintaining a close partnership with the Jewish community of the U.S. The result of all this has been that the scales were traditionally tipped in favor of Israel. Since the Palestine issue is the common denominator uniting all of the Arabs, the United States is seen as the ally of Israel. Only a policy of active mediation in the peace process, like the one carried out by the Clinton Administration, was able to counteract this perception. The abandonment of this role implied a return to the traditional view of things.

In second place, because of the imperatives of its super-power status. During the years of the Cold War, Washington subordinated its relationship with the Muslim world to the dynamics of the East-West confrontation. The resulting inconsistencies caused quite a bit of resentment. Afghanistan is just one of many examples of a country which has been left to its own fate after having fulfilled its purpose in the framework of the larger conflict. After the collapse of communism, the invasion of Kuwait served to establish a new frame of reference, characterized by the permanent presence of U.S. troops in the birthplace of Islamism, Saudi Arabia, and by the bombings and sanctions against Iraq. This, together with its image of being the partner of Israel, is the factor behind the continual friction between the U.S. and the Arab world.

In third place, the ideological clash between a globalization that seeks to homogenize all it touches and an Islamic integration movement that sees every advance of globalization as an expression of barbarism and apostasy. As Huntington correctly noted in 1993, the Muslim world is "convinced of the superiority of its culture and obsessed with the inferiority of its power". To this self-perceived superiority is opposed an unbeatable force, made up of the conjunction of technologies of telecommunications, information and entertainment, which is trying to impose a materialistic Western system of values. What is more, as Benjamin Barber observed, globalization embodies "the very soul of U.S. popular culture". From the point of view of the clash of cultures, the enemy is the United States.

In fourth place, the wish to strike at the deepest aspect of the pride and feeling of stability of a hegemonic power, with the aim of provoking a reaction. A reaction proportional to the magnitude of the wound caused and which may in itself destabilize the international order, particularly the Muslim world.

Given the breach between the government and the populace that exists in so many Islamic countries, a U.S. over-reaction would fan the flames of radicalism, undermining the foundation of moderate regimes.

In fifth place, there was the intent to attack the epicenter of international finances at the very moment when the world economy had entered into a phase of recession. Given the synchronization that is now under way among the different economies of the world and the preponderance of the United States as a factor in global recuperation, the idea was to strike a blow at the economic heart of the world.

THE NEW FACE OF THE WORLD ORDER

On September 11 the international order suffered a strong shock. Its components are still in movement, going through an extremely fluid stage. When the pieces are fitted together again we will find ourselves before a world scenario that will be very different to the one we had known before. It is probable that the arrangement which emerges from this process will have the following characteristics.

In the first place, the United States may have found in the end an adequate replacement for the Cold War, one capable of ordering its priorities, articulating its policies and establishing a framework of coherence for the work of its bureaucracy. Under the pretext of the fight against terrorism it might take the form of containing Islamic radicalism, with an intensity of purpose similar to that which marked the containing of communism. The ideological consistency of this new enemy might allow for a clash of values of a caliber parallel to the dichotomy between capitalism and communism.

In the second place, we may witness the rebirth of the "imperial presidency" in the United States. This came to the fore in periods in which the American people felt themselves threatened by grave external dangers. The essence of this new enemy, capable of striking at any moment and employing the most terrible means, fosters a level of insecurity in the U.S. psyche that demands a strong presidency. This would invert the balance of power which has existed since 1965 between Congress and the White House in the field of foreign policy and clearly favor the latter. At the same time, it would invert the relationship between civil rights and national security imperatives which has been in force since the beginning of the seventies, giving a clear preeminence to the second.

In third place, it may lead to a rebirth of the State and a proportional weakening of the market. Spending in the field of defense, security requirements, the job of reactivating a world economy in recession and the need to provide a safety net of social benefits for runaway unemployment present challenges which only the State can meet. The 130 billion dollar package of incentives for the economy that has been set into motion by the White House is an expression of this new reality. At the same time, limitations on the free movement of goods and persons, due to security considerations, may hinder the expansive force of world trade. The private sector's ascendancy over the public sector will be reversed and the fundamental thrust of technological innovation may pass from the ambit of the productive economy to that of security and defense.

In fourth place, Russia may draw closer and closer to the West, reaffirming the European nature of its Slavic matrix and trying to find some kind of place within the European Union and NATO. Abandoning the idea of a multi-polar world and its "strategic association" with China, it will move towards a framework of alliances that not only set it against the common Islamist enemy but also enable it to respond to its gigantic economic problems. This turn towards the West will not be free of strong frictions with the United States, arising from the growing presence of the latter in its Central Asian sphere of influence.

In fifth place, sooner than later, the emergence of a Palestinian State may become inevitable. The only way of mobilizing Islamic moderates in the systematic and long-term fight against Islamism and, at the same time, destroying the battle standards of the latter would be through support for a Palestinian State. The weakened role of Congress in a foreign policy dominated by the White House and the generalized perception that support for Israel means high costs for the United States would greatly facilitate this shift in position. The great stumbling blocks to its success will continue to be the violence practiced by Islamic extremism, the intransigence of Sharon and his identification of U.S. policy towards the countries that shelter terrorism with the correlation between the PLO and the radical Palestinian movements. Nevertheless, it should be recognized that the seizing of arms coming from Iran and destined for the Palestine Authority did not make this process easy.

THE NATURE OF THE CRISIS

In order to comprehend the nature of the international crisis that has arisen from the September 11 terrorist attacks, we must take the following points into account:

In the first place, the war against terrorism which the United States has declared will have a selective character. In general, such expressions of terrorism as the ETA, the Real IRA, the Colombian guerrilla FARC and the Corsican nationalists would seem to have a low priority in terms of U.S. response. The focus of U.S. attention will be centered upon the terrorism practiced by Islamism. That is, the movement which seeks to make Islam a militant revolutionary ideology and which insists on applying in the twenty-first century the spirit and letter of a religious law enacted in the seventh century.

In second place, Islamism is directed against three groups of enemies: Western values and particularly the phenomenon of globalization, exemplified in both cases by the United States; the moderate and pro-Western Muslim regimes; and finally, Israel. By attacking the United States, it has not only sought to shatter the security of that colossus and make it swallow its pride, but also to provoke the U.S. to over-react in a way that would unleash the anger of the masses of the Muslim world. Through the latter tactic, it seeks to bring about the fall of the more vulnerable Muslim regimes. The particular targets are Pakistan and Saudi Arabia, which would put not only the atomic bomb in the hands of Islamism but also the key piece in the world petroleum equation. Israel would come next.

In third place, the reaction of the United States up to now has turned out to be much more moderate, balanced and structured than one might suppose, taking into account the background of the present government. In fact, up to September 11, U.S. foreign policy was in the hands of the ultra-conservative sectors of the Administration. Time and time again the moderate voice of the Secretary of State was silenced by the hawks in the government. If their opinion had prevailed after September 11, there is no doubt that the conditions that the Islamic extremists sought would have come into being. Fortunately, Powell's approach was adopted, thus confirming the thesis of Robert Kaplan, who has argued that the U.S. military has always been more moderate about the use of force than its civilians.

In fourth place, it is evident that Islamism did not achieve its objective with regard to stirring up the masses of the Muslim world. Their reaction was easily contained and controlled. This, despite the charisma of Bin Laden, considered by many to be the natural heir of Nasser in his capacity to capture the imagination of the Muslim world. Nevertheless, the situation is still in an extremely fluid stage. There are many factors which might bring the tension of the masses to boiling point, striking at the bases of support for the pro-Western regimes of the region. Among them it is worth mentioning the opening of new fronts of action, a radicalization of the Jewish-Palestinian conflict or some unexpected move by Saddam Hussein.

THE WORLD AFTER SEPTEMBER 11

September 11 changed the world. Its impact on the international order was felt on every level and seemed to bring with it a set of evident transformations.

The foreign and defense policies of the United States went through significant alterations. In the first place, the lower priority given to the Strategic Defense Initiative seemed to be an inevitable outcome. The idea of a protective umbrella against enemy missiles requiring multi-billion dollar investments lost support with the emergence of a terrorist threat capable of expressing itself in such a surprising and varied way. This hyper-modern "Maginot Line", essentially static in nature, could no longer compete with the emphasis now placed on intelligence activities and the capacity for tactical mobility. In second place, there was an abandonment of the unilateralism which had characterized the foreign policy of Bush up to then, which now gave way to the building of the complex interweave of alliances that is needed to confront terrorism. The unilateral policy shown by Washington through its refusal to support the Kyoto Treaty, the 1972 Anti-ballistic Missiles Treaty and the pending treaties on biological weapons and small arms, among others, gave way to the need to find as many allies as possible. In third place, the priority given to the war against drugs-trafficking ever since the end of the Cold War was now overshadowed by the demands of confronting a much more dangerous and implacable enemy. Drugs-trafficking only remains significant insofar as it can be linked to terrorism, but even so, it is Islamic terrorism which counts now. This shift implied paying less attention to Latin America, with a lessening of the emphasis given to Colombia.

On an international level there were significant changes as well. The common denominator provided by the fear of Islamic fundamentalism brought the member countries of NATO closer to Russia and China. Russia's enormous vulnerability to this phenomenon, whose most tangible expression is seen in Chechnya, tended to make the points of agreement with the West more important than all of the differences that had marked their relationship. The threat to internal stability represented by the Islamic populations within China, and Beijing's desire to preserve an international economic order which had brought China so many benefits, were sufficient reasons for supporting a much closer approach to the United States and its transatlantic partners.

The U.S. effort to exert diplomatic pressure on or establish a rapprochement with the nations of the Muslim world, with the aim of creating an alliance against terrorism and those who supported it, came to create enormous tensions within the Islamic countries. The ambivalent attitude towards the Islamist movement and terrorism held by many of these states, which had been adopted in order to safeguard their own stability, became every more difficult to uphold. The U.S. policy of forcing them to be "with us or against us" led to unequivocal definitions which undermined the shaky equilibrium that had characterized their regimes.

Finally, the inevitable clash between Islamism and Western pragmatism defined the tenor of the new era. We are talking about a collision course that came to prevail over all other considerations.

THE AXIS OF EVIL

In his first State of the Union address, President Bush coined the phrase "the axis of evil" to refer to the three countries which in that moment symbolized the adversary: Iran, Iraq and North Korea. Those countries thus constituted a sort of higher category of the so-called "rogue states", the position in which Cuba and Libya, among others, are also placed. From the semantic point of view, the term "axis" would not seem to be the most adequate one to describe three states which have little in common and which in no way embody an alliance. Despite this, by defining the enemy in that way President Bush set into motion a dynamic process whose implications, which are highly intermeshed, may be the following:

In the first place, an apparent return to unilateralism, with a smaller influence placed on the policy of alliances. Up to September 11, the foreign policy of the Bush Administration had been marked by a unilateral approach, with an evident undervaluing of the importance of international alliances and treaties. From then on, however, the U.S. President seemed to go back to the path laid out by his father in the time of what was called the "New World Order". That is, the strengthening of a U.S. leadership based on an interweaving of carefully-worked alliances. By defining the new adversaries without consulting his allies and independently of what it might cost them, Bush seemed to have returned to the road of unilateralism.

In second place, the erosion of the domestic consensus on foreign policy and along with it, the possibility of an "imperial presidency". That term is used to denote those periods when the American people feel themselves to be vulnerable to foreign threats which require presidencies that are strong in foreign

affairs. The consolidation of such a presidency nevertheless demands that policies are likely to win the
assent of Congress. By defining an option as aggressive as the one summed up in the postulate of an
"axis of evil", the possibility of a consensual policy
may have been restricted and, in the end, the possibility of an "imperial presidency" as well.

In third place, a strengthening of the military option may appear, with a consequent weakening of
the diplomatic option. The quick triumph in Afghanistan may have made the diplomatic effort that preceded it seem superfluous. One of Churchill's jokes
puts the matter well: "When you work with allies it
sometimes happens that they develop their own opinions".

In fourth place, the balance of power within the
cabinet of President Bush that existed before September 11 may be restored. That is, one in which the
"hawks" are more powerful than the "doves", with
Rumsfeld overshadowing Powell and the Pentagon
subduing the State Department.

It is still too early to reach definitive conclusions,
but Bush's State of the Union message may represent
a return to the state of things as they were before
September 11.

THE REVENGE OF THE STATE

Few times in the course of history had the State
been so undervalued as in the final decade of the

twentieth century. On the one hand, the new can-
ons of international law ignored its primacy and on
the other, its strength was undermined on every front.
On the lower levels of power, it was affected by
uncontrolled ethnic passions and growing regional
autonomies, while, on the higher ones, it confronted
powerful multinational financial bodies, economic
mega-conglomerates and NGO's. In short, it had re-
gressed to what the Australian author Hedley Bull
called a "new Middle Ages".[4] That is, a State in which
the central power saw its traditional power being
diluted in the midst of a growing network of impositions, interventions and interdependencies. What
is more, the explosion of ethnic sentiments gave rise
to a process of dismemberment of big state entities
and the appearance of a large number of new states.
It was not by chance that Ignacio Ramonet came to
speak of the emergence of a "sixth continent", a reference to the twenty-two independent states that
arose from the disintegration of the Soviet Union,
Yugoslavia and Czechoslovakia.

The nosedive of the State was in inverse proportion to the strengthening of the market. The years
following 1990 became the era of money, but of
private, not public, money.

According to *The Economist*, the world has come
to have 425 billionaires. For their part, Sarah Anderson and John Cavanagh, of the Washington, D.C.

---

4. *The Anarchical Society*, London, Macmillan, 1997

Institute for Policy Studies, point out that of the one hundred biggest world economies, 51 are corporations and only 49 are nation-states.[5] In 1983 the central banks of the five richest countries of the world had reserves on the order of 139 billion dollars, while daily transaction on world financial markets were around 39 billion dollars. By the middle of the nineties the reserves of those banks had doubled, while daily financial transactions had multiplied thirty times.[6] To resume, the world economy was based on the expansive force of private capital.

At the beginning of the new millennium, however, things began to change and by the end of the second quarter of 2001, the crisis of the market and private money had become evident. The World Gross Product as a whole seemed to have shrunk for the first time in twenty years and the economies which, as a whole, accounted for two-thirds of world production were in or on the point of a recession. The three great engines of world economic growth during the decade of the nineties had been put into reverse. While, before, their weight had created a fortunate spiral of economic growth (but not of political stability, social justice or financial calm), it was now producing a vicious circle of economic contraction. These driving forces

5. Top 200: *The Rise of Global Corporate Power*, Washington, Institute for Policy Studies, 1999
6. Jeffrey Garten, "The Maniacal Logic of Global Capitalism", Harvard Business Review, January-February, 1997

were the New Economy, the financial markets and globalization.

The terrorist attacks of September 11 did away with the unquestioned preeminence of the market. While, from a strictly economic point of view, the logic of the market itself led it into crisis, the events of September 11 came to represent the reemergence of politics as the fundamental imperative of the new times. In the end, the subject of terrorism is too grave to permit us to continue to think merely in terms of the market. Spending in the defense field, security imperatives, the challenge of reactivating an economy in recession and the need to provide a social welfare safety net for galloping unemployment are problems which can only be solved by the State. So we are seeing the revenge of the State. It remains to be seen whether the State, which has been profoundly hemmed in and insecure in recent years, will be able to deal with the challenges of this emerging reality.

THE GENEALOGY OF ISLAMISM

The term "Islamism" refers to a radical Islam, militant and ideologized, which assigns political ends to religion. The Islamists see themselves as a vanguard force in relation to the Muslim masses, destined to assume power at any cost with the objective of founding a social order entirely ruled by the Koran. In essence, Islamism approaches the Koran through a literal but politicized reading of its norms. Although its earliest expressions go back to 1928 with the creation of the Muslim Brothers movement in Egypt, it was only in 1979 that it showed its first major triumph, with the coming to power of Khomeini in Iran. Today Islamism prevails in Iran (in a more moderate form by now) and Sudan. A short time ago it also appeared in Afghanistan. Algeria, Egypt and Turkey have been subjected to the terrible violence of its subversive strength, in the same way that the West now faces one of its biggest threats in the form of Islamic terrorism. To better comprehend the essence of this movement it is necessary to explore its genealogy.

For centuries the diffusion of the Koran was extended by means of two currents. On the one hand, through the Sufis, popular priests who were an expression of a popular Islam. And, on the other, through the Ulamas, academic clergymen who were an expression of a cultured Islam. While the former undertook a missionary role which brought the Koran to the remotest places, the latter were identified with the elite and the big cities. Whereas the Ulamas preserved the original version of the Koran, the Sufis allowed the Koran to be amalgamated with different local beliefs in order to encourage its dissemination. The Islam of the Ulamas was restrictive, while that of the Sufis was inclusive. The Ulama tendency was an essentially secular one; the Sufi was more concerned with otherworldly things.

In the eighteenth century the Muslim world began to go through a worrying decline. This was seen by the Ulamas as a sign that Islam was in decadence and needed to be cleansed of its popular manifestations in order to return to its former strength. This powerful movement of religious renovation embraced changes that ran from the "holy wars" in the Arab world, West Africa and Central Asia to educational reforms in North Africa, India and Indonesia. The result was a reencounter with the original roots of Islam and the forging of a common Muslim identity. It was, at the same time, a return to a secular and down to earth Islam.

European colonialism and the spectacular expansion of Western power and values brought new ideological challenges to the Muslim world. The response took the form of three great movements: the Reformists, the Modernists and the Islamists. The first, of which the Wahabites of Saudi Arabia are the purest expression, envisaged a greater emphasis on the formulas for religious purification which had been in existence since the eighteenth century. The second was in favor of assimilating Western science and technology and adopting many of its values, as a tactic for overcoming the backwardness of Muslim society. After the First World War it would also emphasize the creation of nation-states and an exchange of positions between women and religion. It argued that women should no longer be confined to their homes, while religion should be considered a strictly domestic matter. The Islamists, alarmed by the failure of the Reformists and the concessions of the Modernists, constructed a politico-religious ideology which called for the overthrow of Western capitalism and socialism and any manifestation of them in the Muslim world. A radical ideology which has given rise to ever more radical actions.

BUSH, THE FORTUNATE

Little was expected of George Bush junior, one of the least impressive world figures that it is possible to imagine, who assumed the presidency as a result of some of the least convincing circumstances in the electoral history of his country. The months following his rise to power did little more than nourish this skepticism. In an incredibly short time he accomplished the difficult feat of bringing about the international isolation of the world's only super-power. On the domestic front, the result was nearly as significant: he humiliated a wavering Republican senator who guaranteed that party's majority in the upper house, forcing him to abandon the ranks of his party. Everything seemed to indicate that he would go down to posterity as George Bush, the Small.

Thanks to Bin Laden, Bush not only found himself but he was also able to achieve what had seemed unthinkable a few months before. That is, a high rating in the gallery of U.S. presidents. Wars or great international crises have surprising effects. Just as they may topple exceptional presidents, they may also lead figures that were thought to be insignificant to the top. They may, as in the case of Lyndon Johnson, cause the spectacular fall of a political heavyweight, with one of the most successful domestic records in the history of his country. But they may also, as in the case of Harry Truman, lead a former shopkeeper from Missouri to the summit of renown.

A major international crisis has the advantage of forcing a definition of priorities, clarifying the agenda of action, giving coherence to the fragmented machinery of bureaucracy, keeping the predatory interests of special-interest groups under control, overcoming party-political divisions within Congress and mobilizing public opinion. A great international crisis may enormously simplify things, provided that one indispensable condition is fulfilled: the presence of a leader with a capacity for decision and the ability to see the broad picture without losing himself in the details. On the occasion of the Iran hostage crisis, Jimmy Carter could have achieved a golden finish to an administration which saw such achievements as the Camp David accords and the Panama Canal Treaty. But his agonizing moral dilemmas and his obsession with details led him into labyrinth from which he could not escape. The "malaise" that Carter attributed to his country was nothing more than his own inability to set a precise course in the midst of the storms of the crisis.

Bush would seem to be especially well-prepared for a situation like the one he now confronts. Being in essence a simple man, he does not easily lose himself in existential dilemmas or analytical complexities. This gives him the advantage of synthesis. But at the same time, as a good Texan, he is not afraid of taking decisions. Little thought has been given so far to what Al Gore as President would have meant for a situation like the present one. A fanatic about details and a worshipper of complexity, he would probably have followed the footsteps of Jimmy Carter. Bush, by contrast, is of the same stock as Truman and Reagan: men without affectations who have a capacity for seeing the woods as a whole, instead of losing themselves in the trees, and capable of being decisive. There is not doubt that Bush has turned out to be a fortunate man.

THE DOOMSDAY COUNTDOWN

When the creators of the first atomic bomb realized the terrible effects of their invention, they announced that the doomsday clock had begun moving inexorably towards the midnight of humanity. When the Soviet Union exploded its first atomic bomb a few years later, that statement seemed to become a reality. Two super-powers, locked into an ideological conflict, found themselves with the capacity to destroy, not only each other, but the whole world in the process. Curiously enough, the balance of nuclear terror which resulted from this led to one of the longest periods of stability in modern history. The nuclear peace managed to last as long as the two great models for political stability of the nineteenth century: the international systems of Metternich and Bismarck.

Obviously, the dynamics of the bipolar confrontation did not enable the world to overcome war. Very much to the contrary, under the shelter of this dual rivalry humanity suffered more than six hundred wars and two million fatalities, as well as the largest creation of arsenals of mass destruction in history. Nevertheless, this only served to highlight the effectiveness of the bipolar system itself, which, despite many opportunities for open conflict, managed to avoid a Third World War. The list of the occasions on which the two super-powers might have been drawn into a full-scale war speaks for itself: Berlin, 1948; Korea, 1950; the demonstrations in East Berlin, 1953; Hungary, 1956; Berlin, 1958-59; the U-2 incident, 1960; Berlin, 1961; the Cuban missile crisis, 1962; Czechoslovakia, 1968; the Yom Kippur war, 1973; Afghanistan, 1979; and Poland, 1981. There is only one reason why the bipolar system turned out to be successful. It managed to keep under control the two routes which most frequently lead countries into war: escalation and the belief that it is possible to prevail in an armed conflict by military means.

The collapse of the Soviet Union enabled many to breathe more easily. Nevertheless, that was the start of our present problems. The vulnerability of Russia's infrastructure of massive destruction set the clock moving towards judgement day again. Since 1992, more nuclear fission material has been stolen from the former Soviet Union than it had been possible to produce in the first three years of the Manhattan Project. In recent years the Russian government has managed to stop 601 illegal transactions in atomic materials, the International Atomic Energy Agency another 376 and Turkey, another 104. As in the world of drugs, however, it is estimated that for every failed transaction there is a successful one. This flow of materials, accompanied by a parallel one of technical "know how", has not only led to a dissemination of nuclear terror but of biological and chemical terror as well. According to the former U.S. National Security Advisor, Anthony Lake, 27 nations have acquired nuclear, biological or chemical armaments since 1998.[7] Will the deterrent logic of mutually-assured destruction apply to this fragmented scenario?

It would seem that the ticking of the doomsday clock is making itself heard with an anguished intensity in recent years.

THE MOST ABSURD OF DECISIONS

In the middle of 1998 India detonated five atomic bombs. This was quickly followed by the setting off of another six by Pakistan. With these events, a nuclear arms race came into being in southern Asia. The nuclear potential of both nations was already

7. *6 Nightmares,* Boston, Little Brown, 2001

known by that time. In 1974, India had symbolically exploded its first atomic bomb, which it labeled a "peaceful nuclear explosion". While this had been done as a response to Chinese threats, Pakistan had no choice but to follow the same path. Nevertheless, although it was general knowledge that India and Pakistan possessed the technology to arm themselves with atomic bombs and missiles whenever they wished, moderation prevailed on both sides. The decision to take a further step, by transforming themselves into nuclear powers, implied passing from the realm of possibility to that of concrete action. Few decisions in history seem more absurd.

In terms of the territorial dispute that divides them, possession of the atomic bomb turns out to be highly questionable. By creating a nuclear arms race, both countries became hostages to the principle of mutually-assured destruction, limiting their military options without increasing their capacity to impose their own will on the opponent as a result. In military terms, it only led them to exponentially increase their costs without receiving significant benefits in return. By taking their capacity for mutual harm to the extreme, they drew a narrow dividing line between rationality and extinction.

Nor did the decision make sense in terms of international status. The idea that nuclear capacity turns one into a world power was already out of date by that time. The fall of the Berlin Wall had meant the end of the supremacy that is measured in politico-military terms, signaling instead the emergence of new codes of power. These new codes have to do with the level of development of a country's economic, financial and communications structure. Despite its gigantic nuclear arsenal and the seven hundred atomic tests realized during the existence of the Soviet Union, it would be difficult to consider Russia as a first-rate power. Its economic limitations and immense domestic weaknesses inevitably condition its international ranking.

A somewhat similar consideration applies to national security. With a population of 955 million inhabitants which is growing by 17 million people a year and will lead it to double its numbers every 38 years, India faces problems of security that are essentially confined within its own borders. In the midst of immense problems of environmental degradation, urban hyper-growth, shortages of water and energy, a collapsed or insufficient infrastructure and caste and ethnic conflicts, the atomic bomb is of little use to New Delhi. It only serves to divert indispensable creative energies and economic resources towards questionable ends. Taking their differences into account, something similar may be said of Pakistan, but the situation there is aggravated by the danger that the Islamists may gain control of the State. In the face of this reality, atomic missiles seem like too lavish toys.

Unfortunately, the genie already escaped from the bottle and the populations of both countries will have to learn to live with the idea of their own extinction as part of their everyday reality.

INDIA AND PAKISTAN: MUTUALLY ASSURED DESTRUCTION

During the four decades that marked the length of the Cold War the non-use of nuclear arms came to be a synonym for self-survival. The nuclear deterrent was seen as a guarantee of the non-use of these weapons and the continual non-use of the weapons as a proof of the success of deterrence. If one thing characterized this period, it was precisely the unusual degree of wariness with which each superpower approached the other, as well as their willingness to grant the concessions that were needed to overcome the risks of an atomic war.

The above does not mean that the use of nuclear weapons has not been considered a possibility in a wide range of scenarios. In fact, on a number of occasions the proposals put forth by the U.S. military establishment turned out to be hair-raising. At the end of the nineteen-forties, General Curtis Le May put forth the idea of launching a preventive nuclear attack against ninety Soviet cities, with the idea of neutralizing that country before it got hold of the atomic bomb. During the Korean War, General Douglas MacArthur proposed annihilating the Chinese forces with atomic bombs and creating a buffer zone of radioactive wastes along the Chinese-Korean border in order to prevent future incursions. In the middle of the fifties certain U.S. war plans contemplated the possibility of eliminating the Soviet Union with nuclear weapons. In each of these cases, however, the opposition of political leaders was conclusive. The sudden firing of the most successful general of the Second World War, MacArthur, was a proof of it.

On the Soviet side as well, the political establishment had a very clear position in this sense. Despite the fact that Stalin began, after the Second World War, to refer to the "inevitable conflict" between capitalism and communism, by the end of his life he had already accepted the notion of a "peaceful coexistence" between the two sides. After the death of Stalin, it was left to Malenkov to publicly declare that a conflict between the two super-powers would lead to the destruction of civilization. Khrushchev would refine this concept by stating that the interests of the USSR and the world revolution would be better served if the existence of the enemy was accepted and there was a respect for the established order. In short, both on one side and the other, great care was taken to scale down the risks involved in the mutually-assured destruction represented by nuclear weapons.

The most shocking thing about the face-off between India and Pakistan at the beginning of 2002 was the facility with which the option of war was proposed and the shallow way in which reference was made to the use of nuclear weapons. The forty to ninety nuclear bombs which India has, complemented by its Agni-2 ballistic missiles, and the twenty-two to forty-three which Pakistan has, together with its Ghauri-2 missiles, are sufficient to turn into real-

ity the celebrated warning given by De Gaulle in
1960: "After a nuclear war, the two sides would not
have powers, nor laws, nor cities, nor cradles, nor
tombs".[8] The combination of nuclear bombs, a territorial dispute and the legacy of previous wars, joined
to the binomial of Islamism and terrorism, is an explosive mixture. Will it be possible to prevent these
two contenders from causing, sooner or later, their
mutually-assured destruction? Or at least that of their
capitals and main cities.

TERRORISM AND WEAPONS OF MASS DESTRUCTION

During the long period of the Cold War the world
was at the mercy of the dynamics of bipolar terror.
Two super-powers, locked into a competition for
supremacy, accumulated weapons of mass destruction with a capacity to annihilate, not only each other
but the rest of the world. A logic that was diabolical,
but a logic nevertheless, governed these dynamics.
In line with the thesis of mutually-assured destruction, both super-powers knew that the destruction
of its rival would lead to its own destruction as well.
In short, there was not only clarity about the nature
of the enemy but also stability with respect to the
governing rules of deterrence. The anguish of know-

8. Speech, May 31, 1960, *Discours et Messages*, Vol. 3, Paris,
   Plon, 1970, p. 218

ing that the world might be blown into pieces at any moment was tempered by the conviction that neither side would be willing to assume the costs of throwing the first stone. In essence, it was a situation marked by a highly rational irrationality.

With the end of the Cold War the world seemed to breathe a sigh of relief, motivated by the belief that with the disappearance of the balance of terror, terror itself would disappear. What many seemed not to understand is that the only thing that really disappeared was the balance, since terror, represented by weapons of mass destruction, had come to stay. The dissolution of the Soviet Union, and the resulting chaos there, had clear consequences. It left an immense staff of technicians skilled in nuclear, chemical and biological armaments virtually available to the highest bidder, as well as a gigantic amount of weapons of mass destruction – and the material to fabricate them – without adequate safeguards. All this in the midst of a political environment marked by mafias and black markets. The end of the Cold War led to a substantial heightening of the levels of anarchy and insecurity. What is more, the page was turned towards a new chapter, in which the threats of mass destruction now came from actors who were much less visible and therefore much more dangerous.

In reality, the only ones who were likely to have reasons to employ weapons of mass destruction against the remaining super-power would be what have been called the "rogue states", with a particular emphasis on the members of the so-called "axis of evil" and terrorists. The logic of deterrence continues to apply to the former and therefore effectively contains their actions. Terrorism, on the other hand, embodies a subterranean threat against which there is no possible chance of deterrence. It is not by accident that President Clinton warned, in 1999, that the United States would be the victim of a terrorist attack with chemical or biological weapons within a period of no more than five years. As far back as March 1995 Clinton had enacted Presidential Directive No 39, which states: "The development of an effective capacity to prevent and deal with the consequences of the use of nuclear, biological or chemical armaments on the part of terrorists constitutes a major priority".

Since September 11 the fear of a terrorist attack with weapons of mass destruction has reached its maximum expression. It may take several forms, although the worst would be the use of biological weapons, composed of live pathogens with a potential to reproduce and mutate in a limitless way. We can only look back on the era of nuclear balance with nostalgia and pray that some remnants of rationalism may still be found in Islamic terrorism.

THE FOREIGN POLICY OF BUSH

Bush, the father, understood that his country could not act alone. It would be difficult for the world to accept that a single super-power may impose its rules on everyone. It was necessary, therefore, to design a mechanism that would allow for the strengthening of U.S. leadership within a framework of collective action. The foreign policy of Bush, the son, represented the antithesis of his father's policy. This, despite having placed in command posts a good part of the team of his father's time. While Bush, the father, believed in a collective action supported by an interweaving of carefully-wrought alliances, Bush, the son, insisted on U.S. unilateralism, with an evident undervaluing of international alliances and treaties. What is more, he revived antagonisms which his father had managed to leave behind.

The foreign policy of Bush touched sensitive points wherever you looked. He infuriated the Europeans and Japanese with his abandonment of the Kyoto Treaty on global warming. He brought relations with the Europeans to the boiling point with the declaration that he was willing to abandon the 1972 Antiballistics Missiles Treaty, without caring about their reservations on the matter; with his unilateral rejection of the proposed accord on biological weapons; and through his opposition to the European defense policy set forth at the Nice Summit.

He further annoyed Russia by ordering the expulsion of 56 Russian diplomats in March 2001, a gesture which had not been seen since 1986, at the height of the Cold War, when Reagan expelled 55 Soviet diplomats. Even more significant, however, was his abandonment of the 1972 anti-missile treaty and Secretary of State Powell's declaration that this policy would carry on even in the face of Russian disagreement.

With China things were even worse. The White House approved the biggest package of arms sales to Taiwan in 12 years; formally declared for the first time that the United States would defend Taiwan if it were attacked by China; labeled China a "strategic rival"; withdrew the status of "strategic partner" which had been given to China by Clinton by virtue of a bilateral trade worth 75 billion dollars; and froze bilateral military contacts, limiting them to exceptional cases. In addition, while U.S. delegations visited Japan, Russia, India and Korea to explain the new program of strategic defense, China was completely ignored.

With the Arab countries tensions also reached their hottest point in years. From the beginning, President Bush made it clear that his involvement in the Jewish-Palestinian conflict would be limited, emphasizing that he would focus his Middle East policy on containing Iraq and Iran. By abandoning its role as the principal mediator of the peace process, Washington not only thwarted any possibility of an agreement, but in doing so it also highlighted its traditional support of Israel. That is, an annual aid packet of 3 billion dollars, as well as permanent support for Israel on the level of the UN Security Council.

Step by step, the present U.S. government wound up alienating the Europeans, Japanese, Russians, Chinese and Arabs. The frenzied march of unilateralism was creating resentments all over the world. As Tom Daschle, Senate majority leader, correctly observed: "We are isolating ourselves and by doing so we are minimizing ourselves". September 11 seemed to have changed everything. From that moment on Bush restored the cardinal points of his father's foreign policy. So it was believed, at least, until he gave his first State of the Union address, where he spoke of the "evil axis", made his allies tremble and sowed the idea of a unilateral action against Iraq. The polemics which arose in the following weeks with the Foreign Affairs Commissioner of the European Union and the Foreign Minister of France seemed to presage a return to unilateralism.

BUSH AND THE STRATEGIC DEFENSE INITIATIVE

Ronald Reagan sought to exploit the insecurity hidden in the soul of the Soviets by fomenting a deliberate state of tension with them. The objective he followed was to put them on the defensive, forcing them to expose their vulnerability and abuse their economic resources. To resume, he attempted to force the Soviets to the limits of their resistance, in order to leave them exhausted. For this he counted upon a very special weapon: the strength of the U.S. economy. Even so, the cost of this strategy was that his country stopped being the world's biggest creditor and became the world's biggest debtor.

A fundamental part of this process consisted of reforming the country's strategic military doctrine with the adoption of what came to be known as the Star Wars program. That is, the idea of a great protective umbrella against enemy missiles. This proposal turned into a real nightmare for the Soviets, who did not have the technology or the economic resources to keep up with the United States in this field. In short, the Russian bear was really exhausted and its weakness would come to the surface with the emergence of Gorbachev, *perestroika* and the final collapse of the Soviet Union. The psychological effect of the Star Wars project was of the maximum importance in this process.

With the end of the Cold War, this famous strategic initiative was shelved and the U.S. returned to the more traditional notion that the best way of preventing an atomic war was to maintain a mutual vulnerability to nuclear weapons, that is, the thesis of mutual assured destruction. Along with this, the 1972 Anti-Ballistics Missiles Treaty ensured the maintenance of the status quo in this field. When the second of the Bushes came to power he decided to revive the idea of the protective umbrella against enemy missiles, with a much more modest version of the former Star Wars initiative. The result was a genuine earthquake in prevailing military strategy, with the resulting awakening of paranoia.

Behind this new idea there lie some legitimate fears about the missile potential of countries which are not part of the conventional political and diplomatic game. Specifically, those nations which the United States has called "rogue states", such as North Korea and Iraq, among others. Nevertheless, the biggest motivation for the new strategy lay in the domestic field and had to do with the need to satisfy the demands of two very powerful sectors: the right-wing of the Republican party and the corporations that depend on military contracts, two sectors which have never recovered from the impact of the ending of the Cold War.

The notion of the protective umbrella is full of significant risks. In the first place, by altering the predominant strategic doctrine, it unleashed uncertainties and fears that may convert themselves into a new arms race. Leaving aside the question of Russia's attitude towards this initiative, the hostile attitude of China has to be taken into account. A China that would react to the U.S. initiative by increasing its arsenal of nuclear missiles would force India to respond, which, in turn, would result in the involvement of Pakistan. In second place, it may lead the United States into a false conception of security, of the "Maginot Line" type, capable of causing multiple political and strategic errors. In third place, it would be completely unworkable in the face of the real danger, Islamic terrorism, which would not recur to nuclear missiles but portable atomic bombs or chemical or biological weapons. This sophisticated technological paraphernalia would be of little use against a suitcase that contains a nuclear artifact or a jar full of highly-destructive pathogens or toxins.

After September 11 the possibility that the latter options may be used has become fully evident. This would make it necessary to substantially reformulate the Strategic Defense Initiative, without diverting to it energies and resources that should be devoted to areas that have a much higher priority. Will the U.S. domestic pressure groups be able to understand this elemental truth?

THE CONFLICTIVE MIDDLE EAST

The Middle East, which guards in its bowels two-thirds of the world's petroleum reserves, seems unable to attain stability. Five basic factors are behind this problem: the Arab-Israeli conflict, the Palestine question, Islamism, the Pan-Arabic movement and ethnic-territorial controversies.

The origins of the Arab-Israeli conflict lie in the period following the end of the First World War, when the British assumed a mandate over the territory of Palestine. That was the starting point for an unchecked Jewish immigration to the region, based on the commitments found in the Balfour Declaration and the demands of the Zionist movement founded by the Hungarian intellectual Theodore Herzl. The 1947 U.N. Resolution 181 adopted a plan to divide Palestine into two states: one Jewish, the other Arab. Israel's declaration of independence in 1948 was followed by a joint attack on Israel by the surrounding Arab countries. As a result of this war, Israel remained in possession of a much bigger territory than the one which had been assigned to it under the plan for partitioning Palestine. To the introduction of a "foreign body" into the region was added the occupation of territories that not had been juridically conferred and the desire for revenge among those who had been defeated by Israel.

The Palestine question had its origin in the impossibility of creating an Arab State in accordance with the prescriptions of Resolution 181, because of the results of the war that followed the independence of Israel. On the one hand, the new Jewish state came to occupy Galilee and the western part of Jerusalem, which belonged to the Arab Palestine. On the other, Emir Abdullah of Transjordan annexed Cisjordan, which corresponded to the State about to be formed, founding on these bases the kingdom of Jordan. Egypt, for its part, took control of the Gaza Strip, which had also been assigned to the Arab-Palestine State. In the Six Days War of 1967, Israel conquered Gaza and Cisjordan, becoming from that point on the central piece of the conflict. The Jews' obsession with ensuring their own security led them to establish settlements in the occupied territories that would create a *fait accompli* difficult to reverse. The Palestine problem has become the common denominator that unites all of the Arab countries, cutting across their immense differences.

Islamism is the expression of a radical Islam, militant and ideological, which assigns political ends to religion. Islamism approaches the Koran on the basis of a literal but politicized interpretation of its norms. The first expressions of it go back to 1928, with the creation of the Muslim Brothers movement in Egypt. Within the Muslim world, Islamism is in conflict with the Reformists of a traditionalist tendency and the pro-Western Modernists. Its objective has been the overthrow of secular Western materialism and all manifestations of it in the Muslim world. The "Sharia", or obedience of religious laws, is set forth as a way to renew contact with Islamic roots in the midst of the alien influence of the modern world and Western culture. In it the Muslim believer will find an answer to his doubts, through precepts that guide all aspects of daily life and provide a shelter of certainty in a world which is full of unanswered questions. It is not by accident that Islamism turns out to be so attractive to broad sectors of the Muslim world.

Pan-Arabism is the result of the artificial and arbitrary process that gave rise to the region's states. Insofar as they emerged from the process of drawing lines on a map, it was not possible to establish an effective identity to uphold them. This search for identity, which met no answer on the level of national units, had to be satisfied in other ways and there were two solutions to the problem. On the one hand, allegiance to the clan, the tribe, the family, and, on the other, to an ideal that would be larger than the individual states: the prospect of a great Arab nation. In accordance with this ideal, which is known as Pan-Arabism, political frontiers are seen as artificial divisions that separate a single nation. This phenomenon has led to the following consequences: the appearance of messianic leaderships which seek to extend themselves over the Arab world as a whole; the practice of intervening in the internal affairs of other Arab states, using as a justification this supra-national concept; the tendency to consider the riches of the region as the communal property of all the Arab countries and the consequent resentments that derive from the impossibility of gaining access to them; the habit of identifying Arabism with Sunnism, that is, of identifying the Arab race with the Sunni current of Islam.

The ethnic-territorial controversies are the product of the artificial way in which the English and French drew the borders of the region after the First World War. Ancient provinces were detached from the ancestral centers to which they had belonged, in the same way that ethnic groups which had the same origin saw themselves divided by the frontiers of the new countries. In this situation, Jordan believed that it had a historic right to annex Cisjordan, just as Iraq believed that it was justified in doing the same with Kuwait. Iraq and Iran have kept up a perennial dispute over the Shatt-el-Arab, while Syria has always considered the province of Mosul, granted to Iraq, to be part of its ancestral territory. From one end of the region to the other these problems repeat themselves, creating frictions and conflicts. At the same time, the irredentist pressure of ethnic groups which feel that they have a right to their own country is strongly felt. Along with the case of Palestine, already mentioned, we also find that of the Kurds, an ethnic group spread over Turkey, Iran, Iraq and Syria.

No other region of the world is more likely to cause major problems for the stability of the international order and world peace.

PARADIGMS

The expression "Cold War", originally used by the Spanish in the thirteenth century to describe their tense relations with the Muslim world, was revived by the famous U.S. elder statesman and economist Bernard Baruch to describe the international order of the post-war world. The term was then popularized by the journalist Walter Lippman, who used it as the title for his most important book. Between 1945 and 1989 the world order was governed by the rules of the Cold War. In accordance with these rules, two great blocks confronted one another in a competition for world supremacy and power. When we followed the happenings in El Salvador or Nicaragua in the eighties, for example, we might have not have known much about the specific details of these conflicts, but we could at least situate them within a familiar frame of reference. We knew that they had to do with yet another chapter of the Cold War. In this sense, the Cold War constituted a paradigm.

The word paradigm is very fashionable nowadays. In essence, it may be defined as a conceptual framework which seeks to explain a process, to define a sense of direction. It is for this reason that, by enabling us to place any local or regional conflict within the context of a contest between the super-powers, the Cold War took on the character of a paradigm. With the fall of the Berlin Wall, its preeminence disappeared. Since then, as Samuel Huntington explained in *The Clash of Civilizations*, new paradigms have appeared, which have challenged the leading role given to the concept of the Cold War during more than four decades. Following the lead of Huntington, we will explain some of these paradigms.

The first and also the most simplistic of the new paradigms that arose after the debacle of communism was Francis Fukuyama's notion of the "end of history". According to this analysis, the world had fulfilled its destiny in the evolutionary process as the result of the homogenization of values and beliefs. The double triumph of democracy and the market economy unified the planet's different regions, granting them a clear common denominator. Although this paradigm has been questioned because of its excessive optimism, many still believe that with the simple triumph of democracy and the market economy the world has become a place that is much safer and much more likely to attain limitless prosperity.

Along with the above paradigm a variety of others appeared. Among them it would be worth citing the one which argues that the cultural factor is gaining supremacy as the contemporary age advances. The exponents of this line of thought include authors like Samuel Huntington, Lawrence Harrison, Thomas Sowell and Roger Peyrefitte, who reaffirm the cultural factor, as the base of the new international reality. Despite their different slants, the common denominator of this paradigm is the importance it gives to conducts defined by custom and rooted values. It is highly curious that Fukuyama himself later embraced the essence of this paradigm. In his book *Trust*, published in 1995, he toned down and reconsidered many of his assertions about the homogenization of values and concluded that the world continues to be a place that is marked by the diversity of cultures.

There is also the paradigm of the "two worlds". That is, the one which seeks to explain the shape of current times through a sharp division between spaces of prosperity and spaces of backwardness and regression. Among those who belong to this school of thought there are authors like Robert Gilpin, Jacques Attalí and Jean Christophe Ruffin.

Another paradigm is that of "chaos". According to this view, the world has entered an era marked by the breakdown of governmental authority; the crisis and secession of States; an intensification of ethnic, tribal and religious conflicts; the consolidation of international criminal mafias; the indiscriminate proliferation of weapons of mass destruction; and the spectacle of massacres and ethnic "cleansing". Among the proponents of these theories we find writers like Zbigniew Brzezinski, Patrick Moynihan, Michael T. Klare and Walter Lacquer. The fundamental difference between those who hold to this line and those who hold to that of the paradigm of "the two worlds" is that the "chaos" theorists believe that the crisis will equally affect the rich and the poor countries, without having the selective character granted to it by the others.

The different paradigms that are employed nowadays encompass a graduated scale, which goes from the "rosy-colored" optimism of Fukuyama's original version to the no-escape pessimism of the believers in chaos. As often occurs, the truth probably lies somewhere between the two extremes. What is more, the true version should include a good many of the assertions found in each of the above paradigms. In the end the danger of any paradigm is that it lays down a route map that is too clear and precise and this inevitably tends to lead to an over-simplification of processes that are always complex.

THE AGE OF MIGRATIONS

Globalization advocates the free movement of goods, ideas and capitals. It evades, however, the spiny question of the free movement of people. For some, globalization carries sources of work to the places where the cheapest manpower is found, therefore serving as an antidote against migrations from the developing countries, which are the natural exporters of human beings. For others, by contrast, it forces whole productive sectors in those countries to lose their economic viability, thus encouraging emigration.

The ever quicker pace of the world economy that results from globalization has left the great majority of developing countries without an adequate capacity of response, creating enormous internal imbalances. In this way it has caused a sharp division between rapid countries which are becoming richer and richer and slow countries which are becoming poorer and poorer. How can we deny that the latter are rapidly turning into exporters of human beings?

The subject of migrations, however, is not discussed in linear terms. For both the developed and the developing nations, the phenomenon of migration is full of ambivalence and has positive and negative elements. It is, in fact, a complex matter.

For the developed nations, the immigration of persons from the slow nations may have plainly negative aspects. Among the most notable of these are the costs in social services and the dangers of transculturation. It is estimated, for example, that in California every immigrant without education represents an average annual cost of 1200 dollars for each native-born household.[9] That is, this is the financial burden which the fully productive inhabitants of the State must bear in the form of taxes paid to maintain services granted to insufficiently productive immigrants. At the same time, the blurring of a society's identity and traditions under the impact of immigration is frequently seen as a negative thing. However, this is closely linked to the level of permeability of

9. *The Economist*, March 31-April 6, 2001

the receptor society and the capacity of integration of the newcomers.

Nevertheless, immigration also has positive effects on these same countries. To the extent that immigrants usually represent two human groupings – those with high and those with low qualifications – they tend to fill gaps in the receptor country. On the upper level they stimulate the dynamism of technological or productive sectors at no cost to the host country. And on the lower, they fill spaces which the inhabitants of the developed countries do not want to occupy. That is, work that is necessary but has a low social status. In both cases a need is fulfilled.

For the developing countries as well, the phenomenon has both positive and negative aspects. The most evident of the former is the remittance of foreign currency to the native country of the emigrant. According to recent calculations made by the Inter-American Dialogue, of Washington, D.C., the Central Americans who reside in the United States remitted 8 billion dollars to their countries in the year 2000. According to *The Economist*, 100 billion dollars are mobilized around the world every year in this way[10]. It is clear, at the same time, that for countries which are submerged in poverty, the export of idle manpower constitutes an important relief of their social pressures.

Among the most negative aspects for the latter, the "brain drain" clearly stands out. The hemorrhag-

10. *Ibidem*

ing represented by this loss of a society's most quali-
fied and productive members is a net loss, with no
counter benefits to justify it.

The subject of migrations is, without doubt, one of
the most complex ones on the international agenda
nowadays. It does not, of course, have the same significance for everyone. For the United States, which
has a virtually full employment and a high degree of
cultural permeability, immigration has different connotations than for the European Union, with 14 million unemployed, or Japan, with its traditional
xenophobia.

BERLUSCONI AND THE
MASTERS OF THE WORLD

In a report on the 35 biggest economies of the
world, the publication *World Press Review* (April 2000)
put in the first rank, along with nations like the United
States, Japan, Germany and the United Kingdom, corporations like Microsoft, General Electric, ExxonMobil
and Walmart. In fact, according to Anderson and
Cavanagh, the world's 100 biggest corporations control 20% of global assets, while of the hundred biggest economies of the world, 51 are corporations and
only 49 are nation-states.[11]

Nevertheless, the above forms a dynamic, not a
static, phenomenon. Due to a systematic process of

11 *Op. cit.*

mega-mergers, there are fewer and fewer corporations but they are ever more powerful. In a great number of productive sectors the five main companies account for more than half of world sales. These oligopolies form what the Italian intellectual Riccardo Petrella has called the "world megasystems".

A few decades ago, John Kenneth Galbraith developed his theory of corporate evolution, according to which the big companies had moved from the charismatic leadership of their founders to technocratic directorates, in which there was no room for outstanding personalities. This is not true of the present situation. If there is one feature we can see today it is the presence in these companies of all-powerful figures who have no reason to envy past business titans like Rockefeller, Ford, Carnegie or Morgan. Figures like Bill Gates, Jack Welch, Stephen Case, Rupert Murdoch, Gerald Levin, Warren Buffet, Ted Turner, Larry Ellison, Andy Grove, George Soros or Kirk Kerkorian symbolize the importance of the individuals who head the corporate world of our times.

These great corporate leaders not only share the same code of values but they also tend to get together in a variety of forums or gatherings. Their values are those which have made their businesses prosper and give support to globalization: the liberalization of trade, privatization, deregulation, the protection of investment, fiscal discipline, etc. To resume, that set of economic rules which lie within the framework of what has been called the Washington Consensus. The ambits within which these leaders meet run from open and broad-based forums like that of Davos in Switzerland to extremely private gatherings.

The combination of gigantic economic power, charismatic leadership, a shared code of values and the capability for association is the key to their capacity to lead the world. It is not an exaggeration to speak of the club of the masters of the world. This club makes its enormous capacity to exert pressure on the nation-states felt in many ways, but it basically does it through two fundamental instruments: finance and multimedia. Any nation-state which questions the code of values of these masters must be willing to assume the costs which such defiance implies in terms of ostracism and pitiless media campaigns.

Curiously, one of the great masters of the world, Silvio Berlusconi, has decided to descend from Olympus and try his luck on the battlefield of mere mortals. A man with a personal fortune of 14 billion dollars, who controls nearly half of the television audience of Italy, owns 50 magazines and some of the major newspapers of that country, as well as a financial, real estate and sports empire, Berlusconi launched himself into the political arena and became a simple government official subject to public scrutiny. Leaving aside the criticisms that may be made about the resulting conflict between public and private interests, which is undoubtedly true, the fact that one of the masters of the kingdom of opacity has decided to chance his arm in open combat cannot fail to be a refreshing spectacle.

WHY A FOREIGN POLICY?

All foreign policy rests on a tripod. This is made up of the attainment of purpose, credibility and effectiveness. A purpose which defines the course to be followed, an international credibility that endorses that course and reduces the obstacles in its way and an effectiveness that makes the implementation of the goals agile and consistent.

The purpose of a foreign policy should be to help accomplish the aims of the prevailing national project by means of international relations. The prevailing national project may be defined as that set of political, economic, social, ethical or other kind of values which is preponderant in a nation at a given time. Such values assume the character of guiding principles for national life and form the foundation on which the political regime which exercises control of the State aspires to justify its legitimacy and continuance. Such a project thus comes to be the formal and substantive expression of a given political regime, which wishes to define, by means of it, its conception of the social order that is desired. Normally, the prevailing national project is usually set forth by means of a fundamental text which grants institutional legitimacy to the ruling political regime. Usually this text will take the form of a written constitution.

The main question under consideration is whether or not a foreign policy is destined to transcend successive political regimes, embodying the permanent aims of the State. What is certain is that the concept of the State is never an objective one. The criteria expressed in the prevailing national project, which are usually upheld by a suitable constitution, determine, so long as the project remains in force, the very nature of the State. Even inherent values like sovereignty, territorial integrity or economic security will tend to be interpreted in terms of the ruling national project.

In foreign policy, it is not enough to have a purpose, you also need to have the capacity to put it into practice. In this sense, the natural aspiration of any State is to find the widest international recognition for its political actions, since such recognition will be directly related to the removal of obstacles to their execution. In other words, within the context of the cost-benefit equation that surrounds any political action, international recognition will tend to reduce costs or increase benefits. Credibility may thus be defined as the potential for external recognition which a State enjoys.

What, however, decides the potential for external recognition? The potential for recognition of a State is directly related to its capacity to impose its policies. As Clausewitz wisely put it, power is simply the capacity to impose your own will on others. A State's degree of credibility in its international relations thus becomes a corollary for its level of power.

What can weak states do in the face of this reality? The answer may be found, paradoxically, in the most cynical words ever uttered about the inequality of power among states. We are referring to the celebrated saying of Stalin, when, mocking the power of the Vatican, he asked, "how many armored divisions does the Pope have?". In reality, the Vatican would not have been able to show a single tank. Nevertheless, it had a high level of international influence by virtue of its moral weight. In other words, the symbiotic relationship that exists between power and credibility has an important flaw: the importance of prestige.

It not was not very long ago that the credibility of the weak was upheld by prestige and that this, in turn, was an expression of moral weight. In the globalized society of present times which has homogenized everything, things, unfortunately, have changed. Today credibility is measured in terms of obedience to the primer that happens to be in fashion. That is, the norms laid down by a famous "consensus", which are upheld by the weight of international finance and an oligopolic multimedia. Nowadays, credibility inevitably tends to turn into a simple matter of sheep who follow the flock.

Effectiveness, finally, is an expression of the instruments utilized by the State in the pursuance of its purpose. Effectiveness thus becomes the faculty for achieving the desired aim. The preconceived idea of the result which one wishes to obtain is, therefore, inseparably linked to the capacity to obtain it.

Both the excessive simplification and excessive pro-liferation of such goals carry dangers. Excessive simplification may be the expression of a reductionist policy, in which a single objective becomes more important than the set of objectives as a whole. It is an extreme that is typical of military dictatorships. This approach substantially limits the flexibility that is required for carrying out a foreign policy in the midst of a complex and dynamic international scenario. Proliferation of goals, by contrast, implies numerous shadings and alternatives, which leads to the loss of the sense of direction. An effective foreign policy there-fore requires a clear and balanced design, which not only achieves a balance among diverse objectives but also defines a sufficiently comprehensible sense of direction. Of course, all these considerations should have, as a frame of reference, the administrative ca-pacity of a nation's bureaucracy and the level of pro-fessionalism of its foreign service.

THE TYRANNY OF THE MINORITY

If one thing characterizes this new age, it is its rejection of the profession of politics. This is a re-sponse to the evident exhaustion of representative democracy. Insofar as citizens no longer feel them-selves to be adequately represented by those who have traditionally exercised this function, they tend to harshly punish their rulers. The problem, how-ever, has to do with something that is more profound than a simple change of old faces for new ones. It is related, instead, to the limits of representation as a system of democratic expression. The citizen wants to have channels which allow him to express his opinions in a more direct manner, without depending on intermediary filters that deform everything. In other words, he wants a non-manipulated participation in the decision-making processes which affect him. The discredit of representative democracy is proportional to the demands for a more participatory democracy.

Representative democracy was well defined by that celebrated phrase of Rómulo Betancourt, former President of Venezuela: "The people in abstract are an entelechy... In modern, organized societies, the people are the political parties, the unions, the organized economic sectors, the trade associations".[12] In other words, what counts is not the citizen as an individual, but the citizen organized around some of the intermediate groupings. The reaction against representative democracy is nothing more than the rejection, by the citizen – individually considered –, of the permanent manipulation of his wishes by such groups. To the extent that these groups became ever more powerful, ignoring the needs of individual citizens as they took on a life of their own and devoted themselves to their own objectives, they stopped being a means and turned into an end in themselves.

12. Cited by Ramón J. Velásquez, "Evolución Política en el Ultimo Medio Siglo", Venezuela Moderna, Barcelona, Editorial Ariel, 1979, p. 238

In the United States, however, this new perception of participatory democracy is not understood. The "Founding Fathers" of that country always warned against the "tyranny of the majority". This view of things had come down to them from Locke and the English liberals of that epoch. From its birth as an independent republic, the United States elaborated an alternative to majority rule, based on the idea of a society made up of counterpoised groups and interests. The essence of government consisted, precisely, of arbitrating these differences, which were considered to be legitimate. This "anti-majority" view of democracy was consolidated, from the middle of the twentieth century onwards, by the emergence of what became known as the thesis of the "elites", which found its starting point in the work of Joseph Schumpeter. The representatives of this school of thought made a distinction between the "democracy of masses" and "liberal democracy", the former being seen as a threat to true democracy. Thus it is that in the United States of today, democracy is conceived of as a proliferation of minorities (interest groups and other kinds of associations), the safeguarding of which is the responsibility of the State.

Despite the strong support for participatory democracy that is now emerging in Europe and other parts of the world, the United States still holds to the notion that representative democracy is the only form of real democracy. The mechanism of referendum, seen by many as a vital defense against the excesses and deformations of political representation, is still considered to be an anathema in the United States. It is not easy to get its citizens to understand that, while respect for minorities is important, it is even more important to prevent all-powerful minorities from willfully manipulating the wishes of the majority. If the tyranny of the majority is a danger, the tyranny of the minority is a much greater one. In short, what is important is that principle which is clearly expressed by Raymond Aron in his book *Democracy and Totalitarianism* : " We always insist that power comes from the people and that sovereignty resides in the people. That being so, what matters above all is the kind of institution that best allows for the expression of the democratic principle".[13]

HOW TO SURVIVE THE WASHINGTON LABYRINTH?

Washington, the capital of the global village and of the United States, is the most fragmented political ambient that you can imagine. The decision-making process that takes place there is penetrated by such a large number of diverse and contradictory interests that it is not possible to expect of it any kind of rationality. Each sector of the bureaucracy, each segment of the Congress, each pressure group, each ethnic group pushes in its own direction, with completely autonomous criteria and selfish purposes. To

13. *Démocratie et Totalitarisme*, Paris, Gallimard, 1975, p. 98

sum up, the U.S. institutional order seems like a gigantic receptor of vested interests, governed by the struggle among forces of the most varied kind.

Nevertheless, this situation, while hazardous in itself, may convert itself into a source of opportunities. In the final reckoning, if permeability is the essence of the U.S. political system, it may be considered both as a threat and an opportunity. The only thing which the system does not forgive is passivity and an ignorance of the rules of its game. An adequate handling of political lobbying therefore becomes decisive.

Each time that one faces an action likely to affect one's own interests, it is necessary to keep in mind a basic method of procedure. The threats that arise from the U.S. political system must be confronted on the basis of a set of essential rules. Among them the following are worth citing :

In the first place, it is necessary to identify the nature of the threat. Is it a "hard" or a "soft" one? This distinction is fundamental, since within any system subjected to multiple demands there often appear numerous declarations of intent which never manage to prosper. Thus, for example, during each congressional period a gigantic volume of legislative bills appear, of which only a very small percentage are feasible. Only those which enjoy a very high degree of political priority will wind up being placed on the agenda of the two Houses of Congress.

In second place, it is necessary to determine how dangerous the source of the threat is. In a country characterized by dispersion and fracturing, you can only determine how representative a segment of power is by taking into account the convergence of interests that coalesce behind it. What are known as the "iron triangles" constitute, in this sense, the most dangerous source of threats. These represent the confluence of interests among a federal agency, a congressional subcommittee and one or more pressure groups.

In third place, it is necessary to identify the potential allies at your disposal. In a society as diversified as that of the United States, any initiative that is taken may affect, simultaneously and for many different reasons, a varied set of actors. Each time that a measure affects one's own interests it is vital to find out who else may be harmed by it, in order to form a joint defensive coalition.

In fourth place, it is necessary to identify alternative decision-making bodies. It frequently happens that the source from which the threat emanates is too powerful to be confronted head-on. To stand up to an "iron triangle" may be a waste of time from the beginning. Such a triangle brings together the federal agency that makes the decision, the congressional subcommittee that funds that agency and the pressure group that finances the political campaigns of the congressmen who make up the subcommittee. This triangle will be immune to external pressures. Nevertheless, there are escape routes. Thus, for example, it is usual to find two or more subcommittees that are able to claim jurisdiction over a certain field of activity. One can try, in this way, to get a "friendly" subcommittee to approve a bill that would neutralize the bill of a "hostile" subcommittee.

In fifth place, it is necessary to concentrate your efforts on those segments of public power that maintain positions that are favorable to one's own. If we assume that the U.S. political system is a receptor of vested interests, we have to accept that rigid and biased points of view prevail in it. Trying to convince a segment of power in the hands of rival interests to accept the validity of your own arguments turns out to be as ingenuous as it is impractical. The time and energy that are required to form alliances therefore oblige one to act with selectivity, so as not to waste either of these two resources.

In sixth place, it is necessary to avoid creating permanent enmities among today's adversaries, since they may turn into tomorrow's allies. The coalitions that are designed to promote the defense of given interests usually recur to flexible "ad hoc" organizational mechanisms. Once the battle that gave rise to the coalition is "lost" or "won", the coalition usually dissolves. In this situation, it is possible that he who opposes you in one battle today may be your ally tomorrow in another, quite distinct battle, and vice versa. Any actor with varied interests will be obliged to play on different game boards and adopt diverse positions.

In seventh place, it is necessary to know how to distinguish between "real" and "nominal" power. In fact, it is fundamental to understand the difference between those who have impressive-sounding titles and those who control real shares of power. On occasions, both things coincide, but it is not always the case. The nominal head of a federal agency may find himself completely isolated and blocked when it comes to the real exercise of his power. Much more useful, in that case, is the strategy of directly appealing to the subordinate bureaucratic channels which in fact control the reins of the agency. In the same way, within Congress itself it is necessary to know the difference between those who in the political argot of Washington are respectively known as "show horses" and "work horses". The former are lawmakers who have a wide reach but a weak grasp and never come to dominate a concrete sector of power. The latter, on the contrary, are those who devote their attention to a specific sector and wind up in full control of it. Even more important, however, is to understand that while legislators "talk", their advisors "work". That is, the advisors are often more useful interlocutors than the legislators themselves.

In eighth place, it is necessary to define a specific tactic for each battle. Each fight is marked by a very particular structure of actors, interests, alliances, balances of power, etc.; therefore, each round of this endless game requires a completely different approach. Thus, there are no "battle plans" of multiple use.

It is essential to learn the rules of the U.S. political game if you want to avoid being crushed by it. It is something that the Israelis, Japanese, Mexicans or Canadians have understood very well.

THE TRIBES OF WASHINGTON

Diverse tribes coexist and give feedback to each other in the capital of the United States. In the first place, there are the public bodies of the federal government: the Executive, the Legislature and the Judiciary. The thousand faces of the Executive power, with its innumerable Departments and Federal Agencies, are headquartered there, which means that there are whole legions of officials. Alongside them circulate the members of Congress and their omnipresent retinue of advisors. In addition to these two, there are the discreet members of the Judicial power, who form a force that is both decisive and little-seen.

Where power exists there inevitably proliferate the political promoters, those who are in charge of gaining the goodwill of the public decision-makers. This activity, which is known as lobbying, derives from the place where it originated: the anteroom or lobby of the Houses of Congress. It was there that those who wanted to present their petitions to the legislators used to gather. Nowadays the large number of lobbyists in Washington corresponds to the great variety of activities that need to be brought to the attention of the political decision-makers. What cannot be obtained through discreet lobbying is left in the hands of public relations and image-building firms, who are responsible for creating a public support which catches the ear of the decision-makers. Along with the lobbyists and public relations experts, there are the lawyers, ready to litigate in the courts to obtain that which is not yielded in a more friendly way.

Another important Washington tribe is the community of specialists. Usually forming part of what are known as "think tanks" or centers of political reflection, their members are dedicated to the systematic investigation of the different fields that correspond to the many political interests that are found in the capital of the world. Basing themselves on the precedent of the Council on Foreign Relations of New York, these centers proliferated with the outbreak of the Vietnam War. In contrast with the Council, which had a bipartisan character and no ideological commitments, the great majority of the think tanks of Washington express party-political conceptions and well-defined ideologies. The community of specialists acts as an indispensable pillar of support for the political decision-makers.

Washington is also inhabited by a numerous family of international financial officials, who belong to the three great institutions that are situated there: the World Bank, the International Monetary Fund and the Inter-Development Bank. They are complemented by the officials and national representatives appointed to non-financial international institutions like the Organization of American States, the Pan American Health Organization and so forth. The above two groups, together with the diplomats, are responsible for giving a cosmopolitan touch to the city. The 172 embassies in Washington compete among themselves to catch the attention of the political world, frequently recurring to the support of lobby and public relations firms.

It was not long ago that Washington was a strictly policy and political city, in which there was little presence of the business world, beyond the inevitable lobbies. Two developments have changed this situation. Since the end of the Cold War, U.S. foreign policy has given priority to the promotion of its economic interests. This has forced the big corporations to move their international affairs offices to Washington. At the same time, the outskirts of the capital have become the home of one of the biggest high-tech parks in the country. Nowadays Washington competes with Boston's Route 128, the North Carolina "Research Triangle" or Austin, Texas to maintain its place as one of the fundamental hubs of the New Economy.

The celebrated 395 highway runs around Washington like a belt, hence it is known as the Beltway. It has come to symbolize a sort of wall that divides a capital immersed in its own dynamics and the activities of its own tribes from the rest of the country. Washington thus shows us a dual character: it is the capital of the global village and, at the same time, a small village of its own.

THE AMERICANIZATION OF JAPAN

If one thing has stood out in the course of Japanese history, it has been the country's capacity to radically change its national project every time that circumstances require it. At the beginning of the seventeenth century, faced by a Western penetration that threatened to alter the foundations of its society, the country decided to isolate itself from all outside influences. For more than two hundred years Japan opted for the route of an absolute autarchy, within the framework of a stratified feudal structure. This era was known as the Tokugawa period.

By the second half of the nineteenth century, the pressures of change within that society had grown so powerful that it was no longer possible to maintain that model. The Tokugawa regime had left a small crack open to the outside world: a Dutch fleet that was allowed to bring its products to Japan once a year. Through this crack filtered Western ideas that inflamed the imagination and the desire for change of the lower ranks of the aristocracy, who were in charge of the actual administration of the State. The attitude of this lesser aristocracy, together with the dissatisfaction of the merchant class, whose economic power was in sharp contrast to its limited political influence, laid the foundations for a radical transformation. Another factor was the realization of what was happening in China, a society whose traditionalism had kept it in the most absolute backwardness and had made it an easy prey for the colonial appetites of the West.

The bureaucrats of the lesser aristocracy and the merchants, each side motivated by its own interests, joined in the idea of rapidly modernizing the country. It was the only way of preventing Japan from suffering the same fate as China. All that was needed was a catalyst that would allow this change to manifest itself. The arrival in 1858 of a squadron of U.S. vessels under the command of Commodore Perry, sent to Japan to demand the opening of Japanese ports to trade with the West, was the spark that set off the revolution. Five years later what became known as the Meiji era began.

During the Meiji era the country entered into the most rapid transformation of institutions and cultural values that had ever occurred in history. The figure of the Emperor, who had been a merely symbolic personage in Japanese life up to that time, rose to the center of the political stage. Under the slogan "Abandon Asia and Enter the West", Japan set itself the task of building a modern economy out of nothing: banks, shipyards, textile factories, steel mills, railways and telegraphs. Within a short time the feudal country of the Tokugawa era was transformed into a nation crossed by railway and telegraph lines, whose institutions adapted themselves to the liberal ideas prevailing in the United States and Europe. The obsession with progress, under Western parameters, meant that Japan would enter the select club of the major world powers by the beginning of the twentieth century. This would inevitably lead to a confrontation with the West for control of the spheres of influences in East Asia. In 1939 the bloody war between Japan and the colonial powers of the West broke out, the precedent for which had been set as far back as 1905 in the Russian-Japanese conflict.

After its traumatic defeat in 1945, Japan reformulated its national project again in a dramatic way, emphasizing its pro-Western orientation but assuming a subordinate role to the United States. The country renounced its hegemonic ambitions and submitted itself to the guardianship of the United States. A model of lifetime employment was also defined and an economy with a civilian character. Freed from the need to assume a heavy burden of military spending, Japan was able to accumulate important surpluses which, after the lapse of several decades, allowed it to enter the club of the great powers once again. This time, however, its membership was limited to the economic sphere.

At the beginning of the nineties Japan seemed to enter another of those great and decisive stages in which it has reformulated its national purpose. The saying that symbolized this new orientation might have been: "Abandon the West and Return to Asia". What was being proposed then was an abandonment of its subordination to the United States and its role as a power with a Western vocation. The emphasis on its Asian condition and the assumption of a clear economic hegemony over the region sought to curb the penetration of the emerging markets of East Asia by the United States and Europe. The benefits which the land of the rising sun might have obtained from the West now seemed to be negligible. The United States and Europe no longer had the capacity to offer Japan what it most needed: the prospect of long-term economic growth. The new gold mine was thought to lie in the Asian economies.

The nosedive of the Asian economies in 1997 and Japan's inability to reverse its own economic recession aborted the emergence of the new national project in its early phase. Recently, there have been signs of a new attempt to reformulate the Japanese national project on the basis of radically different premises. In March 1999, the then Prime Minister Obuchi convoked the leading intellectuals, academics and political leaders of the country to take part in a think tank, with the objective of structuring a set of major national goals for the twenty-first century. This group presented its conclusions at the beginning of the year 2000. Among its recommendations were the following: an abandonment of the parameters of social conformity, of the subjection of the individual to the collectivity and of the system of decision-making by consensus; and the active encouragement of an individualistic spirit that is questioning and open to diversity. In short, the absorption of the idiosyncrasy of the U.S. as the essence of the new mentality.

In any other part of the world such ambitious goals would be considered a matter of mere rhetoric. In Japan, on the other hand, such declarations are often transformed into concrete deeds. Having tried to implant its own economic model as an alternative to U.S. capitalism and aspired to a regional economic hegemony, the land of the rising sun is now abandoning its principles to a globalization with clear U.S. features.

THE WORLD CONTROL OF SOULS

The evolution of the global economy since the Second World War has moved from the predominance of heavy industry, particularly that which is linked to defense, to that of consumer goods and thence the services sector. The services sector, once the poor relation of the world economy, transformed itself into the one which shows the quickest growth and the highest technological sophistication. In 1990, *Fortune* recognized the overwhelming importance which this sector had gained within the U.S. economy, pointing out that it represented about 60% of the national GDP and employed eight out of every ten U.S. workers. Since then the services sector has grown more and more important.

Within the services sector, the trilogy of information, telecommunications and entertainment, that is, multimedia, has become particularly relevant. In his book *Jihad vs. McWorld*, one of the most incisive analyses of recent years, the U.S. academic Benjamin Barber notes that the economy has gone from "goods to services, low technology to high technology, heavy industry to soft industry, the real to the virtual, the body to the soul". Multimedia is, in fact, aimed at the souls of human beings. According to Barber, in

the past capitalism had to take hold of political institutions and the elites in order to control both policies and the ruling philosophy and in this way
construct an ideology that was likely to promote its
interests. In his words: "Today, by contrast, it fabri-
cates, as one of its most profitable products, ideology itself".[14]

Since the nineteen-eighties, multimedia has been
going through a process of concentration of enormous proportions. In his work *The Media Monopoly*,
Ben Bagdikian notes that at the end of the Second
World War 80% of U.S. newspapers were controlled
by independent proprietors but that by 1989 80% of
the country's newspapers had been taken over by
conglomerates. Similarly, he mentions that, while in
1981 twenty corporations controlled around 50% of
the 11,000 magazines that are published in the United
States, by 1989 these twenty corporations had been
reduced to three.[15]

Even more impressive are the findings of an article published in *The Economist*, which analyzed
the process of concentration that is going in the field
of multimedia. The article discussed the seven giants in this sector: Time-Warner-CNN, Walt Disney,
Sony, Viacom, Seagram, Bertelsmann and News
Corporation. These conglomerates are devoted to
the areas of direct, satellite and cable t.v.; movie
production; the record business; the publishing busi-

14. New York, *Ballantine Books*, 1996, p. 77
15. Boston, *Beacon Press*, 1992

ness; the written press; and, in some cases, even Internet itself. According to Christopher Dixon, an expert on multimedia quoted by *The Economist:* "What is being seen is the creation of a global oligopoly. This had already occurred earlier in this century in the fields of petroleum and the automotive industry".[16]

Nevertheless, what is as significant as the process just cited or maybe more so, is the overlapping that is taking place among the above conglomerates. Both Benjamin Barber and the article in *The Economist* highlight the crossover of stock ownership among the seven giants of multimedia. According to the English magazine each of these groups "has its fingers in the other's pie". If concentration is a worrying development, overlapping is even more of a concern, since it facilitates the elaboration of the "ideology" which Barber referred to.

Several years ago the think tank Oxford Analytica published an important book called *America in Perspective.* After studying the influence exerted by the major media of social communication in that country, the book concluded that a small group of them, composed of barely nine corporations (ABC, CBS, NBC, Time, Newsweek, the Associated Press, the New York Times, the Wall Street Journal and the Washington Post), had come to exercise the role of judges of the political process and key in-

16. November 21-27, 1998

fluences in the national agenda.[17] That is, they decided on what had to be decided. What would happen if the seven multimedia emporiums decided to attain the same power on a world level? They would form what might be, in effect, an industry that controls souls.

THE GEOPOLITICS OF THE TWENTY-FIRST CENTURY

After the collapse of communism diverse theories emerged which sought to explain the new course the world might take. The two theses which had the biggest impact were, without doubt, those of Francis Fukuyama, with his theory of the "End of History" and Samuel Huntington, with his "Clash of Civilizations". For the former, the different regions of the world had become unified through their embrace of the values of democracy and the market economy. This homogenization of values and beliefs would transform the world into a more stable and predictable place and, in the end, one less prone to international conflicts. For the latter, on the other hand, the international scenario would regroup itself around seven great "civilizations", which were destined to maintain a permanent conflict among themselves because of cultural misunderstandings.

17. Boston, *Houghton Mifflin Company*, 1986

Having won the support of a great many people for their respective formulations, both authors became the biggest revisionists of their own ideas. Fukuyama has come to recognize his failure to give more importance to the cultural factor and the different ways that people from different regions have of looking at the world. Huntington, by contrast, has recognized that the world is moving towards a multi-polar system made up of a group of regions for which the cultural factor is of minor importance. In other words, Fukuyama has gone from a belief in the predominance of a single culture (the Western, with its belief in democracy and the market economy) to a genuinely multi-cultural vision of things, while Huntington has evolved from the idea of a clash between different cultures to another view, in which the cultural factor only has a vague importance. This being so, the only certainty is that while both authors are busy deciding where the world will finally go, their followers are left in the air and do not know what to believe in.

Some time ago, *The Economist* published an interesting 16-page article about the geopolitics of the twenty-first century, which might well serve as a guide to the confused followers of Huntington and Fukuyama.[18] In its study, that prestigious English magazine argued that the geopolitical map that will come into existence by the middle of the twenty-first century may take the following form:

18. July 31-August 6, 1999

First, culture will acquire the predominant role that ideologies played during the Cold War. In other words, the world will evolve towards a group of regions characterized by their cultural affinity ("culture areas", *The Economist* calls them). Second, each region's subjection to its own culture will vary in intensity. Third, there exists more of a possibility that conflicts will break out *within* a single "culture area" than *between* the different "culture areas". In simple terms, this means that there are more possibilities of conflict within the Islamic or African world itself than of conflicts between these and other regions of the world. Fourth, nation-states will become smaller and smaller, as the result of a growing process of internal division and secession.

According to *The Economist*, these tendencies will lead to the formation of between two to six great centers of world power, which will revolve around cultural affinities. Along with these centers of power there will emerge two or three groups of nations which are also linked to each other by the cultural factor. The latter, however, will not have the strength needed to convert themselves into "centers of power". A further category will be made up of fragmented groups of States that are sunk in anarchy. The reason why there may be between two to six centers of power defined by the factor of culture has to do with the interpretation given to the word culture itself. Thus, for example, there may exist a great "democratic alliance" made up of all those States which follow the ideals of "democracy and the market economy". On the other hand, it might also happen that the United States and its North American sphere of influence (Canada and Mexico) will evolve in one direction, while a united Europe will go in a different one. The six great centers of power may be arranged in the following way: the United States, the European Union, Russia, China, Japan and India, accompanied by their respective satellites. Thus, for example, Canada and Mexico would depend on the United States, just as the Slav world would depend on Russia. Among the two or three groups of countries that would be united by culture but not reach the status of power centers, Latin America, the Islam World and Africa are the likely candidates.

In short, *The Economist* came up with a thrilling geopolitical analysis. It provides us with a surer grasp of things than the intellectual somersaults of Huntington and Fukuyama.

THE RUSSIAN MAFIA

Since the final stage of the Brezhnev period, there was a clear consensus within a wide sector of the Kremlin about the need to undertake an ambitious program of reforms in the Soviet Union. It was left to Gorbachev to carry out this process, which began in 1985. The last of the Soviet leaders opened the pressure cooker, hoping to release the steam that had been building up in a controlled way. His role, however, became that of the sorcerer's apprentice, destined to unleash forces that destroyed everything in their path. First, the East European satellites fell, then the foundations of his power and finally, the Soviet Union itself. In the end, the system could not do without the changes, but at the same time it was unable to assimilate them. It was a system that had exhausted its own possibilities of survival.

The most curious thing of all is that communism might have collapsed ten years before it finally did, if it had not been for the role played by the Mafia. In a society throttled by a sclerotic and totally incompetent bureaucracy, only the black market controlled by the Mafia was able to ensure that the gears would function. The Soviet leadership and the upper strata of the party had learned to coexist with the Mafia, by means of secret deals. The reason was simple: it was the only institution in the Soviet Union that functioned with a certain degree of efficiency. Thanks to the black market, it was possible to circumvent bureaucratic obstacles, enabling the system to create responses in the productive apparatus.

Beginning in 1991, with the final collapse of communism, the Mafia, which had the control of the black market in its hands, was able to abandon its subterranean position and expand as it pleased. In a matter of a mere five years, it came to control forty percent of the Russian economy. In the opinion of Marshall I. Goldman, Associate Director of Harvard University's Center for Russian Studies, by 1995 the Russian Mafia already controlled between seventy to eighty percent of the two thousand banks of the country, as well as forty thousand privatized companies.[19]

Several reasons explain the speed and efficiency of this Mafia takeover of the Russian economy. In the first place, their brutal and indiscriminate use of violence. In second place, the disorganization of the security forces after the collapse of communism. In third place, the endemic corruption that characterizes Russian society. In fourth place, the inflation that was unleashed after 1991 and became consolidated by the middle of the decade. For the rest, the process of privatization, carried out in an accelerated way and without any kind of planning, granted control of companies' stocks to their managers, most of whom already had close links with the Mafia.

If one thing has characterized the Russian economy in recent years, it is the massive transfer of assets to foreign countries. By 1996, a share of Russian wealth, valued at fifty billion dollars and mainly represented by gold, diamonds, precious metals and diverse "commodities", had been illegally exported. Such merchandise, bought with completely devalued rubles and, thanks to corruption, at bankruptcy prices as well, were shipped abroad and sold for hard currency. What is more, the privatized companies themselves had been brutally dismembered, through the sale of their assets to foreigners for the personal gain of their new proprietors. It is not by accident that Russian companies rarely obtain more than a third

19. *Current History*, October 1995

of the profits they earn, the rest going into the pockets of their owner-administrators.

Nevertheless, what is even more worrying is the trafficking of nuclear material that has been going on in recent years. The communist collapse left Russia without an adequate capacity to maintain or control its nuclear arsenals, which has led to the systematic extraction of sensitive nuclear material. The theft of enriched uranium and others kinds of radioactive material has become common: they now have a fixed price in the black market that handles nuclear "commodities". In that field as well, the Mafia has a strong presence and makes spectacular profits.

The Mafia has been occupying an ever-larger space since the final stage of the Soviet regime. Today, its tentacles extend to every corner of Russian society. A handful of large criminal families, whose businesses have become legitimate in recent years, enjoy open pastures in the midst of a country devoid of structure and articulation.

THE COST OF UNCERTAINTY

In his celebrated book *The Lexus and the Olive Tree*, Thomas L. Friedman argues that the current world revolution in the field of information technology constitutes the third great revolution in the history of mankind, after the invention of agriculture and the industrial revolution. In his opinion, we are barely on the threshold of the latest revolution, whose impact on human life over the next thirty years cannot even be imagined today.[20]

In point of fact, the interdependence resulting from the density of the networks of information technology that cover the world today has radically transformed, not only the traditional power of States, but also the very nature of productive processes, financial and commercial activities and the life of societies. What is more, as Robert Keohane and Joseph Nye Jr. point out, the density of such networks now means that small, isolated happenings may have profound catalytic effects, likely to make themselves felt in the most diverse fields and in the most widespread corners of the planet. As in the theories of "chaos", the effects of any isolated action may extend themselves to a world level, with unpredictable effects.[21] As Friedman states, however, we are barely taking the first steps along this revolutionary path.

A concrete example of the world interdependence which isolated deeds create today was found in the so-called Asian crisis of 1997. The bank crisis which occurred in a small emerging market, which Thailand was, spread a financial panic throughout the whole of East Asia. This crisis forced the International Monetary Fund to undertake a rescue program, sending an enormous package of financial relief to the affected economies, and led

20. New York, *Farrar Strauss and Giroux*, 1999
21. *Foreign Policy*, Spring, 2000

to price falls in an infinity of products all over the world. Before confidence was restored, Russia was infected by the crisis, stopping payments on its foreign loans, and the "hedge" funds of the United States took a nosedive, obliging the Federal Reserve Bank to carry out an ambitious rescue plan. Brazil soon caught the disease as well, threatening to take the whole of Latin America down with it – and possibly the rest of the world. It was only after the IMF granted a hefty loan and a major devaluation was imposed, that it became possible to control the Brazilian conflagration. The collapse of the Thai banking system cost the world billions and billions of dollars.

Nevertheless, much more important and significant is the phenomenon of what Friedman has called "the super-powerful individualities". That is, the capacity that isolated individuals now have to affect great world deeds through the information technology networks. Several examples may be cited to support this thesis. On the financial level, we see how individual fortunes are being amassed which make the international reserves of most of the world's nation-states look small in comparison. On the level of civil society, we encounter figures like Jody Williams and Lori Wallach, who have managed to impose their views on powerful States and dominant trends. Williams overcame the opposition of the world's five greatest powers to achieve an international prohibition on the use of land mines, through an e-mail campaign that enlisted the help of more than five thousand human rights and arms-control organizations in different parts of the world. Wallach organized, also through Internet, the coalition of more than 140 groups and NGO's from all over the world that confronted globalization in Seattle, unleashing a wave of protests that is still being felt at every meeting of the global economic elite.

On the other hand, this power of the "super-individualities" is also seen in criminal activities. In 1994, a little-known stockbroker by the name of Nick Leeson mobilized 27 billion dollars in transactions undertaken without the knowledge of his bosses, causing the bankruptcy of the venerable Barings Bank. In the same way, in the year 2000 an obscure bank employee in the Philippines, by the name of Reomel Ramones, infected computers all over the world with the "love virus", causing a panic in governments, corporations and stock markets and nearly 10 billion dollars' worth of damage.

It is not in vain that in the article we have referred to, Keohane and Nye ask whether the "chaotic uncertainty" which the world is experiencing may not be too high a price to pay for higher levels of prosperity. An uncertainty which is barely beginning.

THE ICEBERG EFFECT

In 1965 Gordon Moore, the co-founder of Intel, predicted that computational power would duplicate itself every 18 months. For more than three decades, this assertion, which is known as "Moore's Law", has held true. Nowadays, a personal computer with a cost of less than a thousand dollars operates ten times as fast as a computer which cost 5 million dollars in the nineteen-seventies. By the year 2010, the price of personal computers will have fallen below one hundred dollars and their capacity will make that of current ones look archaic.

The field of telecommunications, for its part, has also witnessed a dramatic fall in prices. Thanks to fiber optic cables, satellites and digitalization, the world has become increasingly integrated, at ever lower prices. When telephone communication was introduced for the first time, in 1915, a three minute call between New York and San Francisco cost the equivalent of 90 hours of work at the average wage. Today, two minutes of work will pay for the same call. When Motorola introduced cell phones in 1984, the unit price of the apparatus was four thousand dollars. At the present time, many cellular phone companies give away the phones in order to get people to sign up for their service.

These two technologies, informatics and telecommunications, have become integrated, giving rise to a world network of interconnections which surpasses anything that might have been imagined only a few years ago. The Internet highways today unite more than 100 million users. By the year 2005 this figure will grow to a billion people and by 2010 it will connect 3.5 billion human beings. Under the impact of the new technologies, frontiers are disappearing and the interrelation among human beings of the most diverse latitudes is acquiring the dimensions of a genuine global village.

The above advances have led to what the writer Frances Cairncross has named "the death of distance". In his view, this has led to "an increase of understanding, an encouragement of tolerance and, finally, the promotion of world peace".[22] Is it so? In 1990, when the tensions that followed the invasion of Kuwait by Iraq were on the point of unleashing the armed conflict, Saddam Hussein used television to address the American people, while George Bush did the same thing for the people of Iraq. Utilizing channels made available by modern telecommunications technology, both leaders were given the opportunity to explain the validity of their arguments to the opposing band. The result? Saddam's message was as incomprehensible to the U.S. public as Bush's was to the Iraqis. Cultural barriers transformed this tele-communicational effort into a mere dialogue of the deaf, in which neither nation was able to understand the meaning of the message directed to it. In short, technology may "kill" the physical distance that separates men, but it will never manage to eliminate the cultural distance.

Michelle LeBaron and Jarle Croker have used the metaphor of an iceberg submerged in water to symbolize culture. That is, as an invisible tissue of mean-

22. The Death of Distance, *Harvard Business School Press*, Boston 1997

ings, beliefs and convictions.[23] That being so, the interconnection among human beings of diverse latitudes that technology accomplishes only takes place at the tip of the iceberg, the part that emerges from the surface of the ocean. This tip of the iceberg would be made up of the shared values of globalization (which run from McDonald's to Nike, the English language to Microsoft, the international financial bodies to Wall Street). In other words, the reign of global "homogenization" proclaimed by Fukuyama. Beneath this tip, however, there lies the gigantic body of the submerged iceberg, represented by the "clash between civilizations" that Huntington refers to. That is, a diversity of cultures that are very hard to reconcile.

When we see things in the above terms, it may turn out that being too close to each other will encourage conflict rather than understanding. Instead of a fully integrated global village, what current developments may be creating is a neighboring house on a planetary scale. The shortage of room to develop one's own identity may well lead to continual quarrels between strangers who live too close to one another.

HIGH POLITICS AND THE ACADEMIC WORLD

The academic world enjoys an immense power within the higher political spheres of Washington.

---

23. *Harvard International Review*, Autumn, 2000

This assertion may be confirmed by means of three criteria of measurement. The first is the active participation of its members in what are known as the communities of specialists. The second is its role in educating the political elite. The third is the dynamic interrelation between the job of teaching and the exercise of important governmental responsibilities.

The members of the academic world are the outstanding exponents of the communities of specialists. As John W. Kingdon points out: "After the pressure groups, the academics, researchers and experts make up the group of non-official actors of most importance in Washington. Signs of their influence are spread throughout the whole political process. The ideas that emerge from academic literature are regularly discussed in congressional and bureaucratic circles. Prominent academics are widely-known figures and their specialized knowledge is permanently called upon by congressional committees and federal agencies, through hearings, meetings and advisory commissions".[24] The representatives of the academic sector fulfill, in fact, a kind of clerical function, responsible for legitimizing "ideas" within the established order. The universities of high prestige and the "think tanks" – like the Council on Foreign Relations, the Brookings Institution, the Carnegie Endowment, the Center for Strategic and International Studies or the Inter

24. Agendas, Alternatives and Public Policies, Boston, *Little Brown and Company,* 1984, p. 57

American Dialogue – are the conceptual leaders of U.S. political life.

The role which the academic world plays in training the public elites is also of great importance. The realm of higher education in the United States embraces nearly 3,000 universities, a figure which has no equivalent in any other part of the world. Nevertheless, this numerical richness occurs alongside a curious concentration of talent in a small number of institutions. From this limited nucleus of universities graduate a disproportionately high percentage of U.S. national leaders. 55% of the country's corporate leadership and 44% of its political leadership are drawn from only 12 universities: Harvard, Yale, Princeton, Columbia, Pennsylvania, Cornell, Stanford, MIT, Dartmouth, Chicago, Johns Hopkins and Northwestern.[25] To the above universities we should add another few, like the California Institute of Technology, Georgetown, Brown, Duke or Berkeley, for example. The above situation creates a sort of natural selection of leadership, at the level of university classrooms themselves. Just as the academic world fulfills a clerical function of legitimization in the realm of ideas, the prestigious universities are responsible for "sacramentalizing" the top leadership of the country.

Finally, we find the phenomenon whereby there is a constant intercross between academic careers and high politics. There exists a sort of "revolving

25. Thomas R. Dye and Harmon Zeigler, *The Irony of Democracy*, Monterrey, Brooks/Cole Publishing Company, 1987

door" between the two worlds, which is always spinning. Scholars from the major universities move into high governmental posts as frequently as former political leaders become part of the academic world. The number of high officials and advisors who have established close links with universities is legion. Among many other names, we might mention the following. Secretaries of State: Dean Rusk, Henry Kissinger, Cyrus Vance, George Schultz, James Baker and Madeleine Albright. National Security Advisors: McGeorge Bundy, W.W. Rostow, Henry Kissinger, Zbigniew Brzezinski, Richard Allen and Anthony Lake. Secretaries of Defense: Neil H. McElroy, Thomas S. Gates, Clark Clifford, James R. Schlesinger and Harold Brown.

To resume, the gigantic influence of the academic world on the government of the United States is unquestionable. Acquiring a systematic knowledge of the country's academic world has become a task of major diplomatic importance for foreign governments.

THE GIANTS OF MULTIMEDIA

According to studies made by a number of experts in 1995, 26.8% of the world GDP lay in the hands of the world's 200 biggest corporations and in a great number of productive sectors the five main companies were responsible for more than half of world production in their respective fields. This situation has only become more pronounced since then, impelled by one of the most characteristic phenomena of our times: the mega-mergers.

As is to be expected, the biggest corporate merger up to the present time has taken place in the field of multimedia. That is, that area where entertainment, information and informatics converge. In fact, nowadays this sector is the equivalent of what the petroleum and automotive industries were at the beginning of the twentieth century. In other words, an oligopolic sector *par excellence*. The merger in question came about through AOL's acquisition in January 2000 of the giant Time-Warner-CNN, at a price of 183 billion dollars. A few weeks before, there had occurred what was until then the biggest mega-merger in that field: the purchase of CBS by Viacom for 37 billion dollars.

Up to a decade or so ago, the sector of social communication media was controlled, in most countries, by domestic companies. The leap towards globalization which has occurred since then in this sector is astonishing. Stimulated by the double process of deregulation and technological advance, it has been producing an ever greater concentration of activities in the hands of an ever smaller group of companies.

The neo-liberal order that rules on a world level was complemented by the advent of fiber optics and digital, satellite and microwave systems. The result has been not only the planetary integration of the sectors of entertainment, news and telecommunication, but also the overlapping of these with the information technology sector.

The multimedia field is dominated by seventy-odd corporations which operate on a global and regional level. They may divided into two large categories: one with a world coverage made up of nine great groups and another which has an essentially regional extension, where the other companies are found. The former category is headed by the gigantic America Online-Time-Warner, which represents the intercross between the biggest Internet services company and the main media and entertainment one. Following this we find Sony, Disney, News Corporation, Viacom, Seagram (now Vivendi-Seagram), Bertelsmann, and, to a lesser extent, General Electric and AT&T, which achieved this rank through the purchases of NBC and Liberty Media. In the second category the leading companies are ones like Dow Jones, Gannett, Hearst and Advance Publications in North America; the Kirch Group, Havas, Mediaset, Hachette, Prisa and Canal Plus in Europe; and Globo, Televisa, Clarín and the Cisneros Group in Latin America. Within this second group the company which has grown the fastest is, without doubt, Hicks, Muse, Tate and Furst, a U.S. corporation which is closely linked to the Cisneros Group in its expansion towards Latin America.

In former times, publishing companies, newspapers and magazines, television stations, radio networks, movie studios, record companies and other media were usually owned by different concerns. Today, such activities and some others which lie within the field of informatics are controlled by giants like the ones we have just mentioned. The reason for this convergent tendency is expressed by a single word: synergy. That is, the capacity to give a maximum strength to each one of these activities through their combined action. Benjamin Barber has described this process in the following terms: "Synergy is a polite way of saying monopoly and, in the field of information, monopoly is a polite way of saying uniformity".[26] In other words, mega-mergers in the multimedia field are leading to what Ignacio Ramonet has called "the single thought".

EUROPEAN ULTRA-NATIONALISM

After the collapse of communism the nationalist phenomenon broke out on the international scene. To begin with, it was centered in the countries of the former Soviet orbit or in the former Soviet Union itself. It was a natural reaction to the long repression of deep-rooted national sentiments in those countries. But in many cases, it was also the response of a leadership which had been compromised by communism and found in the nationalist phenomenon the best formula for renewing its political credentials. Nevertheless, the most characteristic feature of the nationalist movement in recent days is that it is gathering strength in the industrialized world and, particularly, in the European Union.

26. *Op. cit.*, p. 137

After the Second World War, nationalism emerged as a reaction to colonialism and was seen as a counterbalance to the driving force of the developed world. The 1955 Bandung Summit was an expression of this phenomenon, which was championed by figures like Nasser, Tito, Nehru and Sukarno. Nowadays, it is the reverse: it is in the developed world itself that nationalism emerges with greater force. It is a nationalism, however, which has nothing to do with that of Bandung, but closely resembles fascism or the traditionalist authoritarian movements.

A few years ago, in Italy, the Lombardy League led by Umberto Bossi symbolically declared the independence of the Republic of Padania, embracing the northern part of the country, as a way of expressing its rejection of southern Italy. Parallel to this, Italy has seen the growth of a broad spectrum of far-right movements, which run from the neofascist New Force to the National Alliance coalition and emphasize a hostility to immigrants and a nostalgia for traditional values. In France, the National Front founded by Jean Marie Le Pen sticks to its harangue about a "France eternal, peaceful and serene before 'modernity' came to upset everything". It places an emphasis on the defense of traditional values, like the family, work, order and nation. A radical rejection of immigration and the notion of racial superiority are fundamental components of its message. Its strategy, copied from the Islamic fundamentalists, is that of the spider's web. That is, the systematic infiltration of associations, unions, universities, youth organizations and public institutions, with a view to controlling them from within.

In Germany, the Republican party led by Franz Schonhuber is becoming stronger, especially in regions with an extreme right-wing political tradition, like Bavaria, Baden, Wurtemberg and Hesse. The grassroots of this party, for their part, are closely linked with the gangs of skinheads who sow terror amongst foreign immigrants. Another ultra-nationalist option that is getting strong in that country is what has become known as the "New Right", which expresses itself through the positions of top-line intellectuals and journalists, like Botho Strauss, Rainer Zitelman and Karlheinz Weissman. The German "New Right" reaffirms Germany's right to racial exclusivity and a "nationalism without guilt which places the Nazi past in its proper context".

In February 2000, the world focused its attention on Austria, where the Freedom Party of Jorg Heider came to form part of the ruling coalition. After a gradual rise in which it obtained an increasing representation in the Municipal Assembly of Vienna and the local governments of traditionalist provinces like Carinthia, Heider's party was finally able to join the major leagues of Austrian politics. Its strong rejection of immigration and reaffirmation of many of the beliefs of the Third Reich are the ideological foundation of this party, which today accounts for nearly 30% of the national vote. The European Union, alarmed by the potential dangers of the situation, wound up imposing a sort of *cordon sanitaire* around Austria.

There is a curious parallel between the emergence of Islamic fundamentalism, the wild claims for regional autonomy and the far-right nationalist movements. In all of these cases there is a common denominator: the demand for a parcel of the world where you can live in accordance with your roots and traditional principles and thus protect yourself from the uniformity imposed by globalization and the penetration of the foreign. The phenomenon which Europe is experiencing today is another chapter in the fight between the global village and the small village, a fight that will doubtless have a decisive influence on the twenty-first century.

THE NEW MIDDLE AGES

For centuries the international system has been governed by principles whose origins go back to the Treaty of Westphalia. That treaty, signed in 1648 at the end of the Thirty Years War, laid the foundations of the modern State on the basis of two basic notions: the exclusivity of a territory and the exclusion of foreign actors from the handling of internal affairs. That is, territoriality and non-intervention. These two concepts logically led to a third one: the juridical equality among states.

For a long time, the international system that arose from Westphalia was more a matter of what "should be" than what really was. Without doubt, colonialism represented the most glaring violation of its principles. By virtue of such ideas as the "civilizing mission", the "White Man's burden" and even the "Manifest Destiny", the great Western powers ignored the right to an independent existence of States which were considered to be "insufficiently civilized". In his classic work *Colonization among Modern Nations*, Paul Leroy-Beaulieu, the most eminent ideologue of French colonization, argued that the world could be divided into four groups: the member states of Western civilization; the states which were heading in the same direction (mainly Japan); unstable states with a questionable degree of civilization; and "barbaric and savage tribes". Of these four groups, the latter two could be subjected to colonization by the Western nations. In England, in the same period, John Stuart Mill made a distinction between non-intervention in the affairs of civilized countries and the right of intervention in "barbaric countries". [27]

Most of the independent states of Ibero-America, considered to be insufficiently civilized by the great Western powers, were able to free themselves of the colonialist claws because of the Monroe Doctrine. The dissuasive presence of the emerging giant, the United States, served as an important containing wall against European appetites. It was not by accident that it only needed the U.S. Civil War for France to launch herself into the conquest of Mexico.

27. See Hedley Bull, *"Beyond the States System?"*, David Held, Anthony McGrew, Editors, *The Global Transformations Reader*, Cambridge, Polity Press, 2000

Nevertheless, the Monroe Doctrine was barely sufficient. Venezuela, like so many other countries of Latin America, was forced to suffer the consequences of being considered an "incipiently civilized" State. From the loss of a great part of its Guayana region to its exclusion from the 1898 Paris Arbitral Tribunal which defined the future of an important part of its territory, from the 1903 blockade to the foreign intervention of its customs service, Venezuela felt the lash of colonialism on its own skin and was able to vouch for the hypocrisies of the Westphalia system. Nevertheless, for better or for worse, this system defined a "should be" which turned states into the primary hubs of international relations.

Nowadays, it is precisely this nature of the State as the primary axis of the international order which is in doubt. For one thing, the new international law ignores its primacy and for another, its strength is being undermined wherever you look: from below by growing regional autonomies; from above by the supra-national institutions; on the sides, by multinational financial bodies, economic mega-conglomerates and powerful NGO's. In short, we have fallen into what Hedley Bull has called a "new Middle Ages". That is, a State in which the central power is seeing its traditional authority diluted in the midst of a growing web of impositions, interventions and interdependencies. New versions of the empire, the papacy and the feudal lords are hemming in the central power of the State. As we enter into the third millennium we are returning to a political scenario that resembles that of the beginning of the second millennium.

THE INTERNATIONAL SYSTEM AT THE START OF THE MILLENNIUM

The international system at the beginning of the millennium is based on the interrelationship among three sets of fundamental actors, who coexist in the midst of a tense equilibrium. These actors are the states, the multilateral bodies and the private-sector corporations and financial entities. Of these three groups, the first two have a much more symbiotic relationship. In fact, the power of the multilateral bodies rests on the delegation of power and the voluntary renouncement of sovereign spaces by the states themselves. The multilateral bodies may only do as much as the states which cede them power allow them to do. What is more, such organisms are controlled, in most cases, by a small group of states with a great concentration of power. Both in theoretical and practical terms, such organisms wind up being a prolongation of state reality itself. The relationship between states and the world of private capital, on the other hand, is much more complex.

For most of the twentieth century, the State occupied a predominant position. While the big private corporation continued to strengthen itself and become multinational throughout the century, espe-

come multinational throughout the century, especially after the Second World War, it was not in a
condition to compete with the supremacy of the state.
So long as the Cold War went on, political considerations prevailed over economic ones and public over
private matters. In the final decade of the twentieth
century, however, the sphere of the private assumed
priority and the State began to see itself hemmed in
on all flanks.

Never before had the State looked so vulnerable
as in the final decade of the twentieth century. The
new international law was putting more and more
emphasis on such ideas as the right of intervention,
supra-national guardianships, humanitarian rights and
limited sovereignties, all of which coincide in ignoring the primacy of the state within the international
order. For their part, the ethnic and nationalist rivalries unleashed after the fall of the Berlin Wall were
undermining the foundations which upheld state
power. Nevertheless, it has been globalization that
has exerted the greatest pressure on the authority of
states, shaking their very bowels. This has occurred
on two flanks. On one side, there is the technological leap associated with the phenomenon of globalization, which has abolished distance and time. On
the other, there is the very ideology of globalization:
the free market. The cumbersome state bureaucracies, more reminiscent of the nineteenth than the
twenty-first century, were not able to deal with the
technological leap, while at the same time the free
market ideology thrashed them at every turn. The

to take full advantage of the dual technological and ideological phenomenon to consolidate its power base.

The State and the corporation are advancing along different routes. There are more and more states but they mean less and less. The corporations, on the other hand, are fewer and fewer but they have more and more weight. At the end of the Second World War, there were only 51 member states of the U.N, now there are 185. During the last decade of the twentieth century, an average of 3 new states came into being each year. Their recent proliferation is the result of the dismembering of large states and runs parallel to the weakening of the State itself. The corporation has moved along a completely different route. By means of the phenomenon of mega-mergers, the number of corporate actors is becoming ever more reduced. This is tending to form an oligopolic system of gigantic power.

The States and the multilateral bodies will probably wind up joining forces in order to defend themselves from the expansive force of private capital. For this to happen, however, the ideology which accompanies globalization would have to make room for common sense. Let us hope that there will be no repetition of the case of the World Trade Organization's Multilateral Accord on Investments, in which the signatory states sought to grant corporations the unilateral right to sue states for any public policy that might jeopardize their interests.

THREATENED STATE SOVEREIGNTY

As we have pointed out, at the time of its foundation at the end of the Second World War, the United Nations had 51 members. By 1983 their numbers had grown to 158. At the present time there are 185 member states of the U.N. and there will soon be 187. Between 1990 and 1998 an average of 3 new states were created every year. The requirements for joining the U.N. and thus becoming a full member of the international community are as follows: you must have a defined territory, a permanent population, a government and the capacity to conduct its foreign relations. Every member state of the United Nations enjoys the right to have its sovereignty respected in accordance with principles that go back to the Treaty of Westphalia. As we have said, there are two of these: exclusivity over territory and the exclusion of foreign actors from the management of domestic affairs, that is, territoriality and non-interference. These two principles imply a third one: the juridical equality among states.

Curiously, while one trend points to the proliferation of the member states of the international community, another parallel one has to do with growing doubts about state sovereignty. In synthesis, there are more and more states but they mean less and less. This increasing loss of weight of the states may be the result of two different factors. In the first place, the voluntary renunciation of sovereign spaces. And, in second place, the emergence of new tendencies which are ignoring those sovereign spaces. In the first case, the phenomenon is much less serious, since any voluntary renouncement of a right implies the preexistence of that right. In other words, being able to limit your own sovereignty is in itself an affirmation of that sovereignty. When the member states of the European Union renounce their national monetary policies in the name of a monetary union, or when their courts submit themselves to the verdicts of the European Court of Justice, such actions exemplify a loss of sovereignty based on sovereign right itself. The same thing applies when the limiting of this sovereignty is the result of international agreements signed by the states themselves. All this is in harmony with the Westphalia model and does not imply a disregard of its principles. It is much more serious, however, when emerging concepts of international law tend to ignore state sovereignty.

When there is a generalization of the perception, based on the new juridical doctrines, that the right of intervention is viable and feasible, state sovereignty is undermined regardless of the wishes of the states themselves. The danger which derives from this situation is evident. Any intervention in the internal affairs of another State, including armed intervention, requires what might be called a "collective legitimization". That is, the notion that the action is carried out in accordance with norms and procedures that are widely accepted. As the new juridical conceptions to which we have referred gain a wider acceptance, the foundations may be laid for a collective legitimization of the right of outsiders to intervene in the domestic affairs of states.

Two currents of thought about this subject have emerged. On the one hand, there is what might be called the globalization school. And, on the other, there is the realist school. In the view of the former, the members of the international community share rights, obligations, responsibilities and values. Under such conditions, international intervention is fully valid when it promotes or defends certain principles or values. A clear expression of this school of thought is the new humanitarian law. For the realist school, by contrast, the language of the common good hides selfish interests and political calculations, as it has done from the beginning of history. A single example of this may suffice: when intervention is done for humanitarian reasons, more importance may be given to the migratory impact of the affected populations than to the harm caused to the victims.

Be that as it may, there is an elemental reality which should never be forgotten: the powerful make their prerogatives respected through force; it is the weak who require sovereignty to guarantee their survival.

THE EVOLUTION OF THE STATE

The modern State, as a concept and a political ordering, began to develop in thirteenth century Europe. What characterized it was the effort to centralize power in an institution that would embrace all fundamental political relations. Between the seventeenth and eighteenth centuries the notion of the State was based on a mercantilist conception of the economy. Mercantilism specifically promoted the regulation of the economy, for the purpose of strengthening the power of states at the expense of rival ones. It is not by chance that this economic doctrine paralleled the emergence and later apogee of absolutism.

At the end of the eighteenth century both mercantilism and absolutism fell into crisis. The convergence of a market economy in the economic sphere and the state of law in the political sphere created the foundations of a new order. The so-called liberal order, which sought to put precise limits on the State by erecting barriers against the exercise of its power. Nevertheless, instead of initiating the decline of the State, this period saw it acquire a second wind, thanks to the appearance of the nationalist phenomenon. In accordance with nationalism, the citizen owed his fundamental loyalty to the nation-state.

The late eighteenth and early nineteenth centuries are known as the "Era of Revolutions". It is was in this period that there occurred the American Revolution, the French Revolution and the Hispano-American War of Independence, all of which were based on the idea of the supremacy of the nation-state. The thesis of popular sovereignty, which originated with Rousseau, provides the foundations for the consolidation of this new concept of the State. Throughout the nineteenth century the power of the State grew stronger in Europe, riding on the wave of nationalism, and new centralized states, like Germany and Italy, appeared.

The twentieth century would lead the State to extremes that had never been seen before. It would produce the totalitarian "idolatry of the state" of the fascist and communist regimes. In the post-war period, the nation-state became identified with the dismantling of colonialism in Asia and Africa, extending its influence to all parts of the world. For the rest, the end of the Second World War began a period which was characterized by the clash of two powerful states and their respective defense and national security machines: the United States and the Soviet Union.

However, at the start of the final decade of the twentieth century, a genuine cataclysm shook the very foundations of the notion of the State, causing it to suffer its greatest historical crisis. The threats which hang over this ancient and familiar concept are strong and varied. On the juridical, the political and the economic fronts, the survival of the State as a fundamental political organization is in doubt. This was the inevitable result of the collapse of communism, which led to the emergence and acceptance of a whole new set of ideas and paradigms.

As we enter the twenty-first century the State is faced by a gigantic challenge. Will it recover its former preeminence? Or is it condemned to suffer a progressive and inescapable decline?

THE ETHNIC PHENOMENON
AND THE CRISIS OF THE STATE

In the new international reality which emerged since the collapse of communism, the ethnic phenomenon occupies an important place. In fact, it bears a large measure of responsibility for the crisis which the State is going through today. Even before the disease which consumed the Soviet empire started to become evident, a number of states were already being torn up by ethnic conflicts. Nevertheless, the dismemberment of the communist regime that began in 1989 unleashed a fervor of ethnic sentiment, which led people to question the validity of innumerable frontiers all over the world. Today many ethnic groups claim the right to an independent existence, no longer feeling themselves represented by the states of which, for a long time, they formed part. At the same time, ethnic massacres proliferate among groups who are obliged to co-exist beneath the same state roof.

The example set by the reunification of Germany – understood to be the first redrawing of state frontiers in the post-war period –, followed by the dismantling of the Soviet Union, set off a political hurricane of great proportions. Furthermore, the fact that when the Cold War ended the supremacy of supra-national and collective institutions was proclaimed as the foundation of the new world order also had a lot to do with it. This encouraged many ethnic groups to take the chance of facing an inde-

pendent existence, without counting on the binding
or protective power of a consolidated State. The prevailing impression, in fact, was that any mini-State
that appeared on the international scene would be
able to attain economic viability by joining a common market and political viability through the protective umbrella of the mechanisms of collective
security.

Those states which were grounded in a solid national identity were immune to the strong winds that
blew after the fall of the Berlin Wall. For those, on
the other hand, which had a plurality of ethnic identities sharing the space of a single state, the headaches have never stopped. Yugoslavia was the first
to suffer the impact of the new times. In the final
analysis, you were talking about a State made up of
the remnants of two great empires – the Austro-Hungarian and the Turkish – whose ethnic diversity had
turned it into the perfect laboratory for suffering the
rigors of the new reality. In Bosnia alone, 250,000
people died. Russia as well would feel the sting on
its own flesh of the effects of the dismembering of
the Soviet Union that it had propitiated. In Chechnya,
tens of thousands of deaths have resulted from
Moscow's attempts to prevent its secession. In the
former Soviet Union confrontations of an ethnic origin broke out in Moldavia, Georgia, Azerbaijan, Armenia and Tajikistan. In Afghanistan, the Soviet
withdrawal led to a situation in which four ethnic
groups were fighting each other, with the support of
neighboring countries. Further west, in Turkey, the

armed attacks on the Kurdish population still go on.

The states created by the hand of colonialism, which drew frontiers with a total disregard for the underlying ethnic groups, are particularly vulnerable to the destabilizing force of this phenomenon. Africa and the Arab world provide highly-illustrative testimonies in this sense. Curiously, with the exception of the Kurdish problem in Iraq, the Arab world has been fairly remote from the crisis of uncontrolled ethnic sentiments. The problem there is of another kind: Islamism, which has in common with the ethnic phenomenon the search for one's own corner of the universe, where one will be free to live in accordance with one's traditions and roots. In Africa, by contrast, ethnic problems have freely multiplied.

Rwanda and Burundi represent an extreme case of the potential for violence that is found in ethnic conflicts. Between the end of 1993 and the end of 1995 more than one hundred thousand persons died in Burundi as a result of massacres caused by ethnic hate. In Rwanda, eight hundred thousand persons died after the assassination of its President in April 1994. In both cases the clashes between the Tutsi and Hutu groups, which are common to both countries, have been the cause of the massacres. Nowadays, people are even talking about eliminating the artificial borders of both states, in order to create two different nations – a Tutsiland and Hutuland – that would allow these ethnic groups to respectively occupy their own homogenous states. In Liberia, a bloody civil war set diverse factions against each other, each based on a certain ethnic grouping. Wherever you look on the African continent, ethnic identity has become a source of threats to the survival of the states inherited from the colonial epoch.

While it might be useful to extend the list of civil wars and massacres which have occurred in the Southern hemisphere, we should not forget that the survival of several states in the Northern hemisphere is also threatened by the same phenomenon. Canada and Belgium are two particularly relevant examples of the problem we are talking about. In the former, the secession of Quebec is a perennial theme. In Belgium, the heart of unified Europe, the ancestral rivalry between the Flemish and the Walloons hangs like the sword of Damocles over the continuance of that rich country. This, in addition to the emergence of claims for autonomy by the Scots, Bretons, Corsicans, Catalans, Basques, etc.

The ethnic phenomenon has another dimension, which goes beyond the problem of civil wars, slaughters, armed conflicts and refugees. This second dimension lies within the framework of the new orientation of international law, which has made fashionable such notions as the "protection of minorities", "limited sovereignty" and "international guardianships". Take the case of Venezuela and Brazil. More than 20,000 members of the Yanomami indigenous group occupy a territory of about 17 million hectares (equivalent to six Belgiums), on either side of the frontier, where their homelands are protected by "Biosphere Reserves", "National Parks" and "Indigenous Reserves". Under the auspices of the United Nations, a "Universal Declaration of Indigenous Rights" would include the "right to self-determination" for these populations. If we do not keep our eyes wide open, this might be the pretext for establishing international wardships over an area that occupies more than 9% of Venezuelan territory.

THE NEW DIPLOMACY

Although the practice of sending the envoys of one king to the court of another in order to deal with problems of alliances or of war and peace goes back to ancient times, it was not until the fifteenth century, in Europe, that diplomatic missions of a permanent nature began to be institutionalized. It was left to the Congress of Vienna in 1815 to regulate the exercise of diplomatic functions, thus determining their essential norms. In the past, the work of representation, which is characteristic of diplomacy, was carried out with an amplitude proportional to the distance that separated the diplomatic representative from his home country. When an ambassador reached his destination after a journey that might last for weeks and once there, had no way of easily communicating with his government, it was obvious that he had to be granted great freedom of action. From this arose his status as a plenipotentiary, that is, a representative who was granted full powers to realize the negotiations or comply with the instructions which had been placed in his charge.

In our days ambassadors who are accredited in foreign countries still hold the title of plenipotentiaries. But, as often happens nowadays, the title is merely a formal one. In the present epoch of instant communication, of heads of states and foreign ministers continuously traveling, of a host of international summits and meetings at the highest level, few of the former functions of an ambassador survive. Nevertheless, a good many of the diplomatic routines that exist at the beginning of the twenty-first century continue to revolve around fictions inherited from other times. There is a lot in diplomacy that needs to be depurated, refined and made more sincere in order to adapt it to the pace of the new realities.

According to paragraph 1 of article 3 of the 1961 Vienna Convention, the main functions of a diplomatic mission are: a) to represent the accredited State before the host State, b) to protect the interests of the accredited State and its nationals in the host State; c) to inform itself by all legal means of the happenings in the host State and relate them to one's own government; and d) to promote and develop economic, cultural and other kinds of relationships between the two States. Many of these functions have been overtaken by the very thrust of change. Heads of state and foreign ministers frequently communicate by telephone or meet periodically, making the mediation of their representatives less and less necessary. Any information which one wishes to obtain about the internal affairs of another State is immediately available through a globalized media or accessible through Internet. From a handful of major capitals it is possible to maintain a systematic flow of official communications with other states through concurrent embassies, leaving the rest in the hands of the telephone, fax, e-mail and honorary consulates. And so on and so forth.

In the midst of the revolutions in information technology and telecommunications, permanent bilateral missions have lost a good part of their reason for being. This, at least, would seem to be the logical move for states of a middling or minor rank. Globalization submerges us in an international context which presents more challenges and requires us to cover more fronts than in the past, but at the same time, it places in our hands instruments that allow us to have access to the world without leaving our homes. Many of the new courses of diplomacy should be defined in the light of this paradox.

THE EUROPEAN REBELLION

The economic culture of continental Europe shaped itself into distinct variants of the capitalist model. Thus, one speaks of Rhenish, Alpine or French capitalism, each with its particular characteristics. Nevertheless, putting them into a wider context, we may speak of a set of common denominators which have distinguished the economic system of Europe from that of the American-Anglo-Saxon one.

If the liberal American-Anglo-Saxon model is based on what might be called an economy of stock-holders, that of Europe rests on a partnership economy. In the first case, the essence of the model revolves around the need to satisfy the short-term demands of a gigantic number of anonymous stock-holders, who turn their disloyalty to companies into a powerful weapon. The anonymous stock-holder has only one thing in mind: immediate profitability. Any other consideration is alien to him. Under this model, corporations fiercely compete to win the favor of stock-holders, unburdening themselves of all that may weigh down their search for higher yields. Predatory tactics become an inevitable part of a system whose main consideration is the short-term maximization of earnings.

The system of partnership economy, which characterizes continental Europe, is based on the relation of mutual trust that is forged among the diverse actors in the economic process. Corporations, banks and workers establish an organic interweave based on a permanent relationship. Given that this relationship is not a matter of passing circumstance, but a link with a sense of permanence, it tends to emphasize a long-term strategy in which the operative benefits turn out to be reasonably high. What is more, along with economic returns it also takes into account social ones, that is, the price which the system must inevitably pay in order to guarantee harmony and social peace.

These two capitalist models existed side by side for many years, each showing its own virtues and defects. In the end, they responded to different cultural matrixes: different ways of looking at life and deciding what one's priorities are. However, taking the fall of the Berlin Wall as a watershed, in recent years a Darwinian fight for control of world markets has broken out. This is what has become known as globalization. Within the new order which it has created there no longer seems to be any room for considerations other than the maximum yield on capital. In short, it is a matter of a fight to the death for control of the markets, in which those who are less fit are condemned to disappear.

In this new state of things the European system of partnership economy remained without a foundation. Despite a 1.8% annual increase in German productivity between 1979 and 1993, double the U.S. rate, return on capital was only 7% in the German economy between 1974 and 1993, compared to a 9% return in the United States. What can you do at a time when yield on capital becomes the fundamental competitive consideration? Inevitably the Europeans seem to have been left with no choice but to join the liberal Anglo-Saxon model, adopting the predatory practices of the "stock-holders economy". In fact, to meet the demands of a stronger world competitiveness, the Europeans imposed, through the Maastricht agreement, the policy of a single currency. This led them to adopt extremely restrictive fiscal policies at a time when, in the opinion of many experts, they should have concentrated on reactivating their economies.

This process has not been free from hidden costs and surprises. Some years ago, the magazine *Business Week* drew a good picture of the situation: "The competitive pressures of the world economy, joined to the constant sermons of the management gurus of the English-speaking world, have forced Europe into painful reforms, which run from budget cuts to the downsizing of companies. But with unemployment above 12% in Germany and France and economic growth staying below 3% in most of the continent, many Europeans are beginning to cry 'enough!'. Even a part of Europe's managerial elite is questioning the rapid way in which Europe fitted itself into the mould of Anglo-Saxon capitalism".[28]

A generalized sense of frustration is running across Europe and wide sectors of the population believe that the American-Anglo-Saxon formula is contrary to their own culture. Making competitiveness and yield on capital the supreme values contrasts with the traditional criteria of consensus and social cohesion.

What is happening in Europe today is a typical expression of what Paul Krugman has called "the competitive obsession of nations", which leads states to behave as though they were corporations, ignor-

28. February 24, 1997

ing the complexity of social processes. It would appear that these are the inevitable and inescapable costs of global competition. It is easy to anticipate what the political consequences of this new reality will be. Le Pen, Haider, Bossi and the rest of the extreme-right bunch are waiting for them to materialize.

THE IMPORTANCE OF MONEY IN U.S. POLITICS

With every election that takes place in the United States, campaign costs not only increase in a very significant way but the scandals which accompany the subject are increasingly felt as well. It is thus worth the trouble of understanding how the financing of that country's electoral campaigns works. As a result of the high costs which were reached by the 1972 presidential campaign – the most expensive one in U.S. history until then, with investments of 138 million dollars (an insignificant amount compared with the most recent ones) – reforms were introduced in this field in 1974 and 1976. The most important of these reforms was the appearance of the Political Action Committees, usually known as PAC's, which came to transform themselves into the most important institutional development seen in the U.S. political system in recent decades. While the origin of the PAC's went back to 1946, until 1974 they were characterized by the fact that their scope was limited to the labor unions alone. Since the latter date ter date they have turned into the most important mechanism for financing electoral campaigns in the United States. The PAC's are not only able to defray the campaign costs of any candidate, but they also provide any kind of consultant, logistical and operational help to a candidate.

Any corporation, chamber of industry or commerce, ethnic group, ideological organization or association of any kind may form its own Political Action Committee, with the aim of giving electoral contributions and help to their candidates of choice. We thus find PAC's of the corporate kind (the "Philip Morris Political Action Committee" or the "General Dynamics Voluntary Political Contribution Plan") and those drawn from trade and professional associations (the PAC's of the American Medical Association, the American Bankers Association or the National Auto Dealers Association). But there are also PAC's of an ideological nature (the "National Conservative Political Action Committee" or the "Fund for a Conservative Majority"). There also exist what are called the "single issues" committees, that is, associations with a single theme (animal rights, the right to abortion, etc.). There are other ones of an ethnic kind, representing Italians, Rumanians and so forth. The "National Political Action Committee" (NAT-PAC), for example, is one of the 75 that represent the Jewish-American community.

As a result of all this, the PAC's have become the "armed wings" of the U.S. pressure groups, reflecting their different orientations and diversity. As the

Oxford Analytica think tank noted in 1986: "The PAC's give pressure groups a high rank and influence which exceeds all that has been known up to now and this has been achieved at the expense of the political parties".[29] Under this scheme of electoral financing, the loyalty of any legislator or elected public official will be more in harmony with the PAC's than with the political parties. The reason for this is simple and is well explained by the following words of Thomas R. Dye and Harmon Zeigler: "The electorate that matters to a legislator is made up active elites which control the economic resources of his electoral district or state. In an agricultural environment it will be the farmers. In the Southwest it will be the oil men and the ranchers. In the mountain states it will be the mining interests. In the northern part of New England it will be the timber, fishing and granite interests. In the central part of Pennsylvania it will be the steel interests".[30]

In short, any politician who depends on campaign contributions for his survival will try to satisfy those who can finance his career, no matter whether they are business, ideological or other kinds of groups. It is not in vain that many affirm that politicians are now being controlled by interest groups. The curious thing is that when the electoral reform which gave rise to these committees was introduced, the intention was exactly the opposite. That is, to limit

29. *Op. cit.*, p. 327
30. *Op. cit.*, pp. 107 and 108

the amount of contributions that the pressure groups could make, subjecting them to specific regulations. In fact, each PAC may only make a direct contribution of 5,000 dollars per candidate. A direct contribution is understood to be that in which there has been a prior agreement between the PAC and the candidate and where the PAC asks for concrete favors from the candidate in exchange for the money it gives him. The problem is that the conditions of the so-called "indirect contributions" were never regulated, that is, those for which there was no formal agreement between the PAC and the candidate. In this last case there is no limit to the amount of the electoral donation. In practice, however, there is nothing to stop a tacit, instead of an express, agreement between he who gives and he who receives the money. This being so, a voting record in Congress that satisfies the interests of a given pressure group – for example, the tobacco industry – may guarantee enormous campaign contributions for a given legislator, even when the legislator has not made a "direct sale" of his vote. A typical case of this is former presidential candidate Bob Dole, who systematically voted in favor of the interests of the tobacco industry and consistently received favors from it. Among the most respected and at the same time the most implacable PAC's are those of the Jewish community, which not only contribute generously to those who favor the cause of Israel, but also harshly punish those who do not. The center of the organizational matrix which unites the dozens of Jewish PAC's is the celebrated "American Israel Public Affairs Committee" (AIPAC), which keeps a meticulous account of every legislator's voting record on Israel.

As the magazine *Newsweek* correctly observed: "The PAC's have done a lot to convince Americans that politicians may be bought and sold. The PAC's should be abolished".[31]

POLITICAL ACHROMATOPSY

The traditional political division into left and right goes back to the times of the French Revolution. It came from the location of the benches on which the radical and moderate bands sat in the National Assembly. Because of its descriptive facility, the term jelled and it has lasted to the present time. For the rest, bipolar logic was ideal for supporting this distinction. The East was the left, the West was the right and the local and regional conflicts that fell within this pattern were transformed into conflicts between the right and the left.

After the fall of the Berlin Wall, however, this distinction lost any practical meaning. In fact, during the death rattle of communism in the Soviet Union, the old communist apparatus and those who supported it were said to belong to the right, while those who advocated a turn to the West and capital-

31. October 28, 1999

ism were described as belonging to the left. In the same way, the biggest criticisms of free trade – the fundamental paradigm of the right during the long years of the Cold War – came from people like Perot, Buchanan and Le Pen, that is, the extreme wing of the present right. In fact, this is consistent with the view of a liberal thinker like Isaiah Berlin, who regards economic liberalism as left-wing for its opposition to the State power based on the force of tradition, which is of the right. How can we know, then, what is right and what is left in the midst of this whirlpool of new criteria and new interpretations?

Some years ago, one of the most eminent intellectuals of Italy, Norberto Bobbio, undertook the task of interpreting these two classic terms in the light of the new realities. His book *Right and Left* broke all sales records in Europe. The problem is that, after wading through 153 highly-erudite pages, the reader of the book winds up being as confused as he was at the beginning. The closest Bobbio comes to defining where each of these concepts lies is when he tells us that freedom may be equally of the right or the left, while equality is a strictly left-wing ideal. Although the conclusions of this analyst leave us with a lot of doubts, his reflections on the matter turn out to be highly illuminating.

One of the most significant paragraphs in Bobbio's book is the following: "In the ever more complex political universe of the great societies, particularly the great democratic societies, the too sharp separation, the dichotomatic view, of politics turns out to be insufficient... In a plural universe like that of the great democratic societies, where there are many games in play and convergences and divergences are produced that make the most varied combinations feasible, it is no longer possible to speak in terms of antithesis, of alternatives: of right or left; or say that what is not right is left and vice versa. This objection is pertinent but not decisive. The distinction between a right and a left does not exclude the drawing of a continuous line on which, between the initial left and the final right, there exist intermediate positions that occupy the ample space between the two extremes. There is nothing odd about the fact that gray appears between white and black. But the existence of gray does not mean that white and black do not exist".[32]

What Bobbio means here is that the broad gray area has become the dominant characteristic of politics and ideas nowadays. In his thought and action, the contemporary human being inevitably combines positions that are advanced in some respects and conservative in others. It is the distinguishing mark of a society which is evolving with such an astonishing fluidity. As Bobbio correctly observes: "The analytical spirit should not forget that reality is always richer than abstract categories, which must be continually revised in order to include new realities or new interpretations of old realities".[33]

---

32. *Droit et Gauche*, Paris, Editions de Seuil, 1995, pp. 45 and 46
33. *Ibidem*, pp. 26 and 27

To resume, to continue to insist on emphatic classifications between left and right or classify people in this way is the equivalent of suffering from intellectual colorblindness. Achromatopsy, it is worth remembering, is that disease which reduces the visual spectrum of the victim to a world in black and white.

THE UNITED KINGDOM: BETWEEN THE CONTINENT AND THE SEA

The future of the United Kingdom is inseparable from that of the European Union. Great Britain has entered into a long-term marriage with the European continent. There is a lot of history behind this decision. A history of constant comings and goings between the sea which surrounds her and extended her dominion to remote parts, and the European continent facing her coast.

In 1558, the French reconquered the last English possession on French territory: Calais. It was the last prize of the Hundred Years' War, which ended in 1475, that the British had managed to keep. With the fall of Calais an end was put to England's ancient territorial ambitions on the European continent. Henceforth, and except for a limited participation in three European conflicts during the eighteenth century, Britain's continental policy was completely eclipsed. This would drive it into a policy of maritime expansion, which, with the passing of time, would convert it into the greatest imperial power of all time. Nevertheless, turning its back on Europe had its costs. The hegemonic policy of Napoleon at the beginning of the nineteenth century caused Great Britain to violently awake from its insular torpor and find itself subjected to a continental blockade which stretched from Russia to Spain.

In this manner, the English understood that a continent controlled by a hostile power represented a mortal threat. The preceding isolation became untenable and in its place arose what was called the "continental commitment". This was based on the idea that England would not be able to ignore the affairs of Europe. Nevertheless, it limited its participation in such affairs to extreme situations and concrete dangers to the balance of power in Europe. By virtue of such a policy, the English refused to participate in what became known as the "System of Congresses", by which the countries who defeated Napoleon joined together to persecute the liberal and nationalist ideas which had emerged all over Europe.

Little by little, however, Great Britain began to give way to the temptation of politics, participating in European affairs of every kind and forgetting about the limits of its "commitment". From 1826 onwards it followed a long interventionist route, which included initiatives like the following: the defense of the constitutional Portuguese government by British forces; an active support for the cause of Greek independence; intervention in the foundation of the kingdom of Greece; participation in the Russian-Turkish disputes and intervention against Russia in the Crimean War; support for the cause of Italian unification; an active intervention in the framework of Russian, Austro-Hungarian and German relations with Turkey, an intervention that brought England to the point of being involved in a new war; the Mutual Aid Treaty with France; participation in the 'Triple Entente' with France and Russia, against the 'Triple Alliance' of Germany, the Austro-Hungarian empire and Italy; and the Mutual Aid Treaty with Belgium.

In this way, the United Kingdom came to transform itself into an active participant in the squabbles of Europe. The inevitable result of this policy was the loss of a million men on the battlefields of France and Turkey during the First World War. At the end of this terrible conflict, Great Britain incredulously shook its head at the extremes to which its continental policy had driven it. It was the same kind of disbelief which it had felt a century before, when it had contemplated the consequences of its isolation. And if the result of its previous isolationism had been to turn its gaze towards Europe, the result of its continental policy now led it once more into a new stage of isolationism.

This ebb and flow led it to turn its back on Europe and fix its attention on its broad imperial horizons. For the rest, this policy was accompanied by a significant abandonment of the arms race and an emphasis on the economic and social problems of the British people. The country fell into an insular torpor again, turning a deaf ear to the solitary warnings of Churchill, who spoke out against the dangers of a Germany that was becoming more and more powerful. In 1939, a country which had thought that it would be able to maintain itself at the margin of a European conflict violently awoke again, a conflict which was an inevitable and direct result of its previous inaction. Reliving its experience of the Napoleonic epoch, Great Britain had to confront a continent that was overrun by the enemy and endure for two years the weight of a solitary war. It looked like the United Kingdom was inevitably condemned to learn its lessons too late.

The end of the Second World War gave rise to the beginning of its gradual interment of its imperial policy and the renovation of its continental one. This continental policy found its counterweight, however, in a new objective: the Atlantic Alliance. That is, its privileged relationship with the United States and the perception that European security fit within the framework of an alliance with the Americans. The ambivalence of priorities between the European continent and Washington made De Gaulle deeply distrustful of the British and led him to oppose their entrance into the European Community, since he considered them to be a "Trojan horse" of the Americans. In some manner, Britain's close links with the United States were a natural extension of its old maritime instincts.

The United Kingdom continues to move between its commitment to Europe and its special relationship with the United States: between Brussels and Washington. Maintaining, to be sure, a prudent distance from the greater uniformity of criteria and policies of its European partners and at the same time, playing the role of a mature councilor to its transatlantic ally.

THE TRIVIALITY OF POWER

Some words uttered in 1954 by Pierre Mendés-France, then Prime Minister of France, are still famous: he said that it was easier for him to replace the King of Morocco than a minor police official in his own country. This phrase gives a good summary of the paradoxes of power in the midst of a democratic setting subject to diverse institutional restrictions. The ambivalence between the possibilities and the limits of power represents one of the most curious phenomena of our times. Nevertheless, nowhere else does this ambivalence reach the extremes that are seen in the case of the President of the United States. He is, at one and the same time, an all-powerful personage, with the capacity to unleash a nuclear holocaust, and an official hemmed in by an endless number of petty restrictions. Exploring the limits of his office is the best way of understanding the paradoxes of power.

The first of the limitations that is imposed on the President of the United States arises from what happens within the very precincts of the White House.

His close advisors enjoy a great capacity of manipulation. Morton Halperin, a top official of the National Security Council in the days of Nixon, has left us a genial list of the "ten commandments" for manipulating the President. They represent a glossary of the formulas needed to nullify his power: "1. – Withdraw from the President's attention all information that is in conflict with your own intentions. 2.- Only tell the President that which is needed to convince him of the rightness of your own option. 3.- Present your own option in the midst of two plainly unacceptable alternatives, with the aim of giving the President an illusion of choice…".[34] This decalogue of Halperin clearly illustrates the first link in the chain of limitations on his power which bind the Head of State.

Next comes the resistance of the bureaucracy at the level of the Executive Power itself. Reading the memoirs of Nixon, Carter or Kissinger is the best way of finding out about the permanent frustrations of the President in the face of the bureaucratic "ill will" towards carrying out received orders. Listen to Kissinger: "Orders to this effect were given, but our military apparatus resists any interference with strategic doctrine, even when it comes from the White House… When I took up my post, the ex-Secretary of Defense, Robert McNamara, told me that he too had tried to provide the President with more options in strategic matters. He finally gave up, he told

34. Cited by Thomas Dye and Harmon Zeigler, *Op. cit.*, p. 294

me, because of bureaucratic opposition". In another of many similar observations Kissinger writes: "The procedures of the Department of State are well designed to encourage bureaucratic stubbornness. Bureaucratically unpopular orders may be ignored in a variety of ways. Through a clever exegesis, they may be interpreted in such a way that they give a result which is as close as possible to what the Department wanted in the first place; their execution may be interminably delayed; leaks to the press and Congress may sabotage a policy by causing polemics".[35]

In third place, there are the traditional conflicts between the President and the Congress. As a starting point to this situation, we find gigantic gaps in the U.S. Constitution when it comes to defining the respective competences of the Executive and Legislative branches. A constitution that was composed in the eighteenth century, having in mind thirteen agricultural provinces which had agreed to independence, still governs the destinies of the greatest super-power ever seen in history. The result of all this is a gigantic heap of responsibilities that are not constitutionally-assigned, which have had to be defined through a permanent confrontation between the White House and Congress. From Franklin Roosevelt to Lyndon Johnson, the constitutional void allowed for an unprecedented increase of presidential power. Starting in 1965, however, the pendulum swung the other way. It was the start of a congressional on-

35. *Mis Memorias*, Buenos Aires, Editorial Atlántida, 1979, p. 162

slaught which, supported by the silence of the Constitution itself, has imposed one limit after another on the power of the White House.

Another of the links that hem in the exercise of presidential power is the press. In the nineteen-sixties, two historic decisions by the Supreme Court granted a veritable "letter of marque" to the media of social communication in their treatment of confidential matters. The first of these was the case of the "Pentagon Papers". On that occasion the *New York Times* and the *Washington Post* set out to publish secret documents about the management of the Vietnam War which had been stolen from official archives. Opposing the White House's efforts to prohibit the publication of this material on the grounds that it would have disastrous consequences for national security, the Supreme Court upheld the media's right to inform the public. The second of these rulings was the case of the "New York Times vs. Sullivan". In that decision the Court declared that a public official who has been defamed by the press has no right to claim damages, even when the allegations against him may turn out to be false, except when he can prove that the accusations are the result of a "malicious intention". The result of the so-called "Sullivan Rule" has been that the media enjoy a virtual impunity when it comes to destroying public careers. The President of the United States has not been an exception to the exercise of this unlimited power given to the press.

Finally, we find the limits which public opinion imposes on presidential power. In the midst of the permanent conflict seen between the Executive and Legislative powers over the definition of their own areas of competence, the Supreme Court has frequently refused to act as an arbiter. Arguing that most of these disputes are of a "political" and not a "juridical" nature, the Supreme Court has left the resolution of their mutual conflicts to the contenders, without interfering with the results. This has enabled decision-making power to flow towards public opinion, which has become the final arbiter of many of the major institutional debates. In this manner, emotional criteria and simplistic moralisms have been responsible for settling complex political-institutional problems. Within such parameters no room is left for government actions that are not completely transparent and the President of the United States is frequently judged by rules that are more appropriate for a primary school than a world super-power.

An extreme case of the ambivalence between the possibilities and limits of power was seen during the Clinton administration. At the same time that the President of the United States had in his hands the power to order an attack on Iraq, capable of unleashing a dangerous chain reaction, he faced the pressures of the Lewinski scandal. The same all-powerful figure who with a single word could put into motion a devastating war machine lacked the power to prevent his secretary from being summoned before a court to testify about his intimate life, nor could he stop the press from freely talking about his sexual preferences. What is more, he could not avoid being summoned himself to testify about his sexual experiences with a White House assistant. Never before in the history of the great powers had things come to such an extreme. In this case, however, what most stood out were not the paradoxes of power, but the most absolute trivialization of it.

"SEXYGATE"

The United States seems like a gigantic jigsaw puzzle that has not been assembled, like an endless number of loose pieces that are deployed, without order or pattern, on an immense game board. Each sector of the bureaucracy, each segment of Congress, each pressure group, each ethnic group, pushes in its own direction, with a complete autonomy of criterion and selfishness of purpose. Even foreign governments, no matter whether they camouflage themselves behind local ethnic groups or not, have the capacity to pull towards their own side. To this is joined what Erich Fromm has called the "collective neurosis" of the United States, which may be explained by the following words of the journalist Jerry Adler: "In the United States adherence to even the smallest movements is measured in millions of persons. The identity of everyone is politicized, not only in terms of race, ethnic group, religion and language, but also in terms of sex, sexual behavior, age, dress, diet and personal habits". (*Newsweek*, July 10, 1995).

In the face of this reality the media are seen as the last resort, as the ultimate center of power, as the place from which it would be reasonable to expect a thrust towards rationality. Such expectations are not gratuitous. They represent the only factor of power that is relatively homogenous in U.S. society. As we mentioned before, Oxford Analytica made the following observation a few years ago: "The three national television networks (ABC, CBS and NBC), the two major news magazines (Time, Newsweek), the Associated Press (which now has the field to itself due to the virtual collapse of UPI), the New York Times, the Wall Street Journal and the Washington Post: from the late fifties to the eighties these nine organizations (two of which are under the same management), along with the small elite of specialists who have access to them, have enjoyed an immense influence as judges of the political process and key influences in the national political agenda".[36]

For their part, Thomas Dye and Harmon Zeigler pointed out the following: "The true power of the mass communication media consists of deciding on what has to be decided. This may be described as the definition of the national agenda. Those aspects of society which are not considered to be a crisis or a problem by the communication media will never become topics of political decision. Clearly, then, the power of deciding what constitutes a crisis or a problem comes to represent a critical element in the

36. *Op. cit.*, p. 153

political task". Dye and Zeigler add the following. "The top executives of the television networks form a small and cohesive fraternity. They are in permanent contact with the editors of the New York Times, the Washington Post, Newsweek and some of the great press chains, with whom they exchange their points of view".[37]

This being so, in the face of a society like the American one, which is characterized by dispersion, fragmentation and the absence of a joint vision, we encounter a number of social communication media which are extremely powerful and whose main characteristic is their internal cohesion. It is true that both CNN and a number of other press media with a national coverage have appeared since the paragraphs cited above were published. Nevertheless, the essential character of the main U.S. communication media, that of being a "cohesive fraternity", has not changed.

The media elite is not only cohesive, but it also enjoys, by virtue of the very nature of its activity, a global perspective on events. In other words, it has the capacity to pick up the loose and disconnected pieces of a fragmented scenario and present them in an articulated way. Being subject itself to the surplus of available information, this elite must carry out the process of arranging and selecting it in order to focus the collective attention on a specific set of events and figures. This gives it the possibility of carrying out the task which is most needed by a society that seems to

37. *Op. cit.*, pp. 149 and 150

have lost itself in an endless number of small labyrinths: create a mechanism of synthesis.

In short, an elite that has the power to define the national political agenda of the U.S. and which at the same time has the ability to do it in an organic way bears a very public responsibility. The more structured its focus on the reality of the U.S., the more focussed the very life of the nation should be.

In the face of this challenge, however, the major communication media have evaded their responsibility, opting for the easy way out. They have a predilection for what are known as "hot topics" and striking events. A rapid and disjointed succession of isolated deeds constitutes the essence of the prevailing informative process. The above-mentioned Dye and Zeigler give us the following explanation of this: "The criteria for selecting what is newsworthy are not intellectual but emotional. The political or social significance of a story is much less important than its capacity to attract attention; the fundamental requisite is that the stories will not turn out to be boring and that they will manage to catch the interest of people with a short attention span. The tendency is towards the dramatic, the sensational, the extreme... The business of television networks is to attract mass audiences and sell them to the publicity media. To attract viewers, the networks focus news coverage on conflictive aspects, scandals, corruption, confrontation and sex".[38]

38. *Ibidem*, p. 155

The above does not mean, however, that the media assume that their business is entertainment, refusing to define the political agenda of the country. On the contrary, they seek the best of both words: newsworthy entertainment as a formula for increasing profits and, at the same time, the exercise of power which derives from their capacity to decide on what has to be decided.

A typical example is the famous "sexygate" scandal which kept the Clinton presidency in suspense. Curiously, U.S. public opinion, leaving its traditional puritanism aside, wound up declaring, through the different opinion polls, that the intimate side of Clinton's life mattered much less than his presidential performance. Nevertheless, the communication media insisted on transforming the case into a three-ring circus. To resume, this affair contained the fundamental ingredients of a major news story in the United States: sex and power.

While "sexygate" was going on, seeming to turn Clinton into a political cripple, the Asian crisis was threatening to infect Wall Street and the rest of the world, and endanger the global economy. Nevertheless, the U.S. media elite had already decided on what had to be decided, employing its usual criterion: entertainment.

THE NAKED EMPEROR

There has never been much clarity about the precise framework of competence granted to the President of the United States. There is a simple reason for
this: the Constitution that governs that country was
created more than two centuries ago, to fit the circumstances of a handful of agricultural colonies which
had declared their freedom. The drafters of the Constitution of that incipient State could never have imagined the extraordinary political, economic and
demographic evolution that the nation would experience. That being so, the branches of the government
of the United States have had to learn to coexist with
an imprecise definition of their powers.

The lack of clarity in this matter has led to the flour-
ishing of what are known as implicit constitutional
powers. The eminent U.S. constitutional expert Louis
Fisher made the following observation: "When we
venture into the field of the functioning of the branches
of government, we must deal with a surprising range
of competences that are not expressly conferred. They
have been defined in diverse ways: implicit, inherent, incidental, inferred, attached. It is clear that we
are dealing with powers created by custom... In the
end, no matter what the name that is given to them,
the result is the same: the exercise of powers that
have not been granted by the Constitution".[39] In the

39. *Constitutional Conflicts between Congress and the President,*
Princeton, Princeton University Press, 1985, pp. 18 and 19

course of U.S. history, this tortuous terrain of competences that have not been expressly conferred by the Constitution has given rise to heated debates about the nature and the extent of presidential powers. It was during the successive presidencies of Theodore Roosevelt and William Howard Taft, at the beginning of the twentieth century, that the interpretative gap that bedevils these powers reached what was perhaps its fullest expression. Roosevelt, a man with a keen political instinct and a strong sense of authority, affirmed that the President had the right to do all that was not expressly denied by the Constitution and the law. Taft, who was much more of a jurist than a politician, stated that the President only had the right to what had been expressly granted by the Constitution and the law. In other words, for the former all that was not specifically prohibited was allowed, while for the latter all that was not specifically allowed was prohibited. In this subjective interpretation of the orbit of competences, one saw the difference between a strong and a weak presidency.

There have been periods in U.S. history when the prevailing opinion was that the presidency should be strong. There have also been periods in which the majority opinion supported the contrary position. Between the end of the Second World War and 1965, the critical moment of the Vietnam War, there was a broad consensus of agreement about the President's need to enjoy extensive powers. Thenceforth, as a result of the extremes the Vietnam War had led to, there came into being a current of opinion which sought to establish precise limits to the exercise of presidential power.

In the Clinton period, the so-called implicit presidential powers were attacked again. The reasons, however, had nothing to do with another Vietnam. It only needed two women to bring about the downfall of some of the privileges which had been identified with the presidential institution since time immemorial. The scandals revolving around Paula Jones and Monica Lewinsky were behind it all.

In May 1997, the Supreme Court ruled that the lawsuit brought by Paula Jones against an acting President could proceed. This made the exigencies of presidential authority subordinate to the need to respond to a civil action. It now means that any President may be brought to trial during his term of office, by reason of any civil suit – the infinite number of which have become a notorious feature of the U.S. judicial system.

Nevertheless, it was the Lewinsky case which had the most significant implications for the use of implicit presidential powers. Two factors played a role in this. On the one hand, there was the lack of consideration shown towards the institution of the presidency by the Independent Prosecutor, Kenneth Starr. And on the other, there was the determination, on the part of President Clinton and his advisors, to not yield ground without fighting for it, centimeter by centimeter, in the courts. For this reason, it became necessary to unravel the juridical foundation of a number of prerogatives which custom had assigned to the President but which had never been expressly granted. As was to be expected, the courts were not able to find any legal precedents that would support the privileges in question and so proceeded to reject them. The result of all this was that the presidency was shown to be defenseless and the constitutional leader of the country was transformed into an ordinary man.

On previous occasions when presidents had been questioned, as in the Watergate case, the prosecutors had behaved with sufficient moderation and prudence. Richard Ben-Veniste, a veteran prosecutor in Watergate, revealed that those who led the investigation against President Nixon "would never have dreamt" of taking things to the extreme that Prosecutor Starr did. But it is also true that in the past, when their prerogatives were questioned, Presidents preferred to negotiate discreetly, yielding in some cases, so that they would not have to put the juridical-constitutional validity of their powers to the test. By wanting to gain time at any cost in the Lewinsky case, the advisors of President Clinton recurred to the courts and appealed against the adverse decisions. By doing so, they wound up making evident something which many had known but did not wish to recognize: that the Emperor has no clothes.

THE COMING BALANCE OF POWER

In 1998, *The Economist* published an interesting article entitled "The coming balance of power". It set out to forecast the potential power, over the next thirty years, of the world's main countries and regions. Its conclusion was clear: only China would be in a position to tread on the heels of the United States as a super-power.[40]

Making use of the classic factors that determine the foundations of a state's power, *The Economist* came up with a system of comparative scores, extending over the next three decades. According to its ranking, the United States obtained 14 points, China 13 and the other competitors were far behind. Russia itself only obtained 8 points, despite its nuclear weaponry. What is more, said the magazine, China shows a combination of factors that are not found in other countries or regions of the world: a solid national identity, a long-nurtured desire for revenge resulting from humiliations suffered over many years and economic strength. All of this gives it the vocation of a super-power.

What *The Economist* did not analyze was the direction that the relation between these two future super-powers would take. In this sense, the key questions that we have to ask ourselves are: What will become the fundamental reason for rivalry between China and the United States? Could this rivalry lead to an armed conflict?

40. January 3 and 9, 1998

It does not seem likely that the ideological factor will become the key motive for conflict between these countries. In contrast with the ideological confrontation that arose during the Cold War, which postulated the existence of two irreconcilable value systems, this factor does not seem to be the sign of future times. The Chinese have not only set out on the path of capitalism with a strong sense of purpose, but they have also recovered the ancestral pragmatism inherited from Confucius.

Nor does it seem likely that Chinese ambitions towards Taiwan and the U.S. guardianship over it will be the central factor in a possible crisis in the future. The same Chinese pragmatism to which we have referred will surely lead to a peaceful and negotiated settlement between Beijing and Taipei. The Chinese takeover of Hong Kong is a hopeful sign in this respect.

The essence of a future confrontation may revolve around the tensions and rivalries deriving from trade. These, joined to the factors of Chinese nationalism and that country's historic desire for revenge, may become the most probable source of conflict. Stephen S. Cohen, the well-known Berkeley University professor, has been arguing that the perennially unsettled nature of the relations between Washington and Tokyo is on the point of repeating itself in the case of Washington and Beijing. Nevertheless, in contrast with Japan, China is turning into a first-rate military power.

The tensions that China's position as a mass exporter might create would be difficult to handle. Nowadays the dizzy growth of Chinese exports (joined to those of Hong Kong and Taiwan) have led to a 40 billion dollar trade surplus with the United States. Nevertheless, the China of today is barely a pale reflection of what that country might become over the next thirty years. The Chinese leader Jiang Zemin aspires to maintain an average annual growth rate of 6.5% during the next 25 years. This would transform China into an industrial super-power, with a GDP on the order of 5 trillion dollars. China is already a gigantic exporter of goods with a low aggregate value. If it can manage to cure the ills of its state economic system and make its financial system efficient, it would easily be able to mobilize around 400 billion dollars of annual savings, emerging as a rival of Japan, the West and its own neighbors, the Asian tigers, in industries that run from steel to heavy machinery.

Could the competition in trade between the United States and China lead to an armed conflict? Some years ago George Friedman and Meredith Lebard published an interesting book about the Japanese-U.S. rivalry. The book turned into a best-seller in Japan and also achieved big sales in the United States. The thesis advanced by these writers was simple. Japan, as the great importer of raw materials that it is, cannot allow the bloodstream that nourishes its economy to depend on another nation. Especially when this other nation, the United States, has interests that are fundamentally opposed to its own. This would lead Japan to attempt to secure its own maritime supply routes, which would inevitably create the need to have a navy that is able to compete with the U.S. navy.[41]

A rivalry for control of the Asian seas, together with permanent trade tensions, would create a highly emotional situation capable of provoking an armed conflict. According to Friedman and Lebard, in all of the public opinion polls published from 1988 onwards Americans saw Japan as their main enemy, even in the period when the Soviet Union was still in existence. They mention, as an example, a poll carried out by McGraw-Hill, in which 22% of the Americans who were questioned saw the Soviet Union as a rival, while 68% replied that Japan was the biggest threat.

The argument of Friedman and Lebard has already become outmoded in the face of the reality of the Japanese economic crisis. Nevertheless, its premises will be perfectly applicable, and with much more reason, to the case of U.S.-Chinese relations. By the year 2015 China will be importing 7 million barrels of petroleum daily, vital for its economic survival. The need to control the maritime routes along which this vital sap of energy flows will inevitably lead China into a rivalry with the United States, which has always seen the Pacific as a *mare nostrum*. However, in contrast with Japan, China is a military power of great significance, with access to nuclear armaments.

41. *The Coming War with Japan*, New York, St. Martin's Press, 1991

The combination of a power with the extraordinary industrial might of Japan and a first-rate military strength contains all of the elements that could unleash an armed conflict with the United States. Especially when China's nationalism and historic desire for revenge are taken into account.

THE U.N. AND WORLD PEACE

The birth of the United Nations took place within the context of a certain tradition of U.S. idealism. This same tradition which always made President Woodrow Wilson feel so close to God and so certain about the course which world affairs had to follow. It was the same tradition which sustained Franklin D. Roosevelt, when, in the Yalta Summit, he made innumerable concessions to Stalin over Eastern Europe with the aim of winning Stalin's consent to the creation of the U.N. The clearest expression of Roosevelt's idealism is found in a celebrated phrase uttered by his Secretary of State, Cordell Hull, about the role which the U.N. would play. Hull said: "There will no longer be any need for spheres of influence, alliances, balances of power or any other special arrangements like those which, in an unhappy past, nations needed to safeguard their security". In other words, the United Nations would become the guarantor of peace and collective security, without the need for any of the mechanisms employed for those ends throughout history.

It was precisely this extreme idealism, this heavy burden of hopes, that led to the harsh disappointment that later arose with regard to the United Nations. Abba Eban, the famous former Foreign Relations Minister of Israel, referred to this in an interesting article published in the magazine *Foreign Affairs*. According to Eban, the thesis of collective security which surrounded the formation of the U.N. and which was a clear expression of Hull's words did not turn out to be realistic.[42]

According to Eban, the view that the U.N. would be able to ensure world peace was based on six basic precepts, none of which took into account the harsh realities of international life. The first of these is that States would identify their own security with world security and that, in this sense, they would be willing to involve themselves in situations which were remote from their own national interests. The second, that States would have the capacity to achieve agreement on what constitutes an act of aggression in each particular situation. The third, that the aggressor would turn out to be so weak or isolated that it would be possible to confront him with stronger international forces. Fourth, that States, out of their desire to preserve peace and the world order, would be willing to punish their closest allies in the same way that they would their adversaries. Fifth, that States would be willing to renounce their independent power of decision so as to place their armed

42. September/October 1995

forces at the disposal of the U.N. in areas where their national interest was not at stake. Sixth, that public debate within the framework of an international body would become a more effective method of achieving peace accords than discreet negotiation between the interested parties.

In the opinion of Eban, all of the above ignored the intrinsic selfishness of States and overestimated a collective body's ability to achieve peace. It is evident that, although Eban's realism is too extreme, in the end it is a realism that puts in a truer perspective the excesses which surround the ideal of collective security on which the U.N. rests. During the 45 years that followed the creation of this international body it was the agreements reached between the super-powers, not the collective action of the U.N., that managed to achieve peace in most of the situations of conflict.

In fact, the logic of bi-polarity offered the possibility of controlling the intensity and duration of the conflicts created by the Cold War, on the basis of accords between the super-powers themselves. When the tension arising from a local or regional confrontation went beyond certain limits, the United States and the Soviet Union were able to impose a negotiated agreement on the contending parties: it was only after these top-level agreements were made that the U.N. Security Council was able to enter onto the scene as an instrument for carrying out decisions already made. The 1956 Suez crisis, the 1958 crisis in Lebanon, the 1960 Congo crisis, the 1965 crisis on the Indian subcontinent and the 1973 Middle East crisis were evidences of this reality.

The exception to the above rule occurred during the Korean War in 1950. This happened for the simple reason that the Soviet Union's temporary withdrawal from the Security Council allowed the United States and its allies to manage collective security in their own way without the Russian veto. The fact is that if ensuring peace on the basis of the six points mentioned by Abba Eban is extremely difficult, it is even more so when the veto rule applies. That is, when any one of the Permanent Members of the U.N. Security Council can paralyze the Council's actions in order to serve its own interests.

After the profound crisis and subsequent collapse of communism, conditions arose which enabled only one of the members – the United States – to lead collective security. But in this case, once again, the U.N. Security Council came to act as an instrument that merely served aims defined at other levels. Nevertheless, both Washington and the other permanent members of the Security Council soon discarded what, in the times of the first Bush, was called the "New World Order".

As has happened since the eve of history, the great events of the world still continue to be dominated by spheres of influence, alliances and balances of power, and not simply, as Cordell Hull believed, by the activities of a collective body. For the rest, we should not forget the impressive list of peacemaking events which have occurred beyond the sphere of the U.N. from 1945 to the present time. Among these we might cite the following: the end of the Berlin blockade, the Treaty of Rome which established the European Community, the end of the Algerian war of independence, U.S. recognition of communist China, the Salt 1 Treaty, the Panama Canal treaties, the *Ostpolitik* of Willy Brandt, the establishment of Zimbabwe, the Helsinki Conference and the 1990 Conference on European Security and Cooperation, the Egyptian-Israeli peace treaties, the Jordanian-Israeli peace treaty, the Israel-PLO accord and the talks between Britain and the IRA, to name only a few.

STATE AND MODERNITY

In 1802 Hegel wrote one of the most important books of the nineteenth century: *The German Constitution*. In it, the German philosopher called for the formation of a unitary German State as an indispensable condition for the advance of the German people into the modern age. At that time, in fact, Germany was divided into a diverse number of kingdoms, principalities, duchies, ecclesiastical territories and autonomous entities. Within this collection of petty states, Austria and Prussia had not only become the two dominant forces, but they were also the only two territories which embodied true States in the modern sense.

In that work, Hegel made reference to the feudal organization that prevailed in Germany and which recognized and guaranteed to each of its members the right to go its own way. It was, in fact, a right defended by all of them and was based on what was known as "German freedom". For Hegel the "freedom" which was the basis of German disunity was nothing more than an anachronism which had made Germany turn her back on history. An anachronism that had kept Germans in a clear state of backwardness with regard to the great national states of Europe, like France and England. Hegel issued a powerful summons for the formation of a true State. Several decades would have to pass, however, for this ideal to be transformed into a reality. It was only in 1871 under Bismarck's leadership that this unitary aspiration resulted in the creation of the modern German State.

In Italy as well – which, like Germany, was divided into multiple kingdoms, principalities and duchies, in addition to a Papal state – a movement that called for the unification of the country came into being from 1815 onwards. The leading intellectual exponent of this movement, which became known as the *Risorgimento,* was Mazzini. He, in contrast to Hegel, who wrote his works in a language that was shared by all Germans, had to write in French. There was a simple reason for it: there were so many dialects and variants of Italian that a single language comprehensible to all Italians did not exist. After long years of conspiracy and fighting, the Italians managed to emerge from the Middle Ages and join the ranks of "modernity". It was on the basis of the formation of that unitary State that another new creation was able to emerge: a language that was common to all Italians.

When men like Hegel, Bismarck, Mazzini, Garibaldi and Cavour advocated and fought for the establishment of unitary states, they were convinced that the logic of history was behind them. They were certain that, by leaving behind territorial and autonomous divisions that had been inherited from the Middle Ages, their nations would enter the modern age and adapt themselves to the demands of the future. How could they have imagined that, at the end of the twentieth century, modernity would be identified with fragmentation, territorial division, the unleashing of a desire for autonomy and the proliferation of diverse languages within the heart of the State itself ?

These tendencies are not new, of course. In the nineteen-thirties, the Spanish Republic had already tried this path, under the mandate of "modernity". One of the most brilliant minds of Spain in all of its history, José Ortega y Gasset, argued in the Constitutional Courts that there was a need to give free rein to regional autonomies. However, it was with the collapse of communism that this process took on its full strength. In fact, we might well say that the Berlin Wall represented the last bulwark, not only of the political against the economic, but also of the ideological against the cultural.

With its fall, the economy came to occupy the dominant space that had been previously reserved for politics. But, at the same time, with the disappearance of ideological barriers, the cultural phenomenon was able to show its strength and vigor.

For many years the matter of identities, a synonym for the cultural, was repressed in the name of ideological impositions. With the shattering of ideologies, the emergence of the cultural became inevitable. Samuel Huntington speaks of this in the following words: "In the post-Cold War world the most important distinctions between peoples are not ideological, political or economic. They are cultural. Peoples and nations are trying to answer the most basic question which human beings may ask themselves: Who are we?... Peoples are defining themselves in terms of ancestry, religion, language, history, values, customs and institutions. These are identified with cultural groups: tribes, ethnic groups, religious communities, nations... Peoples are using politics not only to promote their interests but also to define their identities".[43]

In this new state of things, the march of history points in the direction of cultural particularities. Each community, each city, each region, seeks to find symbols to define its own being. The reaffirmation of local or regional traditions, dialects and particular customs is the current fashion. Inevitably, this can only happen at the expense of the power and unitary sense of the central states. It is not by accident that so many states bear the enemy within their hearts.

43. *Op. cit.,* p.21

What would Hegel or Mazzini say about this curious return to the ideals of the Middle Ages? How could they have imagined that the same values which were in force at the end of the first millennium would reemerge at the end of the second?

THE DRAMATIC TWENTIETH CENTURY

The opening of the twentieth century was full of hope and optimism about the progress of human civilization. The great technical advances which marked the latter part of the nineteenth century seemed to presage the initiation of an age of permanent improvement in the human condition. Within a very short time, however, these illusions were shown to be false. Never before had the world seen wars, genocides, massacres and excesses of every kind that were as irrationally destructive and costly of human life as those of the century we left behind a short time ago.

From the Armenian genocide to the First World War, from the Spanish Civil War to the massacres of Manchuria, from the Second World War to its corollary, the Jewish Holocaust, from the Stalinist purges and slaughters to the war in Biafra and the massacres of Cambodia – the human race has not spared any effort to display its irrationality and tendency to self-destruction. Now armed with the capacity to eliminate any vestige of his presence on earth, thanks to nuclear, biological and chemical weapons, mankind has become aware, as never before, of the vulnerability of his species.

When only a decade was lacking to culminate the twentieth century and the greatest excesses of destruction and violence seemed to have been left behind, the nineties brought a tragic reminder of the fragility of our rational condition. The ethnic topic has become a detonator of limitless hatred and violence.

Between the end of 1993 and the end of 1995 more than 100,000 persons died in Burundi as a result of the massacres caused by ethnic hatred. In Rwanda, eight hundred thousand persons died after the assassination of its President in April 1994. These killings were accompanied by the forced displacement from their lands of hundreds of thousands of human beings. In both cases the clashes between the Tutsi and Hutu groups, which are common to both countries, were the cause of the massacres. Wherever you look on the African continent, ethnic identity has become a factor that threatens the survival of the states inherited from the colonial epoch and of civilized life itself.

In Europe also the cost in suffering and human lives which ethnic disputes have brought has been gigantic. The dismembering of the state of Yugoslavia revived some of the worst memories of the Jewish holocaust. With its concentration camps, forced displacements of thousands of human beings, ethnic cleansing and indiscriminate application of terror, the conflict brought the subject of racial superiority to the fore again, along with the supposed territorial right which this implies.

Bosnia left a million human beings displaced from their homes and their ancestral territory and two hundred and fifty thousand deaths. If it had not been for the intervention of NATO, Kosovo might have repeated the Bosnian tragedy. The three raised fingers which symbolized the Serb triumph became a sort of modern swastika. The pain and humiliation of the refugees and victims of ethnic cleansing were intensified by the arrogant spectacle of self-declared racial superiority.

The example given by German reunification – considered to be the first redrawing of national frontiers in the post-war epoch –, followed by the dismantling of the Soviet Union, set off a political hurricane of gigantic proportions. Those of the world's states which were based on a solid national identity were immune to the force of the winds arising from the fall of the Berlin Wall. However, for those which had a multitude of ethnic identities sharing the territory of a single state, the headaches have never stopped growing. In cases like that of Rwanda, Burundi, Yugoslavia and the former Soviet Union, this has led to great tragedies.

It is odd, as well, that Europe, the hub of Western civilization, has ended the century with new testimonies to its indisputable laurels in the field of irrationality and violence. At the very moment that the process of European integration and the subsequent monetary and political union formalized at Maastricht seemed to have redeemed the Old Continent from its past excesses, Bosnia and Kosovo were placing it once more at the summit of man's capacity for self-destruction.

Latin America, which is always despised and given a bad reputation for violence, shows one of the least bloody records of the twentieth century. In comparison with Europe, Asia and Africa, the deaths of the Mexican Revolution, the War of the Chaco, the conflicts between Ecuador and Peru and the violence of Colombia, Central America and the Southern Cone seem like minor affairs. The bad name for violence borne by that region is not easily justified when you look at the historical evidence.

If the turn of the twentieth century was marked by hope and optimism about the human condition, the turn of the twenty-first was accompanied by pessimism, disillusion and fear.

YUGOSLAVIA

In the nineteenth century there emerged a movement which sought the union of the Slavic peoples of southern Europe. This movement, known as "Illyrianism", wanted to integrate into a single State the regions belonging to two great empires: the Austro-Hungarian and the Turkish. It was not until the end of the First World War that this idea was able to become a reality. Croatia, Slovenia and Bosnia-Herzegovina, which had just separated themselves from the Austro-Hungarian empire, united with Serbia and Montenegro, which had formed part of the Turkish empire up to the end of the nineteenth century. The kingdom of Yugoslavia was assembled from these loose pieces of the two lost empires.

The Second World War was devastating for that country. In 1941, Yugoslavia was invaded by Nazi troops and broken up into a number of pieces that were shared out between Germany and its allies, Italy and Hungary. Two large guerrilla groups arose to oppose the invaders. One, a pro-royalist force that sought the liberation of Serbia and the other, a communist one that fought for the liberation of the whole of Yugoslavia. The latter was led by the Secretary General of the Yugoslavian Communist Party, Josip Broz, better known as Tito. It was to left to Tito to become the artificer of his nation's liberation.

Yugoslavia emerged from the Second World War in a totally devastated state. In contrast with the other communist regimes of East Europe, which had come into being simply because of their occupation by Soviet troops, that of Yugoslavia had been self-imposed, basically by the force of arms. This give Marshall Tito's government a freedom of maneuver that was denied to the other communist regimes of the region. Inevitably, this also led to a permanent conflict with Moscow.

It was in its handling of ethnic differences that the Yugoslavian model acquired its most characteristic traits. Five sovereign republics that adhered to a confederation were established. These were Slovenia,

Croatia, Serbia, Montenegro and Bosnia-Herzegovina. Later Macedonia also attained the status of a sovereign republic. For its part, Serbia had two autonomous provinces in its territory: Vojvodina and Kosovo. The legislative branch of this Federal State was made up of a Council of Nationalities, which represented the interests of the six Republics and the two autonomous provinces.

This framework of diverse nationalities was able to function because of the exceptional charisma and personality of Tito, who acted as the great arbiter of the conflicting interests. Like a modern King Solomon he maintained a balance among the warring positions, at times inclining his crosier in one direction and at times in the other. His strategy was clear: to prevent one Republic or sector from becoming strong enough to acquire a dominant position that would endanger the stability of the whole. In synthesis, Tito encouraged a negative balance of forces in which none of the Republics would stand out.

After the death of Tito in 1980 the country went through constant ups and downs under the collective leadership which Tito designed to succeed him. Nevertheless, for better or for worse, the unity of the Federation was maintained. The collapse of communism and the nationalist fever that accompanied it brought to the surface the profound contradictions that lay deep in the soul of that State. Henceforth everything would change.

By the end of the eighties there were two extreme positions in Yugoslavia, one represented by Serbia, the other by Slovenia. While Serbia entered into an authentic nationalist revolution, Slovenia went through an accelerated process of democratization. To ensure a strong Yugoslavia, Tito had always believed that it was necessary to keep Serbia weak. Milosevic came to power by playing the card of Serbian revenge. In order to strengthen Serbia the new nationalist leader would end the autonomy of the two autonomous provinces that existed within that republic: Vojvodina and Kosovo. In the first case this was of little importance, since the majority of its population was Serb. In Kosovo, on the other hand, the immense majority of the population was of Albanian ethnicity. Kosovo's reaction to the suppression of its autonomy led to Serbian repression. This was the final straw for Slovenia, which until then had been patient about Serbian excesses and now decided, along with Croatia, to make itself independent of the Yugoslavian Federation. That was the start of the dismemberment of the Federal State, which in the end would be limited to Serbia and Montenegro.

The Yugoslavian armed forces, under Serbian control, tried without success to prevent the secession of Slovenia and Croatia. Thenceforth the attitude of Serbia and Milosevic changed. It if were no longer possible to maintain a united Yugoslavia, ran their reasoning, then it would at least be possible to integrate all of the Serb populations outside of Serbia into a single unit. Thus the thesis of "Greater Serbia" was imposed. On this basis the Serbian regions of

Croatia were annexed. However, when Bosnia also decided to secede, things became much more difficult. The Serbian populations within that Republic were spread throughout the whole territory, living alongside Croatian and Muslim ones. Milosevic and his accomplices came up with a simple answer: the deliberate and systematic application of terror, as a way of achieving the evacuation of geographical spaces that might be occupied by the Serbs. That was the start of "ethnic cleansing". In November 1995, in the face of NATO pressures and the military offensive by Croatia to recuperate the territories lost to Serbia, the Dayton Accord was signed, which put an end to the Bosnian conflict.

The repression of Kosovo which exhausted Slovenia's patience with Serbia in 1991 also wound up exhausting the patience of NATO with regard to Serbia in 1999. The NATO bombardments that drove the Yugoslavian forces out of Kosovo marked the beginning of the end of the Milosevic regime. In October 2000 the dictator was obliged to recognize that he had been defeated in the elections by Kostunica. A short while later, U.S. and European pressure led Milosevic to be brought before the Hague Tribunal, where he faces accusations of genocide. The saga of Yugoslavia has been dramatic and complex – a drama, which in its final stage, recalled the worst excesses of Nazism, that regime which it had fought against so successfully during the Second World War.

ETHNIC SELF-DETERMINATION

When States break up it is like a divorce between a married couple: the way in which it happens is very important. When such a division results from a negotiation between the parties, things usually turn out much better. Czechoslovakia split into two nations without bloodshed or trauma. The Czechs and the Slovaks had reached agreement about defining the mechanisms that would form the basis of their separation. In Yugoslavia, by contrast, things were done with a bad will. The parties did not negotiate. Even worse, the separation was done on the basis of the most dangerous of methods: ethnic self-determination. That is, the principle by which every ethnic group may choose its own destiny by means of referendum. This, of course, without bothering to negotiate with anyone.

Within this frame of reference, the Croats of Croatia voted to separate themselves from Yugoslavia, but the Serbs of Croatia voted to separate themselves from Croatia and join Serbia. The Croats and Muslims of Bosnia voted to separate themselves from Yugoslavia, but the Serbs of Bosnia voted to separate themselves from Bosnia and join Serbia. And so on and so forth. A process of this nature inevitably led to a bad ending. Above all, when the Serbs, who were the strongest, went through a streak of uncontrolled and aggressive nationalism.

In the absence of a negotiated and organized separation it was evident that the mixture of unchecked ethnic claims and Serbian aggressiveness would lead to a catastrophe. Nevertheless, on June 25, 1991, Slovenia and Croatia unilaterally proceeded to declare their independence, after having decided on it by referendum. The United States and the majority of countries belonging to the European Union disagreed with this decision, knowing that it was the first step towards what might turn into an endless anarchy. Given that the international recognition of Croatia and Slovenia would be a decisive factor in the future course of events, they refused to accept their independence, although it was already an accomplished fact. If, in that moment, the European Community and the United States had insisted upon negotiations between the parties as a precondition for the international recognition of those who had become independent in fact, things might have turned out much better.

Nevertheless, the German government set a course of action that came to complicate everything. Its insistence on recognizing the principle of ethnic self-determination as the basis for the independence of those two Republics represented an inevitable counterweight to the idea of a negotiated settlement. The German attitude was the result of symbolic and emotional considerations. On the one hand, it was argued that a country like Germany, which had been reunified on the basis of the principle of a people's right to self-determination, could not deny this right to others. And, on the other, Germany had a long tradition of mutual sympathy with the Croatians, a people who are openly Germanophile.

In this situation, the European Community's attitude towards the independence of Slovenia and Croatia became divided. On one side there was a majority of nations, led by France and England, which insisted on the need to maintain a prudent attitude, arguing that ethnic self-determination alone was not a sufficient basis for independence. On the other side was Germany, which was a firm defender of the principle of ethnic self-determination as the basis for defining the future of Yugoslavia. The United States followed the position of the former nations. That is, those which called for prudence and insisted on a negotiated and organized dismantling of the Yugoslavian state.

On December 23, 1991, going against the views of its European Community partners and the United States, the Bonn government unilaterally recognized the independence of Croatia and Slovenia. The other countries of the European Community were faced with a serious dilemma: they had to decide whether to distance themselves from Germany, and thus endanger the objectives of the political and monetary union laid down in the Maastricht Treaty, or support the German position. They inevitably opted for the latter and on January 15, 1992, the independence of Croatia and Slovenia was recognized by the main Western governments.

From that moment on, ethnic self-determination became the norm to follow and, as was to be expected, anarchy broke out everywhere. When the Croats of Croatia appealed to self-determination to declare their independence, it seemed valid to them. But when it was the Serbs of Croatia who recurred to this mechanism in order to join Serbia, the Croats did not accept it. When the Serbs of Croatia utilized these means to join Serbia, it seemed valid to the Serbs, but when it was the Muslims or the Croats of Bosnia who did it in order to become independent, they no longer accepted it. And thus it went.

That first moment of international recognition of Croatia and Slovenia set a key precedent for the later course of events. In a certain manner it may be said that it was the last chance to prevent the tragedy that later occurred.

THE DECLINE OF THE UNITED STATES

1898 is generally considered to be the year in which the United States joined the club of the great world powers. In that year it was responsible for the military defeat of Spain and inherited from her an empire that reached from Puerto Rico to the Philippines. Nevertheless, as far back as 1880 the U.S. had replaced England as the world's most industrialized nation and was producing 28.6% of the world Gross Industrial Product. In 1914 the well-known news publisher Henry Luce wrote his famous essay, *The American Century,* setting forth an idea which, with the passage of time, would come to be acknowledged by friends and strangers as the expression of an undeniable reality. After the First World War, the United States consolidated itself as one of the five great world powers and at the end of the Second World War it became one of the two great super-powers. By 1945, what is more, its economic superiority was incomparable: the country was already responsible for 50% of the world GDP. With the collapse of communism, which began in 1989, the United States not only won the Cold War but it was also transformed into the sole and indisputable super-power.

There are multiple manifestations of the present hegemony of the United States. It is the embodiment of military power. The budget which the United States destines for armaments is almost as big as the combined total of the six nations that follow it in the list of military powers and double that of the combined total of all of its possible adversaries. It is also economic power. The United States is the command post of the global economy, being the biggest monetary and stock market of the world. Its companies form a third of the world's five hundred largest corporations and account for half of their profits. They dominate the sectors of high technology and high aggregate value, and also those of mass consumption. It is, in addition, institutional power. The United States is not only the seat of the major world organizations, like the U.N., the World Bank and the IMF, it also plays a guiding role in these and other institutions which are fundamental nowadays, like NATO or the WTO. It is, furthermore, diplomatic power. The United States is the great arbiter of world conflicts: Northern Ireland, the Middle East, the Balkans, etc. Its diplomatic influence seeks to put an end to the division of Cyprus and achieve a balance between China and Taiwan, Armenia and Azerbaijan, India and Pakistan, the Tutsis and the Hutus. At the same time, it has managed to align the majority of the world's countries behind its own norms about intellectual property rights, the free movement of capitals, etc. It is also cultural power. From Hollywood to CNN and MTV, from McDonald's to Microsoft and Yahoo, American ideas, habits, values and fashions reign everywhere. Internet itself has an American accent. It is all of that which Joseph Nye has called "soft" power and which manifests itself through multimedia, universities and the world "pop" culture. It is not by accident that the French journalist Sophie Gerardi came to write: "The U.S. hegemony is not a novelty. What is exceptional is that, through a combination of factors, the United States has wound up winning on all the game boards".[44]

Oddly enough, never before have so many theories arisen, from the heart of the U.S. academic community itself, that proclaim the inevitable decline of the United States. In the very moment when the evidence of its power seems to be incontrovertible, these theses, following the footsteps of Paul Kennedy's work *The Rise and Fall of the Great Powers*, argue

44. *Le Monde: Dossiers & Documents*, May 1998

that the United States is beginning to slide down the slope of decadence. Samuel Huntington affirms that modernization has only served to strengthen other, rival cultures and reduce the power of the West and, by extension, the United States.

What is more, the "multi-culturalism" which internally affects the country under the impact of the foreign cultures which penetrate it is considered to be a powerful source of moral and material decadence. It is the same argument, of course, that is held by the U.S. populism exemplified by Pat Buchanan. Robert Putnam reasons that the "art of association", the key to U.S. greatness, is decaying. The people have lost faith in their authorities and institutions, while at the same time their capacity to organize themselves into guilds, organizations or simple sports teams is being lost as well. Arthur Schlesinger Jr., on the other hand, believes that the key to the decline of the U.S. is to be found in an excessive capacity of association, which is leading to the "tribalization" of its society. Lester Thurow declares that the process of globalization is seriously reducing the individual power of states and that the United States is not an exception to it. In his opinion, the U.S. economy not only accounts for a smaller and smaller percentage of the global economy, but it also has a progressively smaller influence in multilateral economic organizations. He adds, what is more, that the appearance of the euro represents the emergence of a currency that will rival the dollar and will have a strong impact on U.S. economic superiority. He argues, at the same time, that the growing economic inequality within the country itself is laying the foundations for serious political and institutional crises. Donald White, too, says that the reduced weight of the U.S. in the world economy is a sign of decline, which is worsened by the fragmentation of its society into ideological, ethnic and pressure groups and the loss of a capacity for consensus about the country's role in the world.

It is highly paradoxical that, in the moment of its greatest glory, the intellectuals of the United States are pondering the country's future with such pessimism.

THE COUNTER-SOCIETY

Several years ago the French sociologist Henri Mendras coined the term "counter-society" to describe all those members of a society who do not or cannot follow the rhythm that society follows. The members of a counter-society would be those who refuse to accept the speed imposed on them by the society they live in. The slow segments of the population of quick nations are the fullest expression of a counter-society.

In the United States two segments that typify the counter-society stand out: the Black and the Hispanic population. In both cases, these groups have turned in on themselves, seeking an identity of their own that distinguishes and separates them from the rest of society. It is a very particular way of dissociating, of divorcing, themselves from the rhythm at which the country is evolving, so that they may live at their own cadences and within their own values. It would seem that both groups want to assert their right to their own small corner of the world.

More and more, a significant part of the Black population is getting into what is called Afrocentrism. This is a movement whose history goes back to the early decades of the twentieth century but which really became strong in the sixties under the inspiration of the famous Malcolm X. Afrocentrism is the counterpart of the Eurocentrism that sought to place Europe at the center of universal civilization. This Afrocentrism tries to reformulate the teaching of history by emphasizing the prominent historical role of the African continent.

There is nothing wrong with signaling the importance of Africa. On the contrary, it tends to demolish many myths and restore Africa to its rightful role in world civilization. The problems start when attempts are made to justify a sort of inverse racism on these bases, by means of which Black culture may consider itself to be not only superior but even self-excluding. In fact, some of the leading proponents of Afrocentrism wish to segregate education in U.S. public schools so as to emphasize the teachings of Africa and discard any expression of "cultural imperialism" – meaning, it is worth pointing out, the history of the West. In a few words, the younger Afro-American generations would have to deal with the challenges of the twenty-first century within a self-imposed cultural ghetto.

In the Hispanic community as well, there are signs of a trend towards turning one's back on the values and customs of U.S. society. Enclosed in themselves, seeking to preserve their own language and traditions at any cost, many Hispanics seem little willing to enter the great melting pot of U.S. society. In contrast with previous immigrations, which sought to copy the habits and customs of the host society as a means of social ascent, an important part of the Hispanic community watches its own Spanish-language television programs, hears its own music, reads its own newspapers and refuses to let itself be influenced by Anglo-Saxon culture. Without knowing it, these Hispanics follow the ideas of the early-twentieth century Uruguayan writer, José Enrique Rodó, who contrasted the humanism of Latin Americans with the overwhelming materialism of the Anglo-Saxons. It was the myth of the Latin spirituality of Ariel against the crude materialism of Caliban. Nevertheless, as in the case of the Black population, this leads to a false sense of superiority which is nothing more than not wanting to accept the challenge of competition. The Hispanics, like the Afro-Americans, enclose themselves within their own counter-society, convinced of their own cultural and spiritual superiority. They do not realize that when they do so, the very swiftness of society will cause them to be left behind.

There is a curious parallel between these slow populations and the revolt of Islamic fundamentalism or the emergence of stubborn nationalisms. In all of these cases there is a common denominator: the need to reclaim a small piece of the universe where one may live in accordance with one's roots. The need to reclaim one's own rhythm of doing things. The need to assert oneself in defiance of the uniformity of values and beliefs.

CONSTITUTIONAL REINVENTION

Every constitution must be preceded by a constituent assembly and a constituent process. Understanding the essence of the constituent process implies having a prior knowledge of the nature of the emerging national project which the process seeks to legitimize. Let us start with the conceptual base. A national project may be defined as that set of political, social, economic, ethical or other kind of values which attains a national priority. Such values assume the character of guiding principles for the life of a country and form the foundation on which a given political regime hopes to articulate its legitimacy and field of action.

A national project may express itself in different ways. It is usually set forth by means of a fundamental text that governs the institutional life of a country, that is, a constitution. It is possible, however, that it may be expressed through other means, such as manifestos, programs, declarations of principles, institutional laws or even a group of policies which, by the very amplitude of their goals, imply a global design intended to transform society.

Among examples of the constitutions which have embodied concrete national projects we find the revolutionary Mexican Constitution of 1917, the presidential-focused Chilean Constitution of 1925, the Constitution of the "Estado Novo" of Brazil of 1937 and the Venezuelan Constitution of 1961. Nevertheless, there have been many alternative ways of expressing a national project, among which we find, for example, the following: the 1789 Declaration of the Rights of Man and the Citizen, which was later incorporated in the French Constitution of 1791; the Soviet Declaration of the Rights of the Working People (January 4, 1918), later included in the 1924 "Fundamental Law" of the Union of Soviet Socialist Republics; or even the "Green Book" of Kaddafi.

The most frequently-used formula is the constitutional one. Constitutional doctrine usually shows two tendencies. The first emphasizes the normative nature of the constitution, that is, its formal, juridical aspect. The second emphasizes the material nature of the same, that is, its substantive character. In the latter, the accent is placed on the role played by political forces in the determination of the principles which give life to the constitutional ordering, this being the expression of the sovereign will. It is precisely this latter vision which we want to single out. That is, the constitution as the embodiment of a national project.

An example of the material tendency to which we have just referred is reflected in a famous address given by José Ortega y Gasset before the Constituent Courts of Spain in September 1931. There, the philosopher, as a member of the constituent assembly, defined a group of fundamental objectives that, in his opinion, had to be incorporated into the new Constitution of the Spanish Republic. His discourse ended with the following words: "If this is not done, the Constitution, which should be pure life, living and fully-active, will drag along corpse after corpse and be burdened with the skeleton of the history that has now expired".[45] It is precisely this idea that a constitution "should be pure life, living and fully-active" which expresses the need for every emerging national project to be shaped into a constitutional text that reflects its exigencies and necessities. This, indeed, is the essence of every constituent process.

It is not by accident, then, that we may, in most cases, follow the evolution of a country's successive national projects through its constitutional history. A clear illustration of this is French constitutional history. From the 1791 Constitution, which sought to reconcile the survival of the monarchy with the predominance won by the bourgeois classes through the French Revolution, to the 1958 Constitution, which established the foundations of a presidential regime, each of its thirteen successive constitutions

45. "Proyectos de Constitución", Discursos Políticos, Madrid, Alianza Editorial, 1974

has been a true reflection of a given national project. We may also cite constitutional texts like the following: the 1919 Constitution of the Weimar Republic of Germany, the 1924 "Fundamental Law" of the Soviet Union, the 1936 Constitution of the Turkish Republic, the 1948 Constitution of the Italian Republic and the 1949 "Fundamental Law" of the German Federal Republic, each of which embodied specific national projects.

Constituent processes continue to be the fundamental recourses which enable states to reinvent themselves periodically within the context of the state of law.

THE AMERICAN PEOPLE

No other people on earth are in the paradoxical situation of being, at one and the same time, profoundly homogenous and profoundly heterogeneous. This homogeneity expresses itself through a sum of common denominators, through the infinite reproduction of the same brands, the same patterns, the same ways of doing things, the same tastes. This heterogeneity, for its part, manifests itself through a profoundly fragmented society, in which signs of ethnic or national identity, intensity of beliefs or participation in groups with a common interest create dividing lines.

The whole of U.S. society is made uniform by baseball, Coca-Cola, apple pie, Mickey Mouse, Santa

Claus, Halloween or Thanksgiving Day. Throughout the length and breadth of U.S. territory you see
the same shopping centers – the malls, with the
same franchise shops, the same names, the same
styles of architecture. Its highways, suburbs, fast-
food restaurants, bookshops, drugstores – all are
standardized. Its hotel chains, each with its characteristic interior designs, procedures and gastronomi-
cal styles, offer a protective nest which allows
everyone to feel that he is close to home, no matter how far away he is from it. In short, when you
know one American locality it seems that you know
them all. A varied but necessarily limited repertory
occupies the whole stage of the country. Americans all seem to be traced from the same pattern.
No other people on earth show such a level of
uniformity. What is more, now that American culture has become globalized, the signs of American
identity form the foundation on which the whole
of humanity is made uniform.

From another angle, however, those who live in
the United States are much more diverse than one
might imagine. The descendants of Greeks still stay
within the intimacy of their family circles, the ambit
of their communities, the old customs of their fore-
fathers. So too do the descendants of the Irish, the
Italians and the Poles zealously conserve their ancestral customs. In the United States, an American
Jew may be loyal, at one and the same time, to the
State of Israel and the nation of Washington, in the
same way that a Greek American feels that he may

be faithful, without any inner contradiction, to both the United States and Greece. In his memoirs, the French intellectual Raymond Aron observed that this double sense of national identity, characteristic of Americans, would be unacceptable in France. A French citizen of different ethnic origin has to fully assimilate French language and civilization before he can be considered part of that human flock.

But the heterogeneity of the U.S. is not limited to the matter of ancestry. The intensity of beliefs causes a fragmentation of society into a virtually unlimited number of special interest groups. These would include groupings of an economic and political character, the single interest groups, the ideological and religious ones, the public interest groups, etc., etc. Usually the head of each coin has its tail and each position has its counter-position. The anti-abortion groups versus the right-to-choice groups, the gun lobby versus the anti-gun lobby and so on through the list. For some, like the well-known American intellectual Arthur Schlesinger Jr., this threatens to create the "tribalization" of U.S. society. That is, the possibility that society becomes fragmented into multiple and incompatible identities. Several years ago, the political analyst Jerry Adler published an eloquent article in the magazine *Newsweek*, where he stated: "In the United States adherence to even the smallest movements is measured in millions of persons. The identity of everyone is politicized, not only in terms of race, ethnic group, religion and language, but also in terms of sex, sexual behavior, age, dress, diet and personal habits".[46]

To resume, U.S. society represents a very curious mixture of homogeneous and heterogeneous elements. This capacity to make everyone alike and at the same time profoundly different constitutes the most outstanding characteristic of U.S. identity. It is in great contrast with a society like the Japanese, where everyone not only looks but also thinks the same. Perhaps it is this paradoxical coexistence of uniformity and heterogeneity that is the secret of American success. That is, the social discipline that results from homogeneity and the individual creativity that results from heterogeneity.

THE TWO SPEEDS

The futurologist Alvin Toffler remarked that the world is divided into two kinds of nations, "quick" ones and "slow" ones. The former are those which enjoy advanced technologies and economies and move towards the future with a clear sense of purpose and a sure rhythm. The latter, by contrast, are those which have lagged behind, both economically and technologically, and struggle in the midst of great economic limitations and grave social problems. For them, the future seems uncertain and full of danger. This distinction made by Toffler is a reflection of the

46. July 10, 1995

reality of the international order of our times, which is characterized by a small number of islands of privilege in the midst of a veritable ocean of uncertainty and backwardness.

A number of years ago the United Nations Development Program (UNDP), in its annual report of 1996, confirmed the assertion of Toffler with solid statistics. In that report we find the following observation: "The world has become much more polarized and the gap between rich and poor has widened. Of the 23 trillion U.S. dollars that made up the world GDP in 1993, 18 trillion dollars belonged to the developed countries and only 5 trillion to the developing countries, where 80% of mankind lives". According to the same report, the 358 billionaires of the world have a combined income that is higher than the combined GDP of countries which shelter 45% of the world's population. It is superfluous to point out that the great majority of these billionaires come from the swift nations.

Nevertheless, not everyone marches at the same rhythm within the swift nations themselves. Within the quick countries there are slow segments of the populations which have not been able to adapt themselves to the velocity of the society of which they form part. This becomes more and more of a reality every day. Up to a number of years ago, it was still possible to speak of nations with a high degree of homogeneity. That is, societies that did not show major differences in the rhythm at which their different members moved. Japan and Germany were good examples of this situation. Today, even the Japanese, considered to be the most homogeneous society in the world, show a profound dichotomy. There is a dynamic Japan, focussed on the outside world and made up of its great transnational companies. But there is also a Japan of slow growth, made up of those sectors which are oriented towards the domestic economy and a large number of small and medium companies which have been left to fend for themselves. While the dynamic Japan has managed to maintain a high level of competitiveness within the world company, the backward part has been shaken to its very foundations. The problem is that barely 30% of the work force forms part of the dynamic country. In fact, a society like the Japanese, which upheld the norm of lifetime employment, now has an unemployment rate that is comparable to that of the other industrialized nations.

The same may be said of Germany. The reunification of Germany caused two very different sectors of the population to coexist within the space of a single state: the West and the East Germans. Those who had lived under capitalism displayed working habits and a sense of initiative that are very different from those of the Germans who had lived under communism. However, over and beyond the dichotomy between the two Germanys that are now integrated, there are the problems that derive from global competition, which have forced the country to dismantle, in a significant way, the platform of social harmony which characterized it for so many years. Today, the breach between those who have and those who have not managed to adapt themselves to the exigencies of the world economy is growing bigger and bigger.

Wherever you look in the industrialized world, the dichotomy between the slow and quick sectors of the population is plainly evident. The latter form part of the 30% of the active population of the three great regions of the developed world which, in the opinion of the former French Prime Minister Michel Rocard, may be labeled as unemployed or "marginalized". To this army also belong the 14 million unemployed that are now found in the European Union.

In the United States there are a large number of economists and academics who have warned about the ever wider gap between winners and losers within their society. Richard Freeman has called the American economy an "apartheid economy", while Lester Thurow has come to ask: "How far may real salaries fall and inequality increase before something explodes within democracy?".[47]

Although the phenomenon of slow sectors of population within swift nations is becoming one of the main characteristics of the globalized order, it should not lead us to ignore the more traditional phenomenon of quick sectors within slow nations.

47. *The Future of Capitalism: How Today's Economic Forces Shape Tomorrow's World*, New York, William Morrow and Company, 1996, p. 75

That is, the niches of progress that exist within backward societies. These societies have their own versions of Wall Street and Madison Avenue, which have always lived alongside the more primitive features of the Third World. What characterizes the contemporary world is that those rapid sectors of the population are going forward at an ever-quicker pace, while their societies are becoming slower and slower.

WHY CHANGE CONSTITUTIONS?

Written constitutions are a relatively recent phenomenon. They arose as a result of the need to encounter an adequate means of guaranteeing the rights of citizens and limiting the power of rulers within the context of the liberal revolutions of the eighteenth century. Up to that time, unwritten constitutions had prevailed. These embodied the collection of fundamental traditions, usages and principles which, taken as a whole, formed a constitutional law based on custom, that is, an incorporeal and timeless one.

Among the typical examples of customary constitutions we find the German constitution that was in use until 1870 or the English one, which is still in force. In his famous work, *The German Constitution*, written in 1802, the philosopher Hegel argued that the ancestral norms which ruled German political and social life had become the greatest obstacle to the emergence of a modern and unified German state. In fact, when the modern German nation was created in 1870, it set out to create a written constitution. For its part, the English constitutional system, as the Italian political theorist Norberto Bobbio points out, is based on the premise that constitutional norms are the consequence and not the source of the rights defined and guaranteed by the courts of justice. Judicial precedents, together with a varied set of texts and acts that were never codified, are what form the foundation of its customary constitutional system. Among the latter we find, for example, the Magna Carta of 1215, the Habeas Corpus Act of 1679, the 1689 Bill of Rights and the 1911 Parliamentary Act. Nowadays, the English Constitution represents the last vestige of a constitutional law based on custom.

The 1787 U.S. Constitution and the 1791 French Constitution represented the two earliest manifestations of written constitutional texts, establishing the foundations for a tradition that would soon spread to other parts. The fundamental reason for having a written text was that it formally proclaimed the rights and prerogatives of the rulers and the ruled. In that sense, written constitutions were born as the expression of a very concrete ideal of society: that based on the idea that national sovereignty resided in the nation.

The U.S. Constitution of 1787 and the French one of 1791 blazed two very different trails. The former would remain intact with the passage of time, transforming itself into a sort of compromise between

English constitutional tradition and written constitutions. In the United States, courts of justice and custom interact with the written constitutional text, forming a very particular amalgam. The French Constitution, on the other hand, was replaced after a few years, giving rise to the tradition in which constitutions may change in accordance with the transformations that occur in a society.

The notion that constitutions may change as a direct result of the evolution that societies go through became the common rule. Since society is a living, dynamic and fluid body, the need to adapt the fundamental law that regulates it to social transformations is accepted. In this way, constitutional law comes to respond to the exigencies of the ruling national project. That is, that set of political, social, economic, ethical or other kind of values which assume the character of guiding principles for the life of a country in a given moment and form the foundation on which the prevailing political regime hopes to base its legitimacy.

It was precisely by virtue of the above principles that what are known as constitutional preambles became generalized after the First World War. Through these the prevailing political-social doctrine that inspired and governed the activity of the state was formally declared within the text of the constitution itself. In other words, instead of keeping within a neutral and timeless context, constitutional law was converted into the expression of the ruling national project, accepting the idea that states may reinvent themselves periodically. This demonstrated the great transformation that had taken place since the times of the customary constitutions.

THE STATE: PROLIFERATION AND CRISIS

The nineteenth century witnessed the emergence of the last great States. It was not only Germany and Italy that made their appearance in that century, but the United States also transformed itself into a great continental State as it realized its manifest destiny. The twentieth century, for its part, displayed not only the maximum expressions of state-idolatry, with the appearance of fascism and communism, but also the emergence of important States that had resulted from the dismantling of the colonial empires. Furthermore, during the fifty years of the Cold War, the world revolved around a system of international relations that was centered upon two great States. The final decade of the century became, however, the era of the decline of States.

Never before had the State been in such a weak condition as it is now. Particularly striking is the dual process of dismantling which affects the State under the influence of globalization and fundamentalism. It is that which Benjamin Barber has called "McWorld vs. Jihad" and Thomas Friedman, "The Lexus vs. The Olive Tree". Under the effects of globalization, States have been shedding themselves of many of the functions which characterized them before, entering into the processes of privatization and withdrawal from public services. It is becoming harder and harder to distinguish States from private corporations and they are becoming more and more ruled by the norms of competitiveness. Ordinary citizens, who are increasingly unsupported and anguished, see that everything around them is coming to be governed by the ethic and exigencies of private capital. The inevitable erosion of the individual's loyalty to the State which results from these changes is reinforced by the erosion of national identity brought by globalization. It is the inevitable consequence of global homogenization. In a certain way, the globalizing phenomenon hammers away at the State from above, like a pneumatic drill. The only thing that can offer resistance to this grinding down of the state are tough cores of surviving identity, that is, fundamentalisms and ethnic claims. But, at the same time, these nuclei of resistance conspire against the State from below, undermining its foundations.

Paradoxically, the crisis of the State has been accompanied by the indiscriminate emergence of new States. The reason for this phenomenon is closely linked to the very crisis of the State. Four central factors may explain the crisis that is occurring. In the first place, there is the activity of tough cores of identity which seek to establish new States that will respond to their particular characteristics. In second place, there is the possibility of finding, on a global level, the elements of complementation and integration that gave meaning to the State in the past. In other words, insofar as States have become integrated on a global level and stopped being self-sustaining units, it is now possible for their component spaces to aspire to an independent existence. In third place, there is the very fact that success in the global economy is not achieved by having a great amount of natural resources but by the quality of their human resources. The more advanced segments and regions within the State are beginning to regard the more backward ones as an unnecessary burden and seeking to rid themselves of them. In the fourth place, thanks to the protection of organisms of collective security and the new international law, the survival of weak States is now possible, which renders unnecessary the protective shell of strong states.

To resume, the crisis of the State is the very source of its proliferation. It is on the core of this crisis that the dual forces of the global and the small village stand out.

WHO WILL DOMINATE EAST ASIA?

The fall of the Berlin Wall and the end of the Cold War brought with them the resurgence of a strong nationalist sentiment in Japan. This was symbolized by the slogan: "Abandon the West and Return to Asia". This idea proposed giving up the role of being a younger brother to the United States and a power limited by the framework of Western objectives. It represented, at the same time, a return to its

Asian identity and the assumption of a clear economic hegemony within the region, curbing the penetration into East Asian markets of the United States and Europe.

In recent years, however, things have changed radically. Japan now looks like a country that is increasingly incapable of assuming a hegemonic role in East Asia. There are various reasons for this new perspective. Some of them are of a passing kind, like the economic recession which the country still suffers from or the gigantic loans tied up in the economies of the region after the 1997 crisis. Others, however, are of a structural character.

Among the latter reasons we might underline the following. In the first place, there is the dichotomy between a dynamic Japan that looks to the outside world and is made up of great transnational companies and a cumbersome and inefficient Japan, made up of a gigantic network of companies geared to the domestic economy. Seventy percent of the total labor force of the country forms part of that inefficient Japan.

In the second place, we should mention its inability to make the leap towards leading-edge technologies. Its economy has remained stuck in the mass production of computers, semiconductors or cars, without being able to enter the post-industrial economy of the twenty-first century. The very nature of its educational system, which emphasizes docility, discipline and the obedience of social norms, has castrated individual creativity, which is the basis of the new economy of knowledge. Japan has touched the roof of its capacity for technological ascent and by doing so, has left without support the famous "wedge-driving" model of regional development. That model was based on the idea that Japan would continually scale higher and higher rungs of the technological ladder, leaving those who were behind it to occupy the places it abandoned.

In third place, its population is growing older at a faster rate than that of any other nation in the world. By the year 2015, every two Japanese workers will have to bear the weight of one who has already retired. This will not only reduce its rates of domestic savings in a dramatic way, but it will also generate chronic fiscal deficits. Japan will be deprived of the economic surplus which has, till now, made its economy strong. The resources to finance its exports and modernize its industry will become scarcer and scarcer.

In short, although Japan will continue to be an important world economic power, its possibilities for imposing itself as the region's hegemonic center look ever more remote. The big question we have to ask ourselves in this respect is the following: what nation will be able to lead the economy of that region? There is no shortage of aspirants to the post, of course. Taiwan, the only one of the Asian tigers whose economy was not affected by the 1997 crisis, wildly proceeded to offer economic aid to its battered partners on that occasion. It is clear, however, that Taiwan will only be able to acquire a modest share of influence in the region. Only the United States and China have or will have the strength needed to assume a hegemonic leadership in the region.

Up to a short time ago, the United States was going through the longest process of economic expansion in recent decades. Although the country is in a difficult phase at the moment, everything seems to indicate that it will soon overcome it. There is no doubt that the United States continues to be the great economic dynamo of the world. Its chronic fiscal deficit has turned into a surplus and its Federal Reserve Board maintains low and stable interest rates. This is combined with a moderate inflation rate, which was 3.3% in the year 2000. Although the quality of the jobs that are created leaves a lot to be desired, the United States is the only place where jobs are still being created.

To resume, the United States may have the economic conditions needed to transform itself into the great energizing factor of the Asian economies. There is, however, one "but" which affects everything else. The Achilles heel of the U.S. economy is the ever-growing gap in its trade balance, the same factor which has turned into the source of U.S. economic nationalism. It would be difficult for the U.S. to be able to convert itself into the dynamo of the Asian economies, taking into account that the low-cost exports from that region are seen as the greatest threat facing the country.

China also shows an exceptionally successful economy and the plans of its leadership aim at reaching the present U.S. GDP within 21 years. That country had a soft landing after the high (and inflationary) growth rates of the 1993-1994 period, managing to maintain, nevertheless, a growth rate that reached 8% in the year 2000. In the same year the inflation rate was only 0.4%. China has begun the process of selling and massively reconverting its state companies, in order to consolidate itself as a fully capitalist economy. At the same time it has been expanding its financial system in a dramatic way.

However, China also has a big "but". While its exports have grown rapidly, its imports have stagnated. The result of this is an ample surplus in its trade balance, which has put a lot of pressure on its commercial partners of the region. If the Chinese economy becomes concurrent, not complementary, to that of the other countries of East Asia, it will be difficult for it to transform itself into a motor of regional growth. It will only achieve it if its own market can absorb growing quantities of products from the region itself.

In conclusion, everything seems to indicate that there will not be a sole economic hegemony over the region. Japan, the United States and China may share this leadership, although the latter country will be probably become the first among equals.

THE UNITED STATES VS. CHINA:
FOREIGN POLICY AND DIPLOMACY

The confrontation that occurred between the United States and China in April 2001 threw into high relief the complexities of foreign policy as well as the subtleties of diplomacy. The former, because in foreign policy the rationality of political decisions is frequently subordinated, as in this case, to a dynamic alien to the very subject that is decided on. The latter, because in diplomacy the slightest accent that is placed on a word or a phrase and the sensitivity of the negotiations that precede this semantic process are decisive in the resolution of delicate international crises.

What was at stake on both sides throughout the crisis that arose as a result of the aerial collision and emergency landing of the U.S. plane in China was something that transcended the objective facts of the incident. For China, the essence of the game was to clarify the balance of power between its hard-line military sectors and those which emphasize economic growth and an approach to the West. That is, between the forces which are closed to globalization and those which are open it. This occurred against the background of the forthcoming Congress of the Communist Party in 2002, which is going to decide about the succession to the leadership of Jiang Zemin. In other words, it was an entirely domestic matter, in which the pro-Western leadership (Jiang Zemin, Zhu Rongji and Qian Qichen) sought to undo the perception that they were weak, with an eye on the coming fight with the hard-liners.

On the U.S. side, what was at stake was the existing balance of power between two sectors that are vital supports for the government: the Republican far-right and the corporate world. As in China, it was the dialectic between the forces of withdrawal and rapprochement. To keep both sides happy, the Bush administration's Chinese policy has sought to maintain a difficult balance between strategic competition and economic complementarity with China. With the plane incident this correlation of forces became even more complicated, due to the appearance of a curious temporary alliance. This alliance united ideological sectors of the Republican right with human rights activists and the labor unions, which traditionally support the Democratic party. This coalition of ideological hawks, human rights protestors and protectionist sectors confronted the U.S. corporate world, which wants to remain friendly with the world's greatest potential market. The Bush administration's response to the crisis was, once again, an attempt to win a compromise between conflicting interests.

If the nature of the game turned out to be essentially domestic in both cases, the means chosen to resolve the crisis were quintessentially diplomatic. That is, the art of semantics. The U.S. government issued a number of statements that progressively approached the apology demanded by China, without actually articulating it. While this was going on, a subtle mediation carried out by friendly countries took place behind the scene, in which an effort was made to find the right inflection to "save face" for both parties.

The incident between China and the United States was inscribed within long traditions of foreign policy and diplomacy. The first being the expression and escape valve of domestic considerations and the second acting as an intermesh of nuances that allows the affected parties to achieve an honorable withdrawal from a crisis.

THE EUROPEAN UNION: THE NEW ROLE OF THE OUTSIDERS

The Christian reconquest of the lands occupied by the Moors in Spain was responsible for the emergence of a militant and intransigent Catholicism, which would play a decisive part in the history of that country. In turn, medieval Castille, hardened by a centuries-long fight against the infidels, had become the most powerful war machine in Europe at the time of the reconquest. This combination of religious fundamentalism and military aggressiveness made Spain the most hated of the European powers. In no other place did the hostility against Spain and the Hispanic reach such heights as in England. This, in part, because the worst excesses of forced religious conversion suffered by that country took place under the reign of the highly Catholic Mary

Tudor, "Bloody Mary", the wife of Phillip II of Spain. For the English, the picture of Spain was always associated with the trilogy of inquisition, intolerance and counter-reformation.

Although English culture never generated such an intense degree of antagonism in Spain, there was another, very clear, reason for Spanish resentment against the British Isles: Gibraltar. Captured by the English and Dutch in 1704, during the War of the Spanish Succession, Gibraltar was officially transformed into an English colony in 1713, under the terms of the Treaty of Utrecht. From then on, proud Spain, which had formerly been the center of an empire on which the sun never set, had to live with a colonial spike driven into its very soul.

It was not by accident that Spain did all that it could to bring about the success of U.S. independence, in the same way that England promoted the independence of Latin America. In short, of all the possible alliances that might have been formed in European territory, an Anglo-Spanish one always seemed to be one of the least probable. Only on exceptional occasions – as in the anti-Napoleonic wars – were both nations able to unite themselves into circumstantial and short-lived coalitions.

Curiously enough, in the Summit of the European Union held in Lisbon in March 2000 there was a strong Anglo-Spanish alliance. It is significant in several ways. In the first place, because it goes in the opposite direction to the tradition which we have mentioned. But there are two other reasons for its importance. One of them is that it represents an alternative to the Franco-German leadership, which ruled since the dawn of the European Community in the nineteen-fifties. The other is that it brings two "peripheral" actors in European integration to a central position in that process.

From the times of De Gaulle and Adenauer, there was an alliance between the French and the Germans based on their mutual dependence, which, in the following decades, would allow them to maintain a powerful leadership over the movement towards European integration. By virtue of their personal affinities and the overlapping of their respective national policies, Giscard d'Estaing and Helmut Schmidt and then Francois Mitterand and Helmut Kohl consolidated this dual European leadership. The absence of a personal chemistry between Schroder and the French leaders, together with the ending of the mutual dependence between France and Germany, has undermined the consistency of a very successful coalition. A Germany that is reunified and accepted by its neighbors no longer needs France so much, in the same way that a France which is more successful in economic terms no longer depends so heavily on the dynamo of the German economy, which, in any case, has been slowing down.

As significant as this crisis in the former leadership of Western Europe may be, equally so is the fact that the two countries which are their potential replacement have traditionally been considered as "peripheral" ones. In fact, the United Kingdom has always kept its distance from the dictates of Brussels, in an effort to keep its own specificity alive. For its part, Spain (which has always lived with the doubt about whether it is authentically European) was a latecomer to European integration. The fact that these two "outsiders" in the European movement have now assumed a leading role means that there may be a profound renovation of this process.

In short, Mary Tudor and Gibraltar are being ousted by the forces of the new age.

THE UNITED STATES: THE POWER OF NEO-POPULISM

In 1963, Samuel P. Huntington wrote a celebrated article in the magazine *Daedalus*. He argued that the fundamental dividing line in U.S. politics was not between the left and the right, but between the "establishment" and "populism". Essentially, this reality has not changed. It is true that the "establishment" has become tarnished since the sixties and that populism has reshaped itself and changed its clothes. Nevertheless, the general lines of thought that shaped both tendencies in the past are still in force and continue to nourish the debate over basic political ideas that takes place in the United States today. Before dealing with the current situation, it might be useful to explore a bit of the history behind the matrixes of thought found in these two currents of opinion.

The "establishment" arose as a cohesive fraternity of individuals who were grouped around the Council on Foreign Relations of New York, an organization founded in the nineteen-thirties with money provided by the Rockefeller family. As an institution the Council had several basic characteristics. In the first place it was "internationalist", that is, it had a world vocation, a sense of presence and an influence on international affairs. It was an internationalism that advocated an active U.S. involvement in world affairs and was opposed to the isolationism that, except on a few occasions, had historically been the dominant feature of U.S. foreign policy. In second place, it was closely linked to the ambit of international business and the sphere of the big banks and multinational companies. In third place, its fundamental ideology was free trade. As Walter Isaacson and Evan Thomas pointed out in an important book devoted to the men of the "establishment": "They were fervent capitalists for whom free trade was a credo. In their minds there was an unbreakable link between free trade and free men".[48]

The typical member of the "establishment" was a man whose career moved between the upper levels of government in Washington, law firms in New York, top executive positions in some important transnational companies, the boards of directors of major foundations with an international focus, like

48. *The Wise Men*, New York, Simon and Schuster, 1986, pp. 32 and 33

the Rockefeller or Ford Foundation, and teaching posts in Ivy League universities like Harvard, Yale or Princeton. They were men who were interested in what was happening abroad and had a global perspective. Men who found no contradiction between the spheres of government and business, who believed that the government should take a leading role in promoting the U.S. corporate presence throughout the world.

Among the big names of the "establishment" there were people like Averell Harriman, Dean Acheson, Robert Lovett, George Kennan, John J. McCloy, Charles Bohlen, James Forrestal or Paul Nitze. Among their major accomplishments were the policy of containment, the Marshall Plan and their strong support for the creation of the United Nations, the World Bank and the International Monetary Fund. In short, the "establishment" always assumed that events beyond the nation's borders were more important to its security than internal ones. They assumed that it could only be through the maintenance of an international environment favorable to U.S. values, interests, capitals and products that the stability of its way of life would be ensured.

The Vietnam War caused the establishment to enter into a deep crisis from which it never recovered. It meant its irreversible eclipse as an institution. However, its values of internationalism and free trade still serve as cardinal principles for a varied segment of U.S. public life. Even after the "establishment" became outdated, Presidents Ford, Carter, Reagan, Bush and Clinton fully supported these ideas.

Populism represents the antithesis of the "establishment" and of the values which nourished it. This movement arose at the end of the nineteenth century as a reaction to the processes of industrialization and urbanization in the United States. In 1870, the United States produced 68,000 tons of steel; by 1890, steel production had reached 4,200,000 tons. In 1865, the United States had 35,000 miles of rail lines; by 1897, the rail network had reached 242,200 miles of lines. In 1860, U.S. industry produced 1.8 billion dollars worth of goods; by 1900, its production had surpassed 17 billion dollars. In 1870, 57% of its workforce was rural and 47% non-rural; by 1900 62.5% was non-rural. By 1910 the number of people in the United States who lived in cities had become larger than the number who lived in the countryside. Populism arose to express the discontent with the social upheavals which had come in the wake of the country's modernization.

The essential philosophy of populism has always been rural and its values have been grounded in small businesses and small towns. It has nationalistic, patriotic and moralistic roots. In geographical terms, its vital sap lies in what is known as the "Bible Belt". That is, those Southern states with a rich tradition of racism and religious fundamentalism. But it also draws on the values of the rural Midwest, with its tradition of cultural inwardness and racial superiority. Populism fully embodies the old isolationist tradition, which does not exclude a patriotic sense of "he who is not for us is against us". The latter sentiment meant wanting to accept the benefits but not the costs of being a great power. Although a century has passed since the birth of populism, it is still in force, nourished by a nostalgia for the America of bygone times and its simple and predictable way of life. Populism has periodically renewed its strength in reaction to the upheavals caused by the processes of change and the need to adapt to new realities.

In the pantheon of the great names of populism we find W.J. Bryan, Democratic presidential candidate in the early twentieth century, who embodied the values of the small farmers and miners who were confronted by an emerging industrial society; Huey Long, the famous Governor of Louisiana in the nineteen-thirties; Joseph McCarthy, who attacked the intellectual and progressive sectors of U.S. society in the fifties; and George Wallace, Governor of Georgia, who ran for President as an independent candidate in 1968. Among the most important figures of populism in recent years there are Ross Perot, Jesse Helms, Tom Ellis, Terry Dolan, Richard Viguerie, Paul Weyrich, Jerry Falwell, Pat Robertson, Rush Limbaugh, Pat Buchanan, Ralph Reed or Newt Gingrich.

In the past decade a "new populism" made its appearance, made up of a broad coalition of organizations and movements like the following:

"America First", led by Pat Buchanan. Its members believe that the end of the Cold War means that the country should abandon internationalism and concentrate on domestic affairs. In their opinion, U.S. participation in NAFTA, GATT and the WTO represents a betrayal of U.S. sovereignty. They attack Wall Street and the multinationals alike. But, at the same time, they display a marked moral and cultural fundamentalism and a virulent opposition to immigration.

"The Third Force", led by Ross Perot. Its adherents share with the above group an opposition to Wall Street, global finances and internationalism. They are also enemies of hemispheric and international free trade organizations. This does not exclude, however, a fondness for the technological.

"The Christian Soldiers", originally led by the evangelist preacher Pat Robertson and then by the young and dynamic Ralph Reed, who later became an executive of Enron. The movement is based on a religious and moral fundamentalism.

"Third Wave Conservatives", led by former Speaker of the House of Representatives Newt Gingrich. As in the case of Perot, its followers combine a liking for the technological with the classic populist message that revolves around a hostility to Wall Street and immigration and a belief in "law and order" and moralistic values.

"Radio Rebels". This is composed of a wide group of far-right radio commentators who have established a gigantic national audience and whose best-known member is the famous radio broadcaster Rush Limbaugh.

"State Rebels". This is a group of highly-organized citizens who have tried to get anti-immigration and politically-extreme proposals approved on a state level. One of their best-known campaigns is to win support for the famous Proposal 187 of the State of California, an anti-immigration measure.

In fact, the Republican Party has been penetrated and strongly influenced by this new populism. It is a process that began in the nineteen-eighties and reached its fullest expression in the so-called "New Right" of that time. It was in that period too that a number of political analysts began noting how the Republican Party, traditionally associated with the cause of free trade and a firm internationalist outlook, was being penetrated by populist ideas. In an interesting article published some years ago, the well-known political scientist Eugene Genovese observed: "The wrongly-named conservative movement is completely undermining the Republican Party. And I use the term wrongly-named because this right-wing coalition is neither philosophically nor temperamentally conservative, but essentially radical".[49] In Genovese's view, populism was infiltrating the Republican Party, bearing within it the germ of its destruction and subsequent replacement. For his part, the political analyst Ernest B. Furgurson remarked that the populist message that was gathering force in the Republican Party was essentially directed towards: "the outsiders of American life, those who

49. *The New Republic*, December 15, 1986

feel socially and culturally displaced and wronged... the fundamentalists, recently organized, who have been kept on the margin of politics for generations, watching with impotent frustration the country's entrance into modern times. Likewise the millions who believe in the elemental patriotism of 'for us or against us' and who wrap themselves in the colors of the flag".[50]

The fundamental reason for the strength which populism has been showing has to do with the fact that many of the traditional values on their agenda spread throughout the whole of the American population. Historically, those values – nationalism, xenophobia, anti-Washington sentiments, isolationism and religious or moral fundamentalism – had been limited to specific sectors of U.S. society. Nowadays, extreme nationalism is the result of the costs that derive from the country's participation in a globalized and highly competitive economy. Xenophobia is a reaction to growing immigration. Several years ago public opinion polls showed that more than 60% of Americans were against immigration. The discrediting of the profession of politics has led to a distrust of all that is identified with the city of Washington as the center of political power. The end of the communist menace has led to the resurgence of a strong isolationist sentiment. Religious and moral revivalism is the result of the permissive morality of a soci-

50. *Hard Right: The Rise of Jesse Helms*, New York, W.W. Norton & Co., 1986, pp. 281 and 282

ety which is willing to satisfy the demands of any organized group, including those which uphold highly polemical positions. In other words, the old values of the populist agenda have, to a large extent, been updated.

In short, the organizational strength and money of the neo-populist coalition have assumed a great importance within the agenda of the Republican Party. It would be misleading, of course, to speak of a party that has been "conquered" by the populists, but it would be accurate to say that it has been profoundly influenced by them. In fact, their different wings form the most visible attack forces, the best organized segments, within that party. No Republican Party candidate for public office may allow himself the luxury of openly confronting the values or structures which they represent. No Republican President, as the case of Bush now shows, can ignore their claims or refuse to give them an important share of power in his administration. Their Political Action Committees, which are in charge of financing their political campaigns, are among the richest and best-organized in the country. Their sway over the communications media is indisputable. Despite all this, however, their coalition continues to be a lax one, lacking sufficient power of cohesion to unite itself behind a single leadership, as was clearly shown by the failure of Buchanan's candidacy a few years ago.

Today, as in 1963, the United States is still divided into two fundamental lines of thought. On one side, there is internationalism and free trade. And on the other, cultural inwardness, economic protectionism and a nostalgia for a simple and predictable past. The proponents of the global village, on the one hand, and those of the small village, on the other.

THE GIANT AMONG THE PYGMIES

During a period of forty years Washington and Moscow were tangled in a diabolical competition for military superiority. How far away those times seem now! If the 2003 military budget proposed by President Bush is approved, his country will be spending 380 billion dollars on defense alone, that is, an amount equivalent to nearly the whole of Russia's GDP, which is 401 billion dollars. This shows the military insignificance of Moscow today, in comparison with its former rival. In fact, barely seventeen nation-states have a Gross Domestic Product higher than the annual defense budget of the United States. Of course, you would not find among them countries like Switzerland, Belgium, Sweden or Austria, whose domestic wealth is smaller than the amount of money that the Pentagon plans to spend on military materiel.[51] The mere increase in defense spending for 2003 is 48 billion dollars, which is the equivalent of the GDP of Hungary.

Put in other terms, this means that the United States would dispose of more than a billion dollars

51. See *The Economist: World in Figures,* 2002 Edition

per day to spend on defense. This will allow it to develop, with the money distributed over several budget items, a new group of tactical fighter planes – like the F-22, the F/A-18 and the so-called "Joint Strike Fighter" – whose total cost will be more than 300 billion dollars. The logical conclusion from all this is that the military gap between the United States and the rest of the world is growing at an exponential rate. According to Lord Robertson, Secretary General of NATO, Europe is on the way to becoming a "military pygmy" compared to its transatlantic ally. Richard Perle, President of the Pentagon's Defense Policy Committee, was even more emphatic when he stated that the European armed forces have reached "a point of virtual irrelevance".

According to *The Economist*, the increase in defense spending foreseen for 2003 represents the biggest rise in the past twenty years.[52] For its part, the French magazine *Le Monde 2* observes that "if this financial rhythm is maintained, as Pentagon studies show, the U.S. defense budget will be 20% higher, in constant dollars, than the average level that prevailed during the Cold War".[53] In other words, U.S. defense spending will be considerably higher than what was seen at the time of its great rivalry with the Soviet Union. It is worth adding that by 1997 the defense budget of the U.S. was

52. February 16-22, 2002
53. March 2002

already as big as the combined total for the six
nations that followed it in the ranks of military powers and twice that of the combined defense budgets of all its possible adversaries.

To resume, the evident concern is that this over-
powering superiority may lead the U.S. to underes-
timate the value of diplomacy and international
alliances and put too much of an emphasis on
uniliteralism and military options.

THE THREE CHESSBOARDS OF POWER

Joseph Nye, Dean of Harvard's J.F. Kennedy School
of Government, wrote an illuminating article in the
magazine *The Economist* in which he analyzed the
essence of U.S. power. In his judgement, a superfi-
cial look at the matter would lead one to conclude
that the breach between the power of the United
States and that of the rest of the world is purely and
simply overwhelming. In military terms, it is the only
nation with a global reach in nuclear armaments and
conventional forces and its spending in these fields
is more than the combined total for the eight countries that follow it in the list of major powers. In
economic terms, the U.S. accounts for 31% of the
World Gross Product, while its cultural presence in
felt in every corner of the earth.[54]

54. March 23-29, 2002

When you take a closer look, however, the reality of the situation is much more complex. According to Nye, power in the current era of global information is like a three-dimensional chess game. In the upper part of the board you find military power. In the middle there appears economic power, which is clearly multi-polar, since the United States competes with other significant players, among which the European Union stands out. Finally, in the lower part of the board there is a complex transnational network of non-government entities. The latter includes many different kinds of players, from bankers who mobilize amounts of money that are bigger than the budgets of many nations to terrorists who shift arms from one country to another or the hackers who are devoted to creating chaos in the world's computers. On this level, obviously, you cannot talk about uni-polarity, multi-polarity or hegemony, because power is highly fragmented. In Nye's view, when you are playing a three-dimensional game it is a mistake to only focus your attention on the upper level, because this may lead you to lose sight of the games that are being played on the lower ones as well as the vertical connections between the three.

This consideration catches the essence of the dynamics that are now in force as a result of the September 11 terrorist attacks. Initially, Washington was convinced that the response to Islamic terrorism involved the building of a complex network of international alliances. This led it to abandon the unilateralism that had characterized Bush's foreign policy up to then and encouraged a much more sophisticated view of international affairs. The lesson that seemed to have been learned from the overwhelming military triumph in Afghanistan was that the U.S. could rely on itself to meet the challenge that had arisen. In the final reckoning, its own military superiority made diplomacy, and the concessions it involves, seem superfluous. In other words, the country's attention is focused on the upper level of the board.

Nevertheless, the real threats to the United States are terrorist tactics like the setting off of a radiological nuclear bomb in the heart of Washington or New York or the spreading of chemical or biological pathogens through the subway or reservoir systems of a big city. The uni-polar military strength of the country would have little or no utility in such cases. The only way of confronting such dangers is through inter-governmental cooperation, alliances and diplomacy. Controlling the theft and trafficking of nuclear, biological or chemical material from the Russian arsenals through international agreements; strengthening cooperation among the world's intelligence services; working to resolve the problems that nourish hatred of the West and fundamentalism in the Islamic world: these are the only kinds of initiatives that are likely to be effective. Unfortunately, it will be difficult to direct such efforts to the required ends while the United States insists on unilateralism and feels itself to be self-sufficient. If you try to respond to the challenges of the lower board by focusing your attention on the upper one, it will be impossible to win the game.

II

THE ECONOMIC VIEWPOINT

PETROLEUM AND ITS NEW SCENARIOS

The petroleum industry is, by its very nature, profoundly uncertain. Vital information for the determining of prices, such as volumes of production, sales, inventories, etc., are only known belatedly. In other words, the market is managed on the basis of what is assumed, not what is known. At times of international crisis, like the one that arose after the September 11 terrorist attacks, uncertainty may reach exponential levels. This is the ideal ambit for speculators. Due to their activities, petroleum prices have fallen to their lowest level in nearly two years. Speculators face two scenarios: one points to the contraction of demand and the other to the contraction of supply. The former is based on the premise of a world recession, while the latter responds to the shortage of petroleum that might result from an aggravation of the international crisis. Up to now speculators seem to agree that there will be a reduction of demand as a result of the recession. For this reason prices have been falling.

The reason why attention has centered on the recession is fairly clear. Before September 11, initial

calculations suggested that the Gross World Product, as a whole, had contracted during the second
quarter of the year for the first time in two decades.
However, what seemed to stop the row of dominoes from falling was the confidence of the U.S.
consumer. Since the United States is the biggest
market in the world, the state of mind that prevails
there turned out to be decisive and 76% of its consumers were convinced that the U.S. economy would
come out from the crisis. September 11 changed
everything. The figures speak for themselves: 144,000
job dismissals were announced after the attacks; there
was a 1.38 trillion dollar fall in stock prices during
the first week of trading after the stock market re-
opened; and the Dow Jones Index fell by 14.3%, the
biggest weekly decline since the Great Depression.
All this detonated a monumental crisis in an industry directly linked to fuels: the aviation industry. In
short, the petroleum market has assumed that demand will fall.

The curious thing is that speculators are giving
little importance to the scenario that foresees a contraction of supply. In the final analysis, what motivated the terrorists responsible for the September 11
attacks was the hope of provoking the U.S. to over-
react so as to detonate the gunpowder barrel of Islamic fundamentalism. A threat that looks particularly
explosive in the case of Saudi Arabia. That is, a country which represents the central part of the international petroleum equation. In that country a powerful
Islamist movement joins hands with the discontent

and unrest caused by the presence of U.S. troops, the collapse of the welfare state and the extravagant expenditure of the royal family.

In Afghanistan, U.S. intervention turned out to be restrained and focalized, thus avoiding the risk of great political repercussions in the region. The big question is: what comes next? Iraq, Somalia, Yemen or Sudan? The game is not over yet. If a gesture of this kind prospers, the match would come dangerously close to the fuse and if Saudi Arabia were to fall, the reduction of supply might turn out to be purely and simply catastrophic.

BETWEEN FASHIONS AND MYTHS

Between 1995 and 1998, the sector of information technology, which barely represents 8% of the U.S. Gross Domestic Product, was responsible for a 35% growth of the global economy of that country. It was on the basis of such figures that the myth of the New Economy was created, that is, of an economy driven by information technology.

According to the advocates of this thesis, the information revolution made its influence felt on all sectors of the economy: manufactures, finances, telecommunications, multimedia, etc. Let us consider the example of manufacturing. From the "know-how" needed to manufacture a product to the ability to keep closely in contact with suppliers and respond to the tastes and needs of consumers, everything depends on information. Even more, the complex logistics involved in globalized manufacturing processes heavily depend on information technology.

It is not an accident that many believe that innovations in the technology of information altered productive processes as a whole, unleashing synergies that energized the entire economy. For those who think this way, such technology not only opens an unparalleled potential for productive efficiency but it also allows for a sustained growth which does not overheat the economy, that is, the end of business cycles.

As always occurs, the optimists had to confront the skeptics. Among the latter there are a growing number of spoilsports who have set out to disintegrate the estimates on U.S. economic growth, challenging the myth of the New Economy by presenting the raw statistics. Among them there is Robert Gordon of Northwestern University. For Gordon, in the past few years the figures for overall non-agricultural production in the U.S. have been pretty disappointing, the only exception being the field of computer manufacture. That sector registered a 42% annual growth rate between 1995 and 1999, which raised the overall averages for the economy. In other words, the reason for the apparent economic growth had little to do with synergies, nor higher levels of productive efficiency, nor the capacity to handle highly complex processes, but was simply due to the sale of a large volume of computers.

Be that as it may, what is certain is that the contraction of the U.S. economy in recent quarters, which was set off by the crisis of the New Economy, left in the attic of broken toys the thesis that business cycles no longer had a place in a world dominated by information technology. As the *Financial Times* rightly pointed out: "Even the most optimistic have recognized that the increased productivity of recent years has turned out to be cyclical and is basically driven by increases in demand and not by fundamental improvements in the economy's capacity to produce in a more efficient way".[1] This *Financial Times* article went even further. After analyzing figures on the revised estimates for U.S. economic growth, published by the U.S. Department of Commerce at the end of July 2001, it came to the conclusion that the growth rate between 1997 and 2000 was lower than had been thought, which also drove down the figures for productivity in the same period. In other words, the success of the New Economy not only had more to do with traditional increases in demand than a revolution in productive processes, but in strict economic terms the actual results were not that impressive either.

As in so many recent cases of economic analysis, no one knows what the exact truth is. Everything turns out to be a matter of fashions and myths.

1. *"A miracle in revision"*, August 3, 2001

THE END OF THE NEW ECONOMY?

Between 1995 and 2000 the growth of productivity in the U.S. economy was around 3% annually. That figure was double the growth rate of the two previous decades, which was 1.4% annually. The so-called New Economy, sustained by technological innovation, especially information technology, was responsible for the growth shown in those years. In fact, in the decades of the seventies and eighties, which were characterized by economic stagnation, technology did not do much to stimulate economic growth, while in the period between 1995 and 1998 the sector of information technology, which barely represented 8% of the U.S. GDP, was responsible for a 35% growth in the global economy of that country.

The success shown by the New Economy led to the popularity of the myth about the infallibility of information technology. In the final analysis, what is known as "Moore's Law", which states that available information technology doubles every 18 months, seemed to guarantee a sustained economic growth. Under the shelter of this myth, there arose a belief in such ideas as the end of business cycles, the capacity to prevent production from surpassing sales and the possibility of maintaining constant levels of investment.

Starting in April 2000, however, the New Economy entered into a process of crisis. The apparently limitless fall of the Nasdaq index for high tech stocks, the collapse of dotcom companies and the gigantic collapse in the sales of giants like the Cisco Corporation have punctured the information technology deity. What is more, the bear market has managed to subdue the bull market of economic growth, plunging the U.S. economy into a new cycle of crisis. Figures published by the U.S. Department of Labor on May 8, 2001 showed that the hourly productivity of the U.S. worker had fallen during the first quarter of that year, for the first time in six years. Even worse, according to results known at the end of 2001, the U.S. economy had already entered a recession in March of that year. The warnings, given a fair time before, by those who were skeptical about the New Economy, among whom Paul Krugman of MIT and Robert Gordon of Northwestern stand out, seemed to have been confirmed. That is, that the notion that a permanent economic growth could be sustained by a sub-sector as limited as information technology was a mirage.

The curious thing is that even in May 2001, when the pessimism about the U.S. economy had become generalized, the two most prestigious economic and business magazines in the world, *The Economist* and *Business Week*, were still presenting an optimistic view of the New Economy. According to them, "Moore's Law" would remain in force for another ten years, enabling prices in the information technology field to fall and this, in the end, would stimulate sustained investments. At the same time, they said, the efficiency given to productive processes by information technology would continue to reduce costs and increase earnings. While *The Economist* predicted a growth in productivity for the U.S. economy of up to 2.5% for the coming decade, *Business Week* reaffirmed its faith in the wisdom of Alan Greenspan, Chairman of the U.S. Federal Reserve Board and the maximum guru of the New Economy. According to both publications, there was no doubt that the bull market would resume its place in the U.S. economy.

FROM SELF-SATISFACTION TO RECESSION

The industrialized world's three biggest economies are in crisis. For the first time in seven years the U.S. economy has not grown and since March 2001, it has technically been in recession. The European Union, for its part, is very close to zero growth, while Japan is in a stage of recession. This is the first time since 1990 that the world's three strongest economies have contracted at the same time. In contrast with the previous occasion, however, most of the emerging economies are now in crisis as well.

With the notable exception of China and India, the main emerging economies have entered or are about to enter into recession. East Asia is taking a nosedive, while the three main economies of Latin America face serious problems. Argentina is going through an economic implosion, Mexico is in recession and Brazil is beginning one. The Gross World Product as a whole definitely contracted during the second quarter of 2001, for the first time in 20 years, and the group of economies that represent two-thirds of world production may already be in a recessive phase.

The causes of the above situation are identifiable. The three great engines of growth of the world economy during the nineties went into reverse. If the strength of these economies created a positive cycle of growth a few years ago, they may be producing a vicious circle of economic contraction now. These engines are the New Economy, the financial markets and globalization.

The New Economy has shown signs of the same speculative excesses that marked previous periods of technological innovation. In addition, the risks involved in the fields of telecommunications and the Internet were played down, in the same way that the true impact of deregulation in the former field was miscalculated. Today the New Economy is being crushed by a gigantic over-investment. The financial markets, for their part, have been falling in past quarters with the same exuberance that marked their growth in previous years. The crisis of confidence and the setbacks that have affected high tech stocks are complemented by the financial problems deriving from mega-mergers. Those who invested in Nasdaq in March 1990 had lost 60% of their capital by the middle of 2001. *Business Week* (August 20-27, 2001) reported a 5 trillion dollar fall in stocks in the United States, while *The Economist* (August 25-31, 2001) reported a 10 trillion dollar fall in global stocks between the beginning of 2001 and August 2002. Globalization, in turn, has caused the evils of one sector or region to be rapidly transmitted to others, as happened in the past with the benefits of the bonanza. The contraction of U.S. imports has virtually acted like a global transmission belt.

Now that the orgy of self-satisfaction that accompanied the boom of the New Economy, the financial markets and globalization has ended, we are seeing the other side of the coin.

THE NEW ASIAN CRISIS

The Asian and Southeast Asian miracle was supposed to last for decades and to transform those regions into the main generators of world economic growth. From mid-1997, however, the economy on which the supposed miracle was founded began to fall down. There were several reasons for the crisis. A too-liberal and permissive financial framework and weak state supervision allowed for a heavy indebtedness, mainly made up of short-term loans. These, in turn, fed important speculative bubbles and encouraged over-investment in sensitive export sectors, leading to a depreciation of prices and the saturation of markets. The whole world was to feel the expanding waves of the Asian crisis. In the final reckoning, the eight Asian and Southeast Asian countries in crisis had accounted

for 15% of world trade in 1996. If we add Japan to
them, the region represented 22% of world trade.

After a few years of tough sacrifice, the above
economies seemed to have recovered their health.
In January 2001 the finance ministers of the region
met in the Japanese city of Kobe, where they gave
free rein to their optimism about the future. According to their calculations, the regional Gross Domestic Product would expand by 5% in the year 2001.
Seven months later a picture that was very different
from their expectations emerged: Japan faced recession again; Taiwan had its lowest growth rate – 1.1%-
in 26 years during the first quarter of that year;
Singapore plunged from a growth rate of 9.9% for
the previous year to an estimated one of 1.5% for
2001; and South Korea, Hong Kong and Malaysia
faced a radical slowing down of their economies.[2]

What were the reasons for this new fall? The answer is simple. The crisis of the New Economy left
Western manufacturers of computers, cell phones
and other electronic paraphernalia with inventories
full of microchips. To give one example: according
to *The Economist* the price of memory chips had
fallen by 80% in the previous months and their global sales had shrunk by 50%.[3] The Asian and Southeast Asian countries had invested so massively in
this sector that the white-dressed workers of the semiconductor factories had come to be a symbol of their

2. *Financial Times*, August 10, 2001
3. August 11-17, 2001.

new age. The crisis of the New Economy began to leave them without an adequate foundation of support. For some countries of the region, as in the case of Malaysia, electronics represents 60% of exports and 42% of the GDP. As *The Economist* correctly pointed out, after a long struggle to abandon their dependence on exports of raw materials that are vulnerable to pronounced cycles, some of these economies have wound up being subjected to the same mono-production cycles. The futuristic picture symbolized by workers dressed in white uniforms proved to be an illusion.

The gravest aspect of the problem, however, is that the region is falling once more into the eternal sin of overproduction. Convinced that it does not matter how low prices fall as long as they expand their market, these economies are continuing to increase their volume of production and are competing for the scraps of the electronic markets. It is the same syndrome that the OPEC Countries suffered from a while ago. The inevitable result will be an aggravation of the crisis of the New Economy.

THE ERA OF MONEY

The present era is the era of money, but of private, not public, money. According to *The Economist*, in its issue for the second week of June 2001, the past decade was the decade of the most exuberant creation of wealth in the history of mankind.

The publication refers to the fact that the world now boasts of 425 billionaires and 7.2 million people who each have an investment capacity of more than a million dollars. For their part, Sarah Anderson and John Cavanagh, of the Washington, D.C. Institute for Policy Studies, point out that the world's 100 biggest corporations control 20% of global assets, while of the hundred biggest economies in the world, 51 are corporations and only 49 are nation-states.[4] The value of the annual sales of each of the world's six biggest transnationals is between 111 and 126 billion dollars, a figure which is only surpassed by the GDP of 21 nation- states.[5]

The swiftness with which this accumulation of money is being produced may be demonstrated by a couple of examples. In 1983 the central banks of the world's five richest countries had reserves on the order of 139 billion dollars, while daily transactions in world financial markets were about 39 billion dollars. By the mid-nineties the reserves of these banks had doubled, while daily financial transactions had increased nearly 30 times.[6] Anyone who invested 100,000 dollars at the beginning of the seventies in the "Quantum Fund" run by George Soros would now be worth 300 million dollars.[7]

4. *Op. cit.*
5. Noreena Hertz, *The Silent Takeover*, London, William Heinemann, 2001
6. Jeffrey Garten, *op. cit.*
7. Noreena Hertz, *op. cit.*

The deregulation and resulting acceleration of the financial markets is behind the impressive growth of private capital in recent times. For many years the supervision and regulation of the financial markets were the keynotes of the capitalist economies. In 1975 the United States initiated a process of gradual deregulation, which took off when Ronald Reagan became President. Thatcher's England, always willing to follow examples of economic liberalization, began the deregulation of its stock market in 1986, which caused what was called the "big bang" of the London Stock Exchange. From then on this new orientation spread all over the place, giving an extraordinary dynamism to financial transactions.

It was by this route that there arrived the period which saw the greatest creation of wealth in history, but it also led to the greatest economic uncertainty. In the past few years the financial markets have shown a succession of high-intensity crises: the 1987 fall on the New York Stock Exchange; the 1993 foreign exchange crisis in Europe; the 1995 Mexican crisis; the crisis of the emerging economies that began in Asia in 1997; and the crisis of the so-called "New Economy" that began in April 2000. On each of these occasions the world had to hold its breath for fear of a domino effect that might have leveled everything. We have thus entered an economic era in which the amount of money that is earned and lost defies the human imagination. During the August 1997 fall in the New York Stock Exchange, more than a trillion dollars were lost and last year, in the single week of April 10-14, 2.1 trillion dollars vanished. Bill Gates, who was worth 92 billion dollars in December 1999, had "only" 51 billion dollars in May 2000 and in a similar fashion, scores of dotcom billionaires were wiped off the map during the same period.

It is worth recalling the last time that great wealth was created: the nineteen-twenties. Everyone knows what happened after that.

THE GREAT INSTITUTION OF THE TWENTIETH CENTURY

In his groundbreaking book, *The Concept of the Corporation,* published in 1946, Peter Drucker argued that corporations had replaced the Church as the most representative institution of modern society. In a recent edition in which it reviewed the great landmarks of the twentieth century, *The Economist* chose the corporation as the great institution of modern times. An institution which voluntarily brought together a great number of persons and combined their talent, knowledge and effort to achieve a common aim.

The arrival of the twentieth century found big companies in the hands of family groups, usually under the control of a charismatic "self-made man" who had risen from obscurity to create a great fortune. Names like Rockefeller, Carnegie or Ford were the embodiment of the company in its structurally incipient stage. As John Kenneth Galbraith has shown, these family owners, desirous of expanding their enterprises, opened their accounts books to scrutiny and recurred to public capital. By choosing this path, they involuntarily encouraged the emergence of what Galbraith called the techno-structure. That is, the creation of a managerial class which directly depended on the stock-holding public and was in a position to replace the family owners as the controlling force of such companies. This process became especially noticeable in the United States.

The big company, especially in the United States, was thus based on the small, anonymous stock-holder and a managerial class that was directly responsible to such stock-holders. Beginning in 1950, this process acquired a new thrust with the appearance of pensions funds. Charles Wilson, the head of General Motors, founded the first of those institutions that year, thus widely enlarging the potential base of stock-holders. By the following year there already existed 8,000 pension funds in the United States. It is worth noting that at the present time the three largest U.S. pensions funds – Fidelity Investments, Vanguard Group and Capital Research & Management – alone control more than 500 billion dollars worth of investments. In this way, industry was tied to finance.

In 1990 the Massachusetts Institute of Technology (MIT) published a famous study in which it concluded that industry and finance did not make a good couple. According to that study, this "has helped center the attention of companies on immediate prof-itability". In other words, all industrial strategy was subordinated to the quarterly earnings reports that had to be presented to Wall Street. In Europe and Japan, industry's dependence on the stock-holding public was much less marked. Towards the end of the eighties there still existed in those countries a greater interdependence between industry and bank-ing, which to a large extent avoided the stock-hold-ing public. In the opinion of many, this allowed for more rational industrial strategies, as well as a much less predatory managerial ambient. The acceleration of the global economy in the nineties began to make these European and Japanese models unsustainable. Everywhere company accounts books began to be made available to the stock-holding public, leading to a greater subjection to the financial world.

In the past few years, three big trends have domi-nated the corporate world in response to the de-mands of global competitiveness. In first place, there is the phenomenon of mega-mergers, that is, the fusion of large companies in the same productive field. By these means a world economy with ever more oligopolic traits is coming into being. The sec-ond trend is that of managerial restructuring – downsizing, re-engineering and so forth. In synthe-sis, it is a process of "creative destruction" that seeks to improve the corporation's competitive abilities and whose usual victim is employment. To make them-selves more agile, companies shed themselves of surplus "fat", which gives rise to massive dismissals.

The third of these trends has restored a practice that was common in the nineteen-thirties: stimulating the managerial initiative of executives through the proliferation of economic incentives. An example of this practice was seen a few years ago, when Bob Allen, head of AT&T, was awarded a substantial raise after laying off 40,000 employees.

The late-twentieth-century corporation has put an emphasis on efficiency but has also shown itself capable of an extreme degree of depredation. If the corporation has replaced the Church as the great social binder of modern life, it is notable that its temples do not preach love, but the survival of the fittest. Its ethics are those of exclusion, not inclusion.

THE THIRD REVOLUTION

The process of globalization which the world is now going through represents one of those great revolutionary periods that irrupt in history every now and again to shake the very foundations of the established order. In terms of its economic impact, the revolution that humanity is experiencing today may be compared to the historical eras of 1760-1830 and of 1880-1930. In the first of these periods, the steam engine and the big textile factories gave rise to what has been called the industrial revolution. In the second, the appearance of electric energy and mass production, created what became known (after Henry Ford) as "Fordism".

Now, at the beginning of the twenty-first century, the dynamo of the new revolution has to do with the technological leap in the fields of information, telecommunications and transport. Productive and financial processes have become integrated on a world scale, causing time and space to lose their traditional meaning. Not in vain has Frances Cairncross coined the phrase which best describes this new reality: "the death of distance". The origin of this third revolution goes back to the nineteen-sixties. Then and in the succeeding decades, the space race consumed enormous amounts of money. Such extravagant spending was frequently criticized as a luxury, considering the problem of world poverty. Nevertheless, the concentrated effort of research and scientific training which it required became the starting point for the unprecedented technological leap which now supports the globalized economy.

The velocity acquired through these scientific and technological transformations, particularly in the past two decades, has led to the transmission of information at the speed of light (300,000 kilometers per second); the "numeration" of texts, images and sounds; the now generalized use of telecommunications satellites; the revolution in telephone technology; the mass spread of informatics in productive and service sectors; the "miniaturization" of computers; and their integration on a planetary scale by means of the Internet superhighways.

This third revolution unleashed an unusual acceleration of the capitalist system. While the Cold

War was in force this acceleration was kept in check by the priority given to politics over economics. The world continued to revolve around parameters defined by the prospect of nuclear war. The fall of the Berlin Wall came to symbolize the fall of the last remaining containing wall against the intense push of the economic. Thenceforth, the unstoppable force of capitalist acceleration overwhelmed the nation-states, forcing them to yield to the dictates of the marketplace. While private capital had kept up with technological advances, creating managerial innovations that allowed the private sector to take full advantage of this revolution, the cumbersome bureaucracies of governments were stuck in a past that was more reminiscent of the 19th than the 21st century.

Never before in history had the accumulation of money occurred as rapidly as in this third revolution. In fact, no one could question the undoubted success of this revolution in terms of the creation of wealth. Nevertheless, the process of globalization based on this third revolution raises critical questions about the resulting social, human and cultural costs. This new era has brought with it a growing deterioration of the rules of the game that supported political and social consensus in a large number of countries. At the same time it has placed in a marginal position not only an immense number of productive sectors but also many nation-states, drawing dividing lines between the net winners and losers. Finally, by virtue of its very speed, this process of wealth-creation has lost all sense of proportion and has entered the realm of adventure.

It is still too early to make a final judgement on this third revolution, but one thing remains certain: the anxieties and stresses which human beings have always felt in the face of great changes have taken on a global dimension in this case.

PARANOIA AND DESTRUCTIVE CREATION

The Lexus and the Olive Tree by Thomas L. Friedman, mentioned above, is obligatory reading matter for the student of globalization. One of the most interesting passages in this book is that in which the author argues that Joseph Schumpeter and Andy Grove are the two most influential ideologues of globalization. Schumpeter, one of the foremost economists of the post-war period, came up with the theory of "creative destruction", that is, the need to know how to destroy everything that is opposed to creative change. Grove, the president of Intel and one of the artificers of the revolution in information technology, popularized the idea that, in the hyper-competitive world of our time, only the paranoid is able to survive. The thesis of Schumpeter and Grove seems, in fact, to have manifested itself on the level of corporations, nations and individuals.

In the corporate world it is well worth mentioning an interesting study published by *Time*, which covers the bloody fight for success and survival in the world of high tech. According to that magazine: "Today's victory only gives you the right to survive so that you can fight again tomorrow... Nathan Myhrvold, who has a Ph.D. in physics and is one of Gates's closest deputies, told *Time* a year ago that 'it does not matter how good your own product might be, because you are only 18 months short of failure'. Myhrvold was wrong. This period has now been reduced to six months and is becoming ever shorter."[8]

It is no accident that, as *The Economist* remarks, the current model for the successful top executive is Jack Welch, former CEO of General Electric.[9] The reason? His emphasis on the need to permanently reinvent your company. Welch brought a kind of corporate cultural revolution to GE, in accordance with which only permanent change, even change for its own sake, can ensure that the company stays competitive. The fact that the need to reinvent yourself seems to have become a condition of survival is also seen on the level of countries. The best example of it is Japan. This country, which presented itself as the great economic power of the twenty-first century a decade ago, has lagged behind in the field of technology. This has been due to a mentality which emphasizes docility, discipline and the submission to social norms. In order to overcome these limitations, Japan is accepting the challenge of subjecting its own ancestral culture to a "creative destruction". The Japanese state is proposing, as a new national enterprise, the abandonment of its

8. September 16, 1996
9. September 18-24, 1999

parameters of social conformity and is actively encouraging its citizens to adopt, instead, an attitude that is individualistic, questioning and open to diversity.

This conviction that one should permanently adapt to technology and the growing challenges of the job market in order to survive is further evidenced on the level of individuals. In the Darwinian society of the present time there seems to be no room for those who are not open to and prepared for permanent change. The inevitable result of all this is the continual anxiety felt by millions of human beings who are subjected to a permanent threat of social exclusion.

Inevitably, of course, not all corporations are willing to follow the example of GE nor all nations that of Japan. What is more, there is an alarming growth in the number of people who have been excluded from the benefits of globalization, which has created a massive dose of resentment. Those who have been left behind are beginning to join themselves into a gigantic defensive alliance. The worldwide process of protests against globalization that began in Seattle in December 1999 is a proof of this. This is the response to the ideas of Schumpeter and Grove.

MEGA-MERGERS: FAILED MARRIAGES

One of the most characteristic phenomena of our times is that, on the one hand, there are more and more nation-states but they are becoming ever less

significant and on the other, while there are fewer
and fewer big private-sector corporations, they are
becoming more and more important. When the
United Nations was founded the world had 51 nation-states. There are now 187 of them and according to the predictions of some analysts, like Brian
Beedham, Editor of *The Economist*, they may surpass 300 by the middle of this century. While all
this has gone on, private-sector corporations, following a trend that started at the beginning of the
nineties, have been going through a process of
mergers that has significantly reduced their number and drastically increased their size. According
to *The Economist*, by 1999 the world value of mergers and acquisitions had risen by more than a third
to reach a level of more than 3.4 trillion dollars.
That is, an amount higher than the combined GDP's
of all of the countries of Latin America and equivalent to the combined GDP's of Great Britain, France
and Holland.[10]

There are many reasons behind this process of
mergers, but all have, as a common denominator,
the need to face up to the challenges of a globalized
economy. No matter whether the idea is to penetrate new markets or new market niches, or to seek
joint synergies in order to become more competitive, the one certainty is that the big corporations
merge with each other for a simple reason: all the
others are doing it. In other words, it is the fashion

10. July 22-28, 2000

of the day and if you go against it you face the risk of being left behind. It is clear that the world economy is becoming more and more oligopolic and that there is a rapid reduction in the number of competitors in each economic sector.

By now, everyone is aware that the great victim of mergers is employment. Every time that two giants merge, thousands of employees become redundant. However, it is only recently that a growing body of literature has come into existence which warns about the dangers that mergers represent for corporations themselves. In the year 2000, *The Economist* dedicated six successive issues to the subject of failed mergers and *Business Week* also gave a wide coverage to the subject. The former publication pointed out that corporate mergers show a higher failure rate than Hollywood marriages. According to *The Economist*, one out of two mergers between companies has led to the destruction of their respective market values.[11] *Business Week*, for its part, stated that barely one in five mergers may be considered successful.[12]

A typical case of a successful merger was the one between Time-Warner and Turner. Nevertheless, for every successful case, there are four which waver between disappointment and outright failure. The latter situation describes the merger between Chrysler and Daimler-Benz. Daimler's 36 billion dollar pur-

11. July 22-28, 2000
12. December 11, 2000

chase of Chrysler in 1998 was said at the time to be one of the most brilliant deals of the year. Today we see that the result of this experience has been the loss of 60 billion dollars in the market value of both companies.

The meager success of mega-mergers should be considered good news, not only for nation-states but also for the man in the street. For the former, because it discourages a process that makes them ever more vulnerable and insignificant and for the latter, not only because it safeguards employment but also because oligopolies are never good for the consumer. In the midst of the advances and retreats of a new era that has still not attained a definitive shape, the trend towards mega-mergers may turn out to have been a passing fashion.

THE HUBS OF THE NEW ECONOMY

The term, New Economy, is utilized to describe the process of sustained economic growth, with very low levels of unemployment and inflation, that characterized the U.S. economy up to a short time ago. High technology is behind the whole process as the fundamental generator of economic growth. Although this high technology is varied, its fundamental component is information technology. The collapse in April 2000 of the Nasdaq index, the main indicator for high tech stocks, raised a profound concern about the strength and sustainability of this New Economy.

The epicenter of this New Economy is Silicon Valley, whose market value was approximately 450 billion dollars in its peak moment. It is there that we find the headquarters of 20% of the world's biggest software and electronics companies, such as Intel, Cisco Systems, 3Com, Sun Microsystems and Netscape, among them. Emerging as an academic-technological community closely linked to Stanford University and intended to rival other communities of the same kind which already existed in Oxford and Bologna, Silicon Valley turned into the main driving force of the U.S. economy in the nineteen-nineties. Paradoxically the headquarters of Microsoft, the great giant of information technology, is not located in Silicon Valley, but in Seattle. The latter city has also achieved the status of a world-leading high tech park. Along with the places just mentioned, we find other critical clusters of information technology. They include the famous Route 128 on the outskirts of Boston; the "Research Triangle Park" in North Carolina; the city of Austin, Texas and more recently, Route 270, which borders the city of Washington and has turned the country's capital into one of the centers of the New Economy. It is from these hubs and others of lesser importance that the expansive force of the U.S. economy radiated.

Although the United States is the world center of high tech, other technological hot spots are found in different parts of the world. Among these we might mention Bangalore, Taipei, Nisshim, Tokyo, Munich, Prague, Cambridge, Helsinki and Tel Aviv, all of which boast of first rate technological or research parks, not only in the field of information technology but also in that of biotechnology or telecommunications. Grenoble, Strasbourg, Nice, Toulouse, Barcelona, Ypres and Frankfurt also stand out as important centers for technological innovation.

Latin America occupies a very small space on the world map of the new technology. Curiously enough, a small banana republic of Central America, Costa Rica, is the only country in Latin America which set out to devote its national energies to finding a place in the New Economy. Costa Rica tried to skip the industrial stage of economic development in order to leap towards a post-industrial economy.

There are serious doubts about the New Economy. For some analysts, its best moments are already a thing of the past. For others, however, recuperation will soon come and with it the high technology of information will still have a very important role to play. This is a fundamental question for all of these hubs of the "New Economy".

FROM THE TELEGRAPH TO THE INTERNET

The phenomenon of globalization is fundamentally based on the network that has resulted from the new technologies of information and telecommunications. Globalization, however, is not a new thing. Throughout the nineteenth century and up to the outbreak of the First World War, it flourished in a world that was interconnected by trade. Then as now, communications and information technologies were an essential part of the process. The telegraph, underwater cables, the creation and development of international news agencies and the transmission of information by means of electromagnetic waves constituted the technological base of that period.

The earliest telegraphs began to be developed in the eighteen-thirties, but it was not until the following decade that the introduction of the Morse Code gave them a practical utility. In the beginning the use of the telegraph depended on overland cables . With the appearance of underwater cables made of copper, beginning in 1850, telegraphic technology began to cross the seas. By 1865, the first underwater telegraph link between Great Britain and India was installed and by the beginning of the eighteen-seventies Europe became connected to America and Asia. By 1900, 190,000 miles of underwater cable permitted world-wide communication by means of telegrams. In 1870 a telegram sent from London took five hours to reach Bombay; by 1924, the time had been reduced to 80 seconds.

The emergence of the international news agencies was another fundamental landmark in the history of globalization. Five major agencies dominated the world scene during this period: Havas of France (now France-Presse), Reuters of England, Wolf of Germany, and the Associated Press (AP) and United Press International (UPI) of the United States. The first of these, Havas, was founded in 1835 and the last two, AP and UPI, in the twentieth century. For a long time the three major European agencies shared the world market by agreeing to limit their activities to certain geographical areas. The appearance of the two U.S. firms meant that five companies shared the world monopoly of news. Thanks to these international agencies, which were based on new communications technologies, news was transmitted from one end of the planet to the other, thus initiating the era of the global village.

The third great development of the period in mention was the transmission of information by means of electromagnetic waves. This innovation was strengthened by efforts to regulate the granting of licenses to use different frequencies of the electromagnetic spectrum. The introduction of radio and radio broadcasting, together with the creation of organizations which ensured a rational use of frequencies, represented a fundamental advance in the field of world communications. The 1906 Berlin conference was the first global effort to organize the use of this immense spectrum.

The new globalization is based on technologies that are infinitely more sophisticated: cable systems that allow for the codified transmission of information; the generalized use of satellites for long-distance communication, usually in conjunction with land-based cable systems; digitalized systems for the processing, storage and transmission of information, etc. The impact of the new technologies has been accompanied by the creation of great mega-conglomerates which cover a vast area that runs from technologies of information transmission to entertainment. The gigantic AOL-Time Warner-CNN is the epitome of the new times. From the invention of the telegraph to the Internet superhighways, the basic foundation of world economic interconnection has always been communications and information technologies.

THE MICROSOFT PARADIGM

Bill Gates and Microsoft recurred to all of the tactics that characterize the monopolist: they pushed competitors out of the market; extended a monopoly over a key area of the business towards parallel lines of activity; and tied the use of products that are vital to the market to the purchase of their other products. Their attempt to control the Internet highways through their "Explorer" program, excluding Netscape's "Navigator" from the highways, led to an anti-monopoly suit that is bound to make history. The Microsoft court case lays bare a whole set of situations that have come to be paradigmatic of the new economic reality. Let us examine some of them.

In the first place, we find ourselves before the paradoxical fact that, at a time when the global economy is becoming ever more oligopolic because of the very imperative of globalization, Microsoft is being punished for having grown too much. The answer to this paradox is found in the following point: while the global economy as a whole has become ever more dependent on the industry of knowledge, this industry has become increasingly dependent, in turn, on a single man and a single company – Gates and Microsoft. In a certain manner, the world oligopolic system cannot allow itself the luxury of letting one company retain so much power over such a vital area.

In second place, the Microsoft case shows how problems arise when nation-states and companies come to be seen as economic entities that are virtually on the same footing. In fact, at a time when the big corporations have acquired an economic dimension that makes them compete with nations themselves (and in reality dominate most of them), state authority is no longer respected. As far back as 1994, the U.S. Department of Justice began warning Microsoft about the sanctions its abusive behavior might unleash. The company, however, loftily ignored these signals, believing that it was too powerful to worry about bureaucrats. The very arrogance with which Microsoft entered the judicial arena, after the U.S. government presented the lawsuit, highlights this fact.

In third place, the case makes evident the risks which the "economy of paranoia" engenders. As we explained, it was Andy Grove, the boss of Intel, who popularized the idea that only the paranoid person can survive in the hyper-competitive economy of contemporary times. Given that his own rise was based on knocking down all rivals who had shown themselves to be vulnerable, Bill Gates is convinced that his own predominance depends on not leaving the slightest chink of opportunity to his competitors. By acting in this manner, he forgot the famous maxim of Henry Kissinger, which states that absolute security for oneself leads to absolute insecurity for others.

In fourth place, the case demonstrates that the new trend in the anti-monopoly fight has shifted from the area of price-control to that of innovation. Traditionally, the concern behind anti-monopoly enforcement had to do with the price-fixing that might derive from a situation in which one or a handful of companies controlled the markets. Nowadays the fundamental consideration is another: to prevent the creation of knowledge, the key to the New Economy, from being concentrated in a few hands. In this way, anti-monopoly cases are overlapping more and more with those on intellectual property rights.

There is no doubt that it is not only in the field of jurisprudence that the Microsoft case has established a landmark. Many of the new rules of the game that govern the globalized economy may derive from it.

THE PETROLEUM MARKET: TRENDS AND PRICES

The international petroleum order has shown a significant set of changes in the past few ears. The new trends in the petroleum industry point to the following developments:

1. The revolution in petroleum has drastically reduced the costs and risks associated with exploration and development. It has granted profitability to areas that were traditionally considered to be non-commercial.

2. Nuclear energy and natural gas have been gaining more and more ground in the energy market at the expense of petroleum. There was a more than 20% fall in petroleum consumption in Europe and Japan between 1973 and 1996. During the same period the consumption of natural gas and nuclear energy rose by around 10% in the two regions.

3. The emergence of the futures markets and other stock-market instruments has radically transformed the commercialization of petroleum.

4. New producers have been attracting a growing percentage of world petroleum investment. The petroleum nationalization programs carried out by the members of OPEC led multinational companies to seek investment opportunities in new countries, in the same way that the end of the Cold War signified the opening up of areas which had been virtually closed to the international petroleum industry for decades.

5. The transport sector is rapidly turning into the fundamental factor in the development of the petroleum industry. The automobile, a means of transport that depends on petroleum, symbolizes the prosperity, individualism and mobility associated with the globalized capitalism of our times. The field of internal combustion engines is responsible and will

continue to be responsible for more than half the growth of the international petroleum industry.

6. Petroleum consumers and producers are tending to come closer in the geographical sense. That is, a rationalization of the market is taking place, by means of which consumers tend to rely on the suppliers who are physically closest to them. By the year 2010, current estimates say, 90% of the petroleum imported to Asia will come from the Persian Gulf, whereas only 5% of the total consumption of the United States will come from the Middle East. Just as the exploitations in the Caspian Sea will be the basic source of petroleum for Europe, so too will the United States be supplied from the Western hemisphere.

The above trends form some of the main pieces of the world petroleum jigsaw puzzle. Nevertheless, judging by the variety of opinions on the matter, they are not a sufficient guide when it comes to determining where petroleum prices will go in the next few years.

Two of the predictions that have been published exemplify this diversity. One position points to a dramatic increase in demand and reduction in supply, which will lead to an era of high prices. Another posits a prolonged excess of supply, with low prices.[13]

13. Quoted by Amy Myers Jaffe and Robert A. Manning, "The Shocks of a World of Cheap Oil", Foreign Affairs, January/February 2000

In the first camp, which follows the tradition established by the Club of Rome in the seventies, we find Colin Campbell, one of the world's most prominent geologists. In a variety of scientific, political and industrial publications, this author and his followers have been arguing that the growth of global consumption of petroleum, driven by the modern industrial growth of the Asia-Pacific region, will create an excess of demand over supply. In fact, they argue, this dramatic growth in demand will coincide with a slowing down of the rhythm of petroleum discoveries. According to this argument, world petroleum production will reach a peak by the year 2003, causing the beginning of the end of the petroleum era and the start of a period of high prices.

A second group, represented by well-known energy analysts like Amy Myers Jaffe and Robert Manning, believes that prices will stay low during the next two decades as a result of a marked and prolonged excess of supply. In their opinion, world demand will have to grow by more than 3% annually to deal with the amount of petroleum that will be pumped onto the market, a figure which contrasts with the average annual growth rate of 1.8% that was registered between 1980 and 1995.[14]

In short, the clear trends we have mentioned do not enable us to create a predictable scenario for prices.

14. *Idem*

GLOBALIZATION:
THREE FUNDAMENTAL CRITICISMS

The globalization process that the world is going through nowadays represents one of those great revolutionary periods that irrupt in history from time to time, shaking the foundations of the established order. In terms of wealth creation no one can question the undoubted success of the model. The criticisms of globalization are of another kind, which lie in the realms of the social, the human and the cultural. But they also have to do with the logic of a process of wealth-creation which, by its very acceleration, has lost all sense of proportion and limit.

Three fundamental criticisms may be made of globalization. It is responsible for the loss of cohesion in societies, the marginalization of countries and productive sectors and finally, the volatility of financial investments. With regard to the first, in a great number of countries globalization has brought with it a growing deterioration of the rules of the game that used to support political and social consensus. Under the impact of a productive competition which has neither frontiers nor restraint and has transformed the reduction of costs into a dogma, there is no longer any room in the world for social considerations. This path tends to lead to a leveling down, whereby the cheapest manpower, or the replacement of manpower by machinery, determines the market survival of producers. Within this scheme of things the web of relations that gave cohesion to whole societies is collapsing. In different parts of the world societies that were known for their high level of harmony are now suffering extreme internal stresses.

The marginalization of a large number of countries and productive sectors is another direct consequence of the globalization process. As Paul Kennedy has correctly declared in his book *Preparing for the Twenty-First Century*: "The enthusiasts of globalization seem to mainly concentrate upon what it represents for the 'triad' of prosperous societies found in North America, Europe and Japan, dedicating little attention to the prospect of marginalization that it represents for the fourth-fifths of the earth's population which is not well-prepared to face up to these new commercial and financial trends".[15] In fact, in a Darwinian global society, in which only the fittest survive, there is not much room for illusion among those who lack capital and technology. Apart from a few competitive niches, it will be difficult for the developing countries to be able to face up to the challenges which this system presents. Nevertheless, it is not only in the developing countries that problems are found. Within the industrialized world itself, whole productive sectors are heading towards a dead end. Economies like the Japanese have been divided into net winners and losers. Authors like Lester Thurow are already warning about the risk of creating a genuine "apartheid" economy in the industrialized countries.[16]

15. *Rio de Janeiro*, Editora Campus, 1993, p.60
16. *Op. cit.*

Finally, it is worth mentioning the volatility of the international financial market in globalization times. Under the shelter of modern communications technology and within the ruling ambient of "laissez faire", the world's stock markets daily mobilize incredible amounts of money. The handling of stock-market instruments that are becoming ever more complex and risky by "yuppies" who are eager for quick fortunes is transforming financial markets into real casinos. Under the stimulus of a piece of good or bad news, billions of dollars flow into or out of countries with an astonishing facility, breaking up their economies and leaving them at the mercy of speculators with a short-term vision.

THE WTO: BLIND ALLEYS

In December 1999, trade ministers from all over the world met in Seattle under the auspices of the World Trade Organization. Outside the conference site, the occasion was marked by the presence of more than one hundred organizations which came to Seattle in order to protest against globalization. Within the meeting itself, the deliberations showed the limits of economic multilateralism. Once agreement on the basic agenda was reached (low tariffs, open markets, etc.) the further advance of the process depended on resolving questions that became ever more specific and controversial. Seattle clearly displayed the numerous blind alleys that mark this process. In essence, the meeting was a war of all against all, which exposed the limitations of an organization whose rules are drawn on a consensus basis.

In the midst of this all-against-all fight, which did not prevent the formation of tactical coalitions among the most improbable allies imaginable, there were conflicts of the most diverse kind. The United States pressured Europe to eliminate its agricultural subsidies. Japan and other countries confronted the United States on anti-dumping norms. The United States struggled with Europe about the regulation of genetically-modified goods. Europe and the United States got into a battle about norms on investment and competition. The developing world fought with the industrialized world about extending the period for implementing the commercial laws required by the Uruguay Round. And so on and so forth. Within this tangled multi-ring circus, two topics, above all, showed the division between the industrialized and developing world in the sharpest possible way: labor and environmental standards.

What do we mean by labor and environmental standards? The prices of products manufactured in the industrialized world incorporate the costs imposed by their domestic regulations on labor or environmental matters. Such regulations are the result of pressures exerted by their trade unions or ecological groups. When the products which originate in other countries are not subjected to similar regulations, it is evident that they enjoy an advantage. In other words, if they were forced to comply with similar standards, the manufactures that come from other latitudes would not be able to compete on equal terms. On the basis of this argument, it is understood that the producers from countries with rigorous standards are implicitly subsidizing the producers from countries with standards that are more lax. By extension, there is also thought to exist a dumping that favors those who have less demanding standards. Seen in this light, there would be a "social dumping" every time that a country does not comply with the stricter labor regulations of other countries and there would be an "ecological dumping" every time that a country does not have to comply with stricter environmental norms.

The developing countries, which found themselves obliged in the past to accept regulations on intellectual property rights which originated in the developed world and to tie themselves to inequitable commitments undertaken from 1986 onwards within the context of the Uruguay Round, stubbornly stuck to their rejection of an imposition of labor or environment norms. The arguments of the developing world showed an unquestionable logic. In accordance with the traditional theory on international trade, the benefits of trade derive, precisely, from the differences that exist between countries. Each country specializes in the production of those goods for which it enjoys comparative advantages, buying from other countries those manufactures which are costly for it to produce itself. The comparative advantages of each country are usually determined by its particular endowment of productive factors: some are blessed with better technology; others, by contrast, with richer natural resources and so the division of production goes. In this way, the differences create equilibrium: the advantages of one country's technology may be compensated by another's low labor costs. If you try to "level up", you not only drive from the market many countries which are unable to keep up with over-strict norms, but you also create a profoundly inequitable ambient. Logically speaking, if you seek to make everyone equal in terms of labor or environmental regulations, then you also have to ensure that everyone enjoys the same access to the technologies, capitals and modern managerial techniques that are available to the industrialized world.

The failure of Seattle showed that it was no longer possible to continue to impose universal standards of conduct on the weak in the name of the currently fashionable economic model (a conclusion that was confirmed in the following WTO reunion in Doha, Qatar). But it also demonstrated the virtual impossibility of getting everyone to agree about everything. In Seattle it became evident that economic multilateralism is full of blind alleys.

THE SECOND GREEN REVOLUTION

An impressive process of technological advance in the field of agriculture took place in the nineteen-fifties and sixties. Based on contributions by international agencies and public capital, it had to do with the development of hybrid crops and the widespread use of fertilizers and new irrigation techniques. The result of all this became known as the "Green Revolution". According to many analysts, the world is now entering into a second revolution in the field of agriculture, thanks to the contribution of biotechnology.

By biotechnology we mean any technique that uses live organisms or processes to make or modify products, improve plants or animals or develop micro-organisms for specific ends. This technology began to develop as a consequence of the notable discoveries relating to the genetic code that were made in the nineteen-fifties. Nevertheless, its full use for commercial purposes came into being in 1980, when the U.S. Supreme Court approved the first patent for a genetically-created creature, which had been developed with the aim of absorbing oil spills in the sea. In 1987, the U.S. Patents and Trademarks Office, for its part, confirmed the right to patent any creature "fabricated by mankind", thus recognizing for the first time that life is a product that may be manufactured.

In its April 12, 1999 issue, *Business Week* dedicated its main story to the subject of agriculture and biotechnology. This article not only referred to the emergence of the second green revolution, but it also spoke of the way that biotechnology is linking the sectors of agriculture and health. According to the magazine, genetic engineering opens up the possibility of fabricating plants which emit their own pesticides or grow in arid or salty soils or produce highly nutritional foodstuffs. Furthermore, the agricultural products fabricated in this way may turn into active instruments for the general improvement of humanity's health. As this revolution advances, we may see, in a not very distant future, potatoes that incorporate vaccines to combat endemic diseases, tomatoes with substances that have been especially designed to fight cancer or cardiac disease, or grains of soy or wheat that are able to produce hemoglobin. In short, a second green revolution whose scope and possibilities would make the first one seem insignificant.

Business Week's exceedingly optimistic view of this combination of agriculture and biotechnology contrasts with the clearly negative one held by Paul Kennedy, author of *Preparing for the Twenty-First Century*, and Jeremy Rifkin, author of *The End of Work*. Both writers issue warnings about the implications of the association between biotechnology and agriculture. For them, the fundamental problem has to do with the possibility of destroying the ancestral relationship between man and the soil in order to create a world in which foodstuffs are produced in closed laboratories. The essence of the process is not that difficult to understand. Once you have the genetic code of whatever vegetable, it becomes like any other manufacture: it would be possible to recreate it on a great scale through industrial techniques. In that way, producing pears or apples would be the same as manufacturing refrigerators or washing machines. As Paul Kennedy wisely points out: "It is one thing to have a tomato that is genetically created to resist disease and which does not quickly rot, and quite another to know that a biotech company can create tomato pulp, orange and apple juice, or tobacco 'in vitro' in a laboratory, without needing to plant crops".[17]

Both Kennedy and Rifkin agree with the argument that, once biotechnology has been let loose in the field of agriculture, there will be no way of controlling its effects. Kennedy declares: "The genie escaped from the bottle and may affect all aspects of our life. What seems much less clear is whether our global society will be able to deal with the economic and social consequences of a large-scale transformation of agriculture".[18]

Rifkin is even more emphatic about the effects of biotechnology: "The new advances in science threaten to do away with open-air agriculture by the middle of the next century. Technological shifts in the production of foodstuffs are leading us to a world without farmers, with unforeseeable consequences for the 2.4 billion persons who depend on the soil for their survival... Hundreds of millions of farmers throughout the world face the prospect of being permanently eliminated from the economic process".[19]

17. *Op. cit.*, p.87
18. *Idem* p.92
19. *O Fim dos Empregos*, Sao Paulo, MAKRON Books, 1996, p. 137

There is an immense distance between the rosy view presented by *Business Week* and the overwhelming pessimism of Rifkin and Kennedy. Only time will tell us who is right.

THE DISAPPOINTMENTS OF GLOBALIZATION

The year 2000 became a turning point for the phenomenon of globalization. Although some of the factors that set off this situation originated in December 1999, it was in the course of 2000 that proliferating trends made evident the disappointment evidenced by globalization.

In the first place, there was the unleashing of a chain of widespread protests which, beginning in Seattle, have taken place at each and every one of the meetings held by the elite of the global economy. London, Washington, Philadelphia, Los Angeles, Prague, Melbourne and Gothenburg – throughout the year all displayed the anger of the organized mass protests against globalization. Up to a short while before, it had been generally believed that the imperatives of globalization had filled the space that corresponded to politics. Some writers, like Thomas Friedman, came to speak of the "golden straitjacket" placed on nation-states by the globalizing phenomenon. The mass protests organized by an endless number of non-governmental organizations began to checkmate the international financial agencies, forcing the nation-states to reaffirm the weight of political considerations. For the first time it became evident that, without the express or tacit support of the nation-states and the determination of the financial agencies, globalization could find itself without a real support.

Seattle also showed that the World Trade Organization was in crisis. Economic multilateralism had come to transform itself, as we have said, into a war of all against all, without an effective arbitrator to regulate it. In addition to the conflicts we have mentioned above, the tensions created by cases like bananas, movies and genetically modified organisms threatened to unleash a genuine trade war between the United States and the European Union.

In third place, the so-called "New Economy" showed its limitations and vulnerabilities. Throughout the nineteen-nineties it was thought that the technological innovations characteristic of the U.S. economy would guarantee a process of continual expansion that would do away with the business cycles of the traditional economy. After the collapse of the Nasdaq index in April 2000 it became clear that the "New Economy" was not only subject to the same rules as the old economy but also that it was much more volatile. Both *The Economist* (December 9-15, 2000) and *Business Week* (October 9, 2000) warned that the spiral of economic growth generated by the "New Economy" ran the risk of turning into a vicious cycle of slow-down and crisis.

Finally, the year 2000 exposed the failure of the mega-mergers. For many years it had been thought that the greater the degree of fusion among the big corporations, the stronger would grow their competitive strength, thus giving dynamism to globalization. In that year, however, an extensive body of economic and management literature began to underline the high percentage of failure that marks this process of business integration. What is more, during that time many of the marriages between companies ended in scandalous divorces.

ECONOMIC GROWTH AND CULTURE

Following the end of the Second World War and the start of the process of dismantling colonialism in Asia and Africa, the notion of "development" became fashionable. According to this philosophy, that group of nations in the southern hemisphere which later came to be known as the "Third World" were in a condition to reach the level of progress that characterizes the rich countries. To achieve it, all that needed to be done was to comply with a set of well-defined requisites: the injection of capital, the supply of technical and material resources, the design of plans for economic growth, etc, etc. In short, by reproducing and concentrating into a sort of compressed package those processes which had created prosperity in the Northern hemisphere, the reasoning went, it would be possible to bring prosperity to the backward nations as well. In the nineteen-fifties, some proponents of this idea, like W.W. Rostow, even came to draw diagrams that set down the stages of economic growth in a mechanical way. How easy it all looked!

As usually happens in these cases, a "spoilsport" had to appear. In this instance it was the economist and sociologist Gunnar Myrdal. In his books *The Asian Drama* and *The Challenge of World Poverty*, he set forth an undeniable reality: there are cultures which are not apt for development. Their beliefs, ways of life and mental attitudes may become gigantic obstacles to the achievement of higher levels of material wealth.

In reality, this idea that culture determines attitudes towards material progress was not a new one. As far back as the beginning of the twentieth century Max Weber had formulated a thesis, within similar parameters, that turned out to be fundamental for understanding the evolution of capitalism in the West. The originality of his thought lay, precisely, in the affirmation that culture acted as a conditioner of economy. And not the other way round, as Marx had argued.

Weber, of course, had concentrated on a particular kind of culture: the one that arose from the Protestant revolution in northern Europe. Characterized by what he termed the "Protestant ethic", it was made up of men who did not consider work as a means to an end but as an end in itself. That is, it revolved around a human being who, motivated by compulsive tendencies of a religious origin, anxiously sought to obtain material success.

What Myrdal and Weber had in common was the idea that the role of the economy is subordinate to culture. Nevertheless, there was a fundamental difference between them. Weber dealt with the question of why some people seemed destined to become rich, Myrdal with why others seemed destined to stay poor. In the final reckoning, they were talking about two sides of the same coin.

Following the stance of Mydral, another "spoilsport" made his appearance. It was the U.S. sociologist Oscar Lewis, who, after studying the reasons for the material backwardness of the "Chicano" population in the United States, coined a term which was dramatic in itself: "The culture of poverty". Among the causes for its existence were such factors as the following: the lack of a participatory and organizational stimulus, the absence of a civic spirit, a fatalistic view of life, a tendency to live in the present without making a diligent effort to construct a future, the perception of wealth as something magical rather than the natural result of hard work, a low level of initiative in the resolution of one's own problems, a parochial view of events, a high degree of dependence on solutions handed down from above, etc, etc.

It has to be said that the "culture of poverty" is in no way exclusive to the Chicano community of the United States. Without setting out to do so, Lewis came up with a precise description of the cultural traits of an immense mass of people who live in the Third World, particularly south of the Río Grande.

Unfortunately, the conclusion is clear: while some are born into a culture which pushes them forward, for others culture is a heavy burden which weighs them down.

Curiously, the belief that it is feasible to attain economic growth and perhaps development itself by following a clear-cut recipe is now becoming fashionable again. Everywhere you look, the norms of the Washington Consensus are being trotted out as a suitable formula for overcoming the structural limitations of developing countries. The formula, of course, does not take into account cultural considerations, nor the need to strengthen cultures through the parallel creation of a civic awareness.

Nevertheless, the proponents of the "cultural" thesis have not been idle. In different parts of the United States and the developed world a powerful current of thought which emphasizes the fundamental importance of culture in economic affairs is beginning to make itself felt. Authors like Samuel Huntington, Lawrence Harrison, Francis Fukuyama, Alain Peyrefitte, Thomas Sowell, Robert Putnam and Benjamin Barber form the vanguard of a movement that reaffirms the cultural as the basis of economic and political processes.

THE DOLLAR VERSUS THE EURO

Throughout the nineteenth century and in the beginning of the twentieth the gold standard was the epicenter of the world economy. That era ended with the Second World War. After the Bretton Woods Conference of July 1944 the U.S. dollar became the new axis of international finance.

At Bretton Woods a fixed parity was established between the dollar and gold, with a value of 35 dollars an ounce. The United States agreed to convert its paper money into gold and pay it, at the fixed parity, to any foreign central bank which solicited such payment. On these foundations the international accounts of the post-War period began to be designated in dollars, not gold.

In August 1971, President Richard Nixon decided to end the convertibility of the dollar into gold. The metallic reserves of that country were no longer able to back up the amount of dollars in circulation. Despite the earthshaking effect of this on the international financial order, the industrialized world agreed to maintain the dollar as the central currency within a floating system. The result was that the United States was able to maintain the benefits of a dollarized international order without having to assume the responsibility which this implied in terms of gold reserves. In reality, no other currency was capable of filling the place held by the dollar and in the absence of a better alternative, Washington held onto its privileged position free of cost.

The benefits which the above situation have brought to the Giant of the North are evident. A single example will suffice to prove this point. Some years ago there was a dramatic fall of the dollar against the yen and other currencies and those who held foreign reserves in U.S. dollars wound up losing up a third of their real purchasing power. This, however, did not cause any kind of run against the dollar, as might have been expected. The reason? There was nowhere else to go. The European currencies, taken individually, turned out to be too weak to allow for the influx of hundreds of billions of dollars, while the Japanese market was too regulated and closed to turn the yen into a viable alternative. In that situation, the owners of trillions of dollars in international reserves were forced to suffer gigantic losses in the real value of their reserves, without having any other options.

In 1991, however, something occurred which could change the whole situation. In December of that year the Treaty of the European Union was approved in the Dutch city of Maastricht. Its reason for being was evident. With the collapse of the Soviet empire and the reunification of Germany, the delicate balance of power upon which the European Economic Community had been built was upset. Germany threatened to become too powerful and the nationalistic instincts of that country, which had always been latent, presaged a new resurgence. To deal with this danger Helmut Kohl and Francois Mitterand came up with the same solution: redefine the terms of the European Community. They had, nevertheless, different reasons for doing so. Kohl wanted to strengthen his country's links with Europe in order to keep the nationalistic feelings of his fellow-citizens in check. Mitterand, on the other hand, wanted to strengthen Europe in order to keep Germany itself in check. It was on these bases that the Maastricht Treaty arose.

Maastricht established three central pillars for the structure of the European Union: a common currency, a joint foreign policy and a common system of justice. The creation of a single currency, the euro, was the fundamental step of the process. Towards that end a set of concrete requisites was established, which had to be met by all signatories, as well as a precise time period to comply with them. The date established for the entering into force of the first phase of the euro was January 1, 1999.

In order to comply with the terms imposed by the euro, the members of the European Union had to adapt rigid policies of fiscal austerity. Controlling public budgets turned into the battle cry of most of the European governments. Many experts, among them the billionaire and philanthropist George Soros, thought that this strategy of fiscal austerity was a historical contradiction. So long as unemployment remained the biggest problem in Europe, threatening a nationalistic-minded rebellion against European integration and globalization, fiscal rigidity, he argued, would only worsen the situation. In fact, in Europe itself many agreed with the opinion of Soros, seeing the euro as a threat to political and social stability.

In the course of 1997, however, things took a sudden and surprising term. The "mayonnaise" of the euro began to congeal and everywhere the opposition to it showed signed signs of yielding. In June of that year, for the first time, more than 50% of the Europeans who were polled said that they were in favor of a single currency. The eternal enemies of the euro – like the French socialists, the German social democrats and even the British laborites – went though a "conversion" and eventually became convinced of its virtues. By now, the euro has become an everyday reality in twelve countries of the European Union.

Reactions to the emergence of the single European currency were not slow to emerge. Lester Thurow saw the appearance of the euro as the biggest threat to the economic supremacy of the United States. In his words: "the most significant change in the economic position of the United States will come with the introduction of the euro in 1999. For the first time since the Second World War, investors and financiers will have a viable alternative to the dollar and the venerable greenback will have become just another currency".[20] For its part, the well-known Swiss bank, Julius Baer & Co. of Zurich, issued the following statement: "The appearance of the euro is going to modify the global monetary scene to an extent that has not been seen since the dollar replaced the pound sterling as the currency of reference more than sixty years ago".[21] The significance of the euro is that an alternative currency to the

---

20. *Harvard International Review*, December 1997
21. *El Mercurio*, March 7, 1998

dollar will have serious consequences for the U.S. economy. In the past, as Yale University professor Diane Kuntz points out: "The United States was accustomed to treat the multilateral financial institutions as branches of the Federal Government".[22] In the future, the United States will no longer be able to continue borrowing with impunity. With the advent of the euro the rest of the world will show itself to be much less disposed to subject itself to the dollar, which will make it ever more difficult for that country to finance its gigantic trade deficits on the basis of credit. As Thurow indicates: "The United States will not be able to continue maintaining a trade deficit once the euro makes its appearance: the funds to finance this deficit will not materialize". Will the twilight of the dollar era have begun?

THE PLAGUE OF THE ROMANTICS

The U.S. academic James P. Pinkerton has called the ecologists the great romantics of this epoch. But just as German romanticism was put at the service of Bismarck's "realpolitik", so too have the ecologists become one of the biggest bastions of support for protectionism, both of the right and the left. In the United States, these "romantics" have allied themselves with the ultra-conservative right,

22. *Foreign Affairs*, July/August, 1995

as represented by a Pat Buchanan or a Ross Perot, in opposing NAFTA and free trade.

Ecological protectionism constitutes – there is no doubt about it – one of the most powerful barriers erected by the markets of the developed world. In the name of environmental idealism there are walls that genuinely block international trade. It may be useful to analyze this subject a little.

Between 1945 and 1979 trade among the developed countries was progressively liberalized, in large measure due to multilateral accords on tariff reduction. The average tariffs of these countries fell from 40% in 1957 to 4% in 1994. Nevertheless, the markets of the industrialized world are as protectionist as they were in the past, or even more so. This, however, is a question of a new type of protectionism that no longer recurs to the classic method of tariffs and trade quotas. Nowadays, the new barriers to free trade have to do with such things as minimum standards on quality, the threat of anti-dumping and anti-subsidy measures, phyto-sanitary restrictions, etc. Within this potent arsenal of weapons available to the new protectionism, the vigor of ecological measures especially stands out.

Among the many varieties of ecological protectionism, we could point to some like the following: ecological "dumping", new environmental standards that regulate the whole life cycle of a product, the so-called "precautionary" principle for environmental damage, ecological labeling, etc. Let us have a quick look at them.

"Dumping" is the name given to price discrimination between countries, or alternatively, the practice of selling for export at less than cost price. The difference between the two prices is known as the margin of "dumping". At the present time, many industrialized countries have coined the term "environmental dumping" to describe the lower production costs that obtain in a selling country by virtue of its looser environmental standards. In this way, the country with higher standards believes that it has the right to penalize products originating from countries with laxer environmental standards, because such products turn out to be more competitive.

The developing countries, who are the ones which usually pay for the consequences of these policies, must face enormous costs if they wish to adjust their manufacturing processes to the environmental standards of the world's more industrialized countries. A recent example of this was seen in Chile: its state mining companies were obliged to carry out a decontamination program which, between 1997 and 2000, represented more than a billion dollar investment in treatment plants, filters and similar measures. This was a prerequisite for the continued sale of their processed minerals to the industrialized world.

Another measure which is beginning to be put into practice are the new ISO 14000 environmental standards, which regulate the whole life cycle of a finished product. In line with these standards, in order to enter some markets of the industrialized world, foreign producers have to guarantee that the final product has been "clean" during all the phases of its manufacturing process. What is more, they must guarantee that the product will continue to be "clean" in the final stage of the cycle, when it is disposed. In this way the norms seek to identify all possible environmental impacts in the productive chain, from the conversion of raw materials into manufactures to transport and distribution to the consumer, and including the maintenance, recycling and final disposal of the product.

Thus, for example, if you set out to analyze a car manufactured in Venezuela or Peru or Egypt, you may have to consider everything from the quality of the iron ore utilized for the steel panels of the bodywork to the "purity" of the glass in the headlamps, and even the biodegradable capacity of its components. You often reach the extreme of requiring the seller of the product to prove his capacity to guarantee its environmentally-friendly recycling and final disposal.

The "precautionary" principle is another of the mechanisms that is beginning to be widespread, particularly within the European Union. According to this principle, even when it is not possible to establish a cause-effect relationship for the environmental impact of given products or substances, restrictive measures may be imposed in order to prevent eventual damages to health or the environment. In other words, even in the absence of scientific evidence, substances or products may be prohibited or given a restricted market access on the basis of a mere suspicion of risk. In this manner, he who wishes to introduce his product to that market must frequently assume the costly burden of proof with respect to environmental quality. Orimulsion, a trademark fossil fuel fabricated from natural bitumen that is produced by the Venezuelan state oil company, is one of many Third World products which have had to follow this difficult path.

"Green" or "ecological" labeling means that the producer has to include information about diverse environmental aspects of his product on his packaging in order to satisfy the environmental sensitivity of the consumers. This not only covers warnings about its negative features, such as the fact that it may be inflammable, but also its biodegradability, the energy-efficiency of its manufacture, its "friendliness" towards the ozone layer, etc. These labels are also used to incorporate environmental information that relates to the whole life cycle of the product: the content of its materials and packaging, its capacity for recycling, the volume of previous products waste incorporated into the new product, etc.

This group of environmental regulations and norms has a devastating effect on exports originating in the developing countries. What possibilities do Haiti or Ethiopia have of competing in such conditions? Furthermore, are countries like Colombia or Peru prepared to face up to the complexities of ecological protectionism? The alliance between the ecologists of the developed world and the domestic industries of the same countries threatens to become one of the worst plagues of fair international trade. It is the plague of the romantics.

THE END OF TRUST

With growing strength a common denominator is coming to mark economic and sociological literature and the language of the politicians. This is the subject of trust as an essential element for the development of nations. On the Old Continent the name of Alain Peyrefitte stands out among those who advance this thesis. In his two latest books, *The Society of Trust* and *Economic Miracles*, this author argues that trust is the fundamental reason why many nations have been able to leap forward to prosperity. A synonym for this quality is the capacity for collective understanding, the capacity to forge social links based on harmony. Two of the most notorious politicians of present-day Europe, Tony Blair and Leonel Jospin, have used a discourse that points in the same direction. Blair coined a term that has been come famous in contemporary political language: society of "stakeholders". Purely and simply, this means a society founded upon the solidarity among the different groups and sectors that compose it. Jospin, for his part, has referred to the need for a "new pact of trust" among his fellow-citizens of France.

On the other side of the Atlantic, a long list of intellectuals and management theorists have been emphasizing the same approach. Authors like Peter Drucker, Charles Handy, Jeffrey Pfeffer and Thomas Teal have stated that the future competitiveness of the U.S. corporation depends on reinventing an atmosphere of trust between employers and employees. For their part, academics like James S. Coleman and Robert D. Putnam have been arguing that the trust factor is the key to social prosperity. Even Francis Fukuyama, one of the two intellectuals who has had the most influence on the post-Cold War world, devoted his latest book to this subject. The thesis of his *Trust* is closely akin to that of Peyrefitte, in the sense of affirming that those cultures which value social harmony turn out to be the most successful ones in economic terms.

In reality, this argument is not that novel. As far back as the beginning of the twentieth century, Max Weber had emphasized the importance of the trust factor in his groundbreaking work, *The Protestant Ethic and the Spirit of Capitalism*. One of the essential arguments of that book was that the capacity for spontaneous association on the basis of reciprocal trust proved to be a key to organizational innovation and, in the end, the creation of wealth. Although this idea is not a novelty, the popularity it has attained in current day intellectual, management and political circles is surprising. Alain Peyrefitte coined the phrase "the ethos of trust", to describe the factor that upholds the process of wealth-creation that occurs in certain societies. Francis Fukuyama reused the term "social capital", originally invented by James

P. Coleman, to express the capacity of individuals to work together in groups or organizations for the purpose of reaching common objectives. This "social capital", based on the aptitude for consensus and trust, is set forth as the essential condition for productivity and economic health.

It is paradoxical, however, that this matter of trust has attained such a central place in the academic and political thought of our times, when it is precisely its absence that most notoriously characterizes the global economy. Everywhere you look, the one thing that stands out is the egoism shown by individuals, organizations, sectoral groups and nation-states, as a consequence of the demands that derive from the market economy. The consensus and sense of harmony found in inter-sectoral relations, formerly a characteristic of the economies of continental Europe, are now on the point of extinction. The path towards the euro has led to the "flexibilization" of labor conditions, an approach that threatens to destroy values and styles of life that were inseparable from their societies. In East Asia, particularly in Japan and South Korea, the old ethic of social harmony and the guarantee of life-time employment have disappeared as well. The rate of unemployment in Japan is now more than 5.6%, while in South Korea it surpasses 7%. The small and medium Japanese business enterprise, a key element in its economy and its main generator of employment, is being mercilessly overrun by the banks and the big corporations. In all parts and on all continents, the combination of technological progress based on automation and the widespread abandonment of norms on social protection is causing anguish and discontent. Distrust is the law of the day. Investors distrust the government, bosses distrust the workers and the workers distrust bosses, the government and society in general. Everyone distrusts everyone. One after another, the world's stock markets fall, sweeping away whole countries and regions, under the impact of this generalized crisis of trust. Any day now, we might wake up to hear that the international financial system has collapsed as a result of this situation.

In his above mentioned book, Fukuyama, who had proclaimed the "end of history" as a result of the world implantation of the free market, has turned into a strong critic of a market economy which does not respect cultural diversity. By imposing utilitarian selfishness as the order of the day, the globalized economy caused the loss of the collective solidarity and the social harmony that ruled entire societies for such a long time and became paradigms to be followed. The costs of this loss are beginning to make themselves felt.

BETWEEN THE MACRO AND THE MICRO

In 1995, John Cavanagh and Frederic Clairmont, respectively research director and researcher of the Washington, D.C., Institute for Policy Studies, pointed

out that the world's 200 hundred biggest corporations held 26.8% of the global GDP. They also found
that in a large number of industrial sectors, the five
main companies were responsible for more than half
of production.[23] Since that time this trend towards
the concentration of world wealth in the hands of a
reduced number of companies has been growing in
a rapid way. The main reason for it is what have
been called mega-mergers. That is, the fusion of two
large firms within a given sector.

In this way, a world economy is being formed
which shows clear signs of oligopoly. In every one
of the economy's diverse sectors, fewer and fewer
companies control ever larger market shares. In the
aviation industry, the merger between Boeing and
McDonnell Douglas has reduced the number of
manufacturers of large-capacity aircraft to two:
Boeing-McDonnell Douglas and Airbus. In the field
of consultants and auditors, the six world giants of a
few years ago are now only four. In the field of
social communications and entertainment, seven
mega-conglomerates have consolidated themselves.
The same pattern repeats itself in one sector of the
world economy after another, forming what the Italian intellectual Riccardo Petrella has called "world
mega-systems".[24]

In the opinion of some analysts, this trend tends
to benefit consumers, since the increase of scale cre-

23. Maniere de Voir 28, *Le Monde Diplomatique*, November 1995
24. Maniere de Voir, *Ibidem*

ates a reduction of final prices. For others, however, the excessive power of the oligopolies inevitably turns into price fixing and a reduced number of options for the consumer. If we follow classical economic theory, the very essence of an oligopoly would be defined by the latter premise. But, leaving aside this dilemma, the process in question has an influence on an additional factor: employment. Productive "rationalization" eliminates the duplication of effort and functions, allowing for the "liberation" of a great number of unnecessary jobs. It is not surprising that the "flexibilization" of labor, a heated subject at the moment, parallels the phenomenon of mega-mergers.

Nevertheless, it is highly curious that the other main business development of our day is the success of the small and medium company. On a much more modest level, of course, these kinds of companies have proven to be a successful model in the era of the globalized economy. The north-central part of Italy, particularly the Emilia-Romagna region; the state of Gujarat in India; the successful decentralization of production processes in Spain; and even the vitality evidenced by modest companies under the franchise system in the United States itself are important examples of this trend.

How have small companies been able to achieve such high levels of competitiveness, often challenging international firms? In small companies there is no dispersal of resources, useless and redundant functions do not exist, decisions are rapid, the company's objectives are concentrated upon a single market niche and the control of only one technology, attention is paid to the quality of the product and the company directly answers to the client. In contrast with big companies, the characteristic of this model is that it generates a lot of employment. By way of example it is worth mentioning that small and medium companies are responsible for between 60-80% of employment in Latin America.

In the era of the globalized economy it would appear that only the macro- and the micro- companies are able to find their own place. Those who occupy the ample middle ground seem to be condemned to absorption or disappearance.

WHOSE FAULT WAS IT?

In 1997, the economies of East Asia entered into a profound crisis. The two most successful economic models of the world – the Asiatic and the market economy one of Anglo-Saxon origin – suddenly found themselves in the dock of the accused. For the Asian economies, where the crisis was unleashed, the other side was guilty. From their point of view, the crisis would never have occurred if they had not liberated and deregulated their markets in order to live up to the liberal model. For the followers of the market economy, on the other hand, the Asian band had been responsible for the crisis. In their judgement, the irrational use given to borrowed funds was what had set off the recessive spiral. On one side and the other, an effort was made to distance oneself from the supposed guilty party. Malaysia, Hong Kong, Taiwan, South Korea and even Japan itself began to take measures that would isolate or protect themselves from Western influences. It was not by accident that people wound up speaking of an Asian stampede from the Anglo-Saxon model. The market, for its part, wanted to unlink itself as much as possible from the Asian economies. In fact, the damage caused to the latter by the flight of capital was out of all proportion to the mistakes which the region had made. Who was right?

For a long time the Asian model had been governed by very particular rules. In the first place, Asia set an economic course based on growth "towards outside", that is, an exporting-oriented system. In second place, it efficiently combined free enterprise with state planning. This encouraged a partnership relation between private capital and the State. In third place, it recurred to a process of regional economic complementation whose main axis was Japan. As the Japanese increased the level of complexity of their exports, those who were behind it came to occupy, in a staggered way, the more backward lines of industrial production. In fourth place, it placed more of an emphasis on technological adaptation than technological innovation. Instead of advancing by means of invention it recurred to the adaptation of other nations' technologies. In fifth place, education and domestic savings were given high priority. The percentages their budgets dedicated to education were among the highest in the world, as were their rates of personal savings.

There is no doubt that the above model was successful. Lee Tsao Yuan, Director of the Singapore Institute of Political Studies, read an interesting paper at the 1997 Asia-Pacific Economic Cooperation forum in Santiago, Chile, entitled "Growth of the Asian Economies". In it he underlined the following growth rates for the world's regional economies during the period 1965-1990: the New Industrialized Economies of Asia (Hong Kong, Taiwan, etc.) grew by 6.7%; the members of the Association of Southeast Asian Nations (Indonesia, Malaysia, etc.) by 4.7%; the industrialized countries of the Organisation for Economic Co-operation and Development by 2.7% on average; the Middle East by 2.5%; South Asia by 1.7%, and Latin America by 0.8%. In accordance with World Bank figures, cited in the paper, during the period 1975-95 East Asia reduced its number of poor from 716 million to 435 million people, a figure without precedents in human history. At the time that the Asian crisis broke out, the region enjoyed stable internal prices, a substantial fiscal surplus and high coefficients of internal saving and investment. That is, all of the macroeconomic factors necessary for a stable development.

How could such a successful system enter into crisis in such a boisterous way? The availability of and massive access to foreign capital, resulting from a market inundated with liquidity and the liberation of its domestic financial systems, led to an enormous indebtedness. As Alan Greenspan, Chairman of the U.S. Federal Reserve Board pointed out: "It is evident that these economies could not absorb such a tidal wave of funds". The abundant supply of cheap foreign funds raised assets prices, which increased their nominal value and allowed borrowers to accede to new and bigger loans. This, as is natural, tended to raise the price of assets even higher. On this basis great speculative bubbles were fed, particularly in real estate and on the stock market. In 1995, the U.S. dollar began to be revalued against the other currencies. Given that the economies of the region, with the exception of Japan, had currencies that were tied to the dollar, these currencies became dearer than those of their competitors. This affected their exports and increased their deficit in current accounts. These factors, together with the uncontrolled rise in stock and real estate prices, began to alarm the big speculators. When George Soros and his counterparts decided to get out of the region, panic broke out in the market. Inevitably, the great speculative bubbles burst, one after another. In a matter of months hundreds of billions of dollars vanished and one hundred million human beings fell back into poverty.

Who was at fault? There is no doubt that both sides should be blamed. It is evident, however, that none of this would have occurred without the existence of a market flooded with liquidity, in which a caste of professional creditors become paranoid in the face of any bit of bad news. By liberating their markets and placing themselves in the hands of such people, the Asian markets made themselves vulnerable to uncertainty. It was the Asian model that became discredited in the eyes of the world, as the market economy triumphantly emerged from the crisis in a strengthened position. Henceforth it would be said that the model that was a rival to the market economy had proved to be a failure.

MARKETS IN CRISIS, COUNTRIES IN BANKRUPTCY

For many years supervision and regulation were a dominant note in financial markets. It was the inevitable reaction to the excessive freedom which had led to the 1929 crash on Wall Street. On May 1, 1975 this trend began to reverse itself. It was on that date that the United States initiated a process of gradual deregulation. The acceleration of financial transactions within this new ambit of liberalization began to worry a number of analysts. Among them was the winner of the Nobel Prize in Economy James Tobin, who issued a warning in 1978 about the excessive agility that the market was acquiring. In his judgement, it was necessary "to put a bit of sand in the gears to keep things in check". He thus proposed a 0.5% tax on financial transactions every time that capitals crossed a border. Instead of following his advice, the U.S. stock market sped up its process of deregulation when Reagan came to power.

Margaret Thatcher followed his example with the deregulation of the British stock market in 1986, causing the so-called "big bang" on the London Stock Exchange. The trend then spread to others parts of the world and by 1987 the world's major stock markets, functioning without pause 24 hours a day, were showing daily exchanges of 150 to 300 billion dollars.

While euphoria took hold of the markets, the financial bubble was getting more and more inflated. It only needed the emergence of some bad news for the entire system to stagger. On October 19, 1987, the world's stock markets were beset by panic. The news that the U.S. trade deficit was bigger than had been predicted and the rise of interest rates in Germany were sufficient to shake the foundations of the market. In a single day, the Dow Jones index lost 508 points. A trillion dollars vanished from Wall Street as a result of that crisis. The invasion of Kuwait in 1990 gave rise to a new crisis in the markets, but it was less violent than the previous one.

Despite these warnings, the market continued to grow and overheat itself more and more. One of the fundamental reasons for it was the increase in monetary liquidity. The inflated price paid by Chancellor Helmut Kohl to finance the unification of Germany, and the money tossed away by the U.S. Federal Reserve to save that country's financial system from the great losses incurred by banks and savings-and-loans institutions, towards the end of the eighties, were among the factors that detonated this process. The well-known U.S. financial analyst Jim Rogers came to speak of "a global sea of liquidity".

While all this was going on, most natural resources had been losing their value in the international markets of the past decades. In this situation, the increase of monetary liquidity has coincided with a sharp decline in the prices of tangible goods. This has become a powerful stimulus for the creation of a world economy based on intangible values. That is, an economy of paper money. More than a trillion dollars flow through daily transactions on the world's stock markets. Inevitably, the concept of the value of money runs the risk of losing all meaning. The combination of a paper-money economy of astronomical dimensions and the multiplication of financial instruments that are making the markets ever more complex is leading to levels of abstraction that are beyond the comprehension of the human mind.

One kind of financial instrument, what are known as derivatives, has become especially dangerous. Combining higher mathematics with a traditional sense of gambling, and relying on the help of supercomputers, more and more complicated models of derivatives investments are being invented. George Soros, the patriarch of financial speculation, has come to affirm: "The explosive growth of derivatives instruments brings great risks. There are many of them and some turn out to be so esoteric that the dangers involved cannot be adequately understood even by the most sophisticated investors"[25] The billion dollar losses generated by these stocks in the nineties speaks for itself.

Some years ago the world saw a palpable example of the extremes which this process is leading to. At the time that President Clinton was receiving world attention by opening a 20 billion dollar credit line to save Mexico from collapsing, an anonymous speculator in Singapore, by the name of Nick Leeson, was mobilizing 27 billion dollars behind the back of the board of directors of his company, London's Barings Bank. When the gamble failed, the 1.3 billion dollar loss led to the disappearance of Barings, one of Britain's oldest and most prestigious financial firms. This contrast between a visible economy in which chiefs of state are subject to public and political controls, and an invisible economy with no controls in which subterranean beings make decisions of this magnitude, is one of the most notorious characteristics of the globalized order.

Many people are now insisting upon the need to supervise and regulate the markets before it gets too late. It is not by chance that George Soros has stated: "The financial markets are inherently unstable and susceptible to bankruptcy, unless you make stability an explicit objective of governmental policy".[26] The well-known economist and former French Primer

25. Byron Wien and Kritzina Koenon, George Soros, *Rio de Janeiro*, Editora Nova Fronteira, 1995, p.305
26. *Ibidem*, p. 113

Minister, Raymond Barre, stated the following in the Davos World Economic Forum a few years ago: "We cannot leave the world in the hands of a band of irresponsible 30 year-olds who only think about making money". These warnings should be taken into account now that the frenzy of the markets has led entire countries into or on the edge of bankruptcy. Hundreds of millions of human beings are becoming more and more dependent on the financial calculations of a few overbearing yuppies. If things carry on as they are, this paper economy will be set alight in the least expected moment, causing a global financial crash.

THE BULL'S VACATION

The animals that symbolize Wall Street are the bull and the bear. The bull is a synonym for a market in expansion, while the bear represents a fall in stock prices. From 1990 onwards the market lived under the aegis of the bull. In April 2000, however, the collapse of Nasdaq gave the first sign that the bear was approaching.

The figures reached by the U.S. economy during the nineties were impressive and are only comparable to the expansive period of the nineteen-sixties. By the end of the nineties inflation barely reached an annual rate of 1.7 %, unemployment only touched 4.5% of the work force and the growth of the GDP stayed at 3.5%. Furthermore, the economy defied the inverse correlation between unemployment and inflation which economists postulate, that is, the idea that when one falls the other rises. During the nineties unemployment and inflation fell in a simultaneous way. The U.S. economy became so successful during this period that not even the experts were in agreement about the reasons for it. Alan Greenspan, Chairman of the U.S. Federal Reserve Board, spoke of the "x factor", when referring to an economic phenomenon which no one could precisely describe but whose effect was undeniable. Others, like Princeton University Professor Alan Blinder, spoke of the "luck factor", when analyzing the cluster of fortunate coincidences behind the boom: a fall in the prices of petroleum, computers and the cost of medical care, together with an increase in the value of the dollar. The more optimistic observers, for their part, preferred to believe in the birth of what was called a "New Economy".

Among those who declared that the United States had entered into the era of a New Economy, we may cite the magazine *Business Week,* which devoted many articles to the subject. According to the magazine, the country had crossed the threshold of a stage of prosperity that would guarantee a sustained annual growth rate of 3% for an indefinite number of years. In accordance with this theory, technological advances had changed the rules of the economy, guaranteeing a long period of expansion. For *Business Week,* the impressive technological development being shown was the culmination of many years of research in diverse fields of knowledge, an enterprise that was now showing results. From the revolution in informatics to the revolution in biotechnology, the foundations had been laid for gigantic accumulations of capital.

Nevertheless, looking beyond the growth and stability that characterized the U.S. economy in the nineties and the immense potential offered by technology, many analysts were not so optimistic about the future. The economist John Makin, of the American Enterprise Institute, recalled that golden ages like those which arose in the U.S. in the nineteen-twenties and in Japan in the eighties, had ended in crisis.[27] In an interesting article, Michael Mandel argued that historical experience shows that periods of rapid technological progress and growth in productivity lead to economic volatility, not stability. He further declared that there were worrying parallels between the twenties and the nineties, since in both cases the economy became over-dependent on a single sector: the automobile industry in the first case and high technology in the second.[28] A similar conclusion was drawn by Paul Krugman of MIT and Robert Gordon of Northwestern University. Milton Friedman himself, the great guru of the market economy, came to predict in 1998 that the United States would face an economic recession in the following year.

27. *Quoted by Fortune Americas*, July 20, 1998
28. *Business Week*, August 24-31, 1998

Starting in April 2000, the forecasts of the pessimists began to be fulfilled, a situation that became more evident by the second quarter of 2001. Friedman's only mistake had been to anticipate the outbreak of the recession, but it did arrive in the end. Nevertheless, there are still many who insist that the bear's visit is only a temporary one and that we will soon see the return of the bull. Only time will tell who is right. The only certainty is that, after a decade of frenzied activity, the bull has taken a well-earned vacation.

THE EURO: THE NEW FACE OF EUROPE

At the beginning of May 1998 the heads of states and governments of the European Union, meeting in Brussels, approved the list of countries which would form the first circle of users of the euro, the new European currency. Of the fifteen nations which make up the European Union, only eleven would participate in the initial stage of the process. The United Kingdom, Sweden, Denmark and Greece did not join this monetary union. For the first three, it was a voluntary decision that meant deferring their adherence to the euro for a while, while Greece was excluded because it had still not fulfilled the preconditions for entrance. The Brussels meeting also decided to create a Central European Bank, which would assume the responsibilities traditionally held by the central banks of the member nations.

A two-stage program was undertaken for setting the euro in motion. In the first, which ran between January 1, 1999 and December 31, 2001, the euro was transformed into the common European currency. However, its use was limited to non-cash exchange mechanisms like checks and bank transfers and giros; during this transition period the different national monies continued to freely circulate. The second stage, which began on January 1, 2002, has seen the placing into circulation of bills and coins denominated in euros and includes a six-months grace period for the definitive elimination of European national currencies.

According to Jean-Michel Quatrepoint, the euro was born as a result of "volition and impotence". Volition to prevent a reunified Germany from becoming too powerful or alternatively, distancing itself from the West. Impotence in the face of Europe's inability to establish its own political space, taking into account the collapse of the Communist block and the emergence of the United States as the world's sole super-power.[29] In short, the euro was advanced as an adequate formula to ensure the continuance of European integration in the midst of the challenges that had arisen from the end of the Cold War.

Two broad and contradictory visions expressed the polarization that seemed to mark analysis of the new Europe that would come into being with the introduction of the euro. For some, the Old Conti-

29. *Le Nouvel Economiste*, April 24-May 6, 1998

nent had begun an era of prosperity, freedom and economic power that would lead it to rival the United States and surpass Asia. For others, however, it opened an era of profound uncertainty, liable to lead to great political and social upheavals.

Among the former there were not only the promoters of the euro (European political leaders and European Union bureaucrats) but also important U.S. economists, like Fred Bergsten, Director of the Institute for International Economics, and Lester Thurow, the MIT guru. According to the former, the pole of prosperity which the new European currency represents would produce massive transfers of international reserves, which might vary between 500 billion and 1 trillion dollars. For the latter, the euro would be the starting point for the decline of the U.S. economy, a strong rival to the dollar capable of attracting great amounts of money. Among those who thought that the euro would be the source of endless political and social conflicts and crises there were not only European trade union leaders, but also leading intellectuals and economists. Some, like the well-known French sociologist Emmanuel Todd, said that the euro was the biggest strategic error that Europe had made since the signing of the Versailles Treaty in 1919. Others, like Harvard economics professor Martin Feldstein, warned that the euro would set off a stage of great national conflicts, capable of generating large-scale violence.

Between the black and white views that seemed to mark the debate about the euro, there existed, however, a gray middle ground. In fact, the euro did set into motion a process of economic reconversion throughout the length and breadth of Europe. It unleashed a wave of mergers, plant closures, lay-offs, easing of labor guarantees and relocation of companies. As is logical to suppose, all this may bring, as a consequence, high levels of unemployment and profound social and cultural disorders. Nevertheless, the result of this process of restructuring may change the face of the European economy, enabling the continent to deploy its full competitive capacities. On the financial front, the European currency may transform itself into a solid and attractive alternative to the dollar and on the productive, it may reshape the map of Europe by encouraging a high degree of specialization. All of this accompanied by the consolidation of a strong economy of services.

While, as we have seen, the picture is not a black-and-white one, it is certain that the euro represents a high-stakes bet. The big question that needs to be resolved is whether the transition to a much more competitive economy will be able to compensate for the profound alteration of values and ways of life which is implicit in this process. The euro has already become a reality as the freely-circulating currency of twelve European countries, including Greece among them. It has passed from its initial phase, when only major companies did their accounting and trading in this currency, to one of general use. From now on, the views of the optimists and pessimists can be measured in terms of a factual experience.

FROM THE OLD TO THE NEW GLOBALIZATION

The phenomenon of economic globalization is not a new one. In fact, we could say that it began five centuries ago. Ever since Europe set out to conquer the supply routes to Asia and Africa, which led Vasco de Gama to round the Cape of Good Hope and Christopher Columbus to accidentally discover America, a willingness to globalize has been evident in history. The Spanish and Portuguese, who pioneered this process, were soon equaled and surpassed by the Dutch, the English and the French. The "Indies Companies" of those three countries transported the raw materials that came to feed the machinery of capitalism. With the objective of making the exchange of merchandise and the trade in capitals and money more dynamic, the London Stock Exchange was created in 1694, transforming that city into the capital of world finance. By the beginning of the nineteenth century the circulation of capitals and merchandise throughout the planet had reached an exponential development. Stimulated by the revolution in production, transport and communications, goods were manufactured and sold on a world scale.

In Europe, France and Germany challenged the hegemony of Great Britain, while the United States, Japan and Russia appeared as the emerging economic powers of the rest of the world. This very economic competition would become one of the sparks that set off the First World War in 1914. Thenceforth everything changed. The world economic scene was characterized by a marked fragmentation that would last until the end of the Second World War and whose effects would continue to be felt until the end of the nineteen-seventies. The Reagan-Thatcher revolution initiated a process of deregulation that was later complemented by the end of the Cold War and the surprising acceleration of technology. In this way, the world has entered once more into a global integration, a reencounter with a past vocation that had been abandoned after 1914.

Nevertheless, the globalized world of today is not the same one that Adam Smith knew. Nowadays, countries do not exchange wool for wine. Instead, they are interwoven through worldwide productive networks, within which a single final product contains components that may have been made in the most diverse latitudes. It is difficult, for example, to speak of the nationality of a vehicle, when its different components are manufactured in a dozen countries. Nowadays information is transmitted at the speed of light and the cost of shipping and transport has been radically reduced. The result of all this a world economy that is homogenized and unified down to the smallest details. An economy in which a shift in budget policy, a salary rise or a change in government thinking, taking place within the sovereign territory of one country, may lead to an instantaneous and massive flight of capitals. In fact, it only needs one expression of concern about the policies carried out by a given country for the information to instantly circulate among investors on the five continents. As soon as Reuters flashes the news of the analysts' mistrust on the computer screen, investors all over the world immediately proceed to withdraw their capitals from countries which believed themselves to be sovereign and to enjoy autonomy over their own actions.

In the globalized economy of today we see two pretty frequent occurrences that Adam Smith could never have imagined. The possibility of sudden and devastating crises in given countries or regions, and the enlargement of such crises to a world scale by means of an inexorable "domino effect". With an astonishing facility, a nation-state or a whole region may, from one day to the next, fall victim to the ill-will of investors. Because the world economy is so intermeshed, the shock waves from these cataclysms with a localized epicenter usually expand to the four points of the planet, making themselves felt over and over again. It is not in vain that George Soros made an observation that would make anyone's hair stand on end: "If people like myself can make governments fall, it is because there is something in the system which is not working well". What Soros omitted to say is that when one domino falls, it is capable of taking the entire row down with it. This being the situation, we have grown accustomed to live with a succession of nerve-wracking economic crises.

THE GREAT DEBATE

The economic history of the twentieth century was dominated by the great debate between the State and the market. During the first and last decades of the twentieth century the market prevailed over the State. In the long intermediate period between the two periods, it was the State which imposed its rules. It has been a cyclical phenomenon. The State acquired its expansive strength from the attrition of the market, and then, many years later, the market similarly drew strength from the weakening of the State.

In most of the world, the triumph of the State did not, of course, mean the abandonment of the market, but only its subordination to the State. In the industrialized world of the West, Latin America and other regions of the world, a mixed economy prevailed, in which the State played a clearly dominant role, but without stifling the market as a result. The mixed economy was based on a basic set of game rules: regulation, planning, industrial policy, state property and a Keynesian fiscal management. The success of this model, in terms of economic growth, was unquestionable in the United States, Western Europe and Latin America. By the beginning of the nineteen-seventies, however, the inflationary pressures that were evident everywhere began to expose the first cracks in the model. The sudden increase in petroleum prices that took place in 1973-1974 – a development that some called a "crisis" and others a "boom" – wound up shaking the very foundations of the mixed economy model. Two economic phenomena – inflation and unemployment which had hitherto been regarded as mutually exclusive, now emerged at the same time, to form what became dubbed as "stagflation".

As the seventies wore on, many critiques of the mixed model appeared, virtually out of thin air. Furthermore, the two most distinguished exponents of the free market model, Von Hayek and Friedman, were awarded the Nobel Prize in Economics, in 1974 and 1976, respectively. To all this was added the foreign debt crisis, which was evidenced by the sixfold increase in the indebtedness of the Third World countries between 1972 and 1981. Henceforth it was inevitable that the International Monetary Fund would transform itself into a partner of the debtor countries, imposing its recipes and credos on their domestic policies.

The early eighties saw the appearance of the Thatcher revolution, shortly followed by the revolution of Reagan. The IMF became a fundamental part of this process and the thrust towards a market economy began to make itself felt in all parts. In turn, the fall of the Berlin Wall at the end of that decade came to represent the collapse of the last containing wall holding back the consolidation of a world free market. A group of economists and schools of thought which, for most of the century, had been relegated to second place, now turned into the new icons of the economic Olympus. Names like Von Hayek, Friedman, Stigler and Lucas; universities like Chicago and to a lesser extent, Los Angeles and Rochester; and economic think-tanks like the Mont Pelerin Society of Switzerland were transformed into the central hubs of the emerging economy. After being ostracized for a long time, these solitary preachers of the "truth", now triumphant, brought with them the fundamentalist style which had enabled them to hold onto their convictions during their exile in the desert. This was the style which would impose itself all over the world.

As had happened a hundred years before, the arrival of the new century coincided with the rule of the market economy. How definitive this situation is remains to be seen. As the number of people who are excluded from the benefits of this economy rapidly grows, forming a genuine counter-society of rejects, it is clear that the market economy has many enemies. No one doubts the evident success of the free market in activating the economy. Nevertheless, this occurrence and its great corollary, globalization, have caused the disappearance of networks of social support and traditional certainties, thus creating profound anxieties. The opposition to what has been called the "single thought" is making itself felt with a growing intensity and every meeting of the international economic elite is now the occasion for a pitched battle. What is more, the crisis of the New Economy and the political imperatives deriving from the September 11 terrorist attacks are beginning to raise serious questions about the predominance of the market.

One does not have to be an advocate of Keynes to see the sense of the criticism he made of Von Hayek in the nineteen-thirties: "You greatly under-estimate the practical value of compromise". It is the attempt to reach such a compromise which is most noticeably absent now. That is, a model in which the State would act as an arbiter of the economy, defining the rules of the game that give guarantees to the market, and at the same time encourage the inclusion of the rejected.

THE NEW MAP OF PETROLEUM

The international petroleum scene has gone through fundamental transformations in the past two decades, especially in the past ten or twelve years. These changes have made life more difficult for the OPEC countries. They have not only presented them with new challenges and greater competitive de-mands, but they have also brought onto the scene actors who were practically unknown a few years ago. It is worth looking at some of these new devel-opments.

New producers have been absorbing ever higher percentages of world petroleum investment. As a result of the nationalization programs carried out by the member countries of the OPEC, international oil companies sought new investment opportunities in countries like Norway and the United Kingdom. In the same manner, the end of the Cold War led to the opening of new exploration sites in countries like the former Soviet Union, China and Vietnam. In many of these countries a desperate need for money, technology and marketing know-how led to a change of laws and regulations, with a view to attracting an influx of foreign companies and creating a climate suitable for long-term investments. Since 1980 the petroleum multinationals have invested more than 350 billion dollars in new areas, without making equivalent investments in the OPEC countries.

Nuclear energy and natural gas are gaining a growing share of the energy market. The fall in petroleum consumption in Europe between 1973 and 1996 is an evidence of this. Some analysts, like Majid al-Moneef, president of the "Energy Team" of the Gulf Cooperation Council, believe the decline was 26%, while others, like Fadhil J. Chalabi, director of the London Center for Global Energy Studies, say that it was 21%. During the same period, petroleum consumption in Japan fell by 23%. Simultaneously, the consumption of natural gas in Europe rose by 11% in the same period and that of nuclear energy by 12%, while in Japan that of natural gas rose by 10% and nuclear energy by 14%.

The emergence of the futures markets, as well as of other stock market instruments, has seriously affected OPEC's influence over the market. The stock market, cash market, "International Petroleum Exchange" (IPE), "New York Mercantile Exchange" (NYME), computerization, deregulation and the 24 hour a day negotiation of petroleum sales have been strengthened by the massive inflow of futures coverage funds to the stock market.

The revolution in recent years of petroleum technology has radically reduced the expenses and risks associated with petroleum exploration and development. It has given profitability to areas that were formerly considered to be high-cost ones. Such developments have led to a rapid reduction in the world demand for OPEC petroleum. Such advances as horizontal drilling, what is known as "seismic 3-D", informatics and the improved recuperation of petroleum have caused many marginal fields to become commercial ones. By way of example we can cite the growing success rate in oil explorations. In Norway, the percentage of successful finds rose from 15% in 1993 to 40% in 1997, while in the Netherlands it rose from 20% in 1993 to 75% in 1994. In a similar manner, the rate of success for petroleum drilling among the seven largest world companies is now on the order of 60%. Thanks to these technological advances, the exploitation of small and difficult deposits is becoming ever more accessible and there is less dependence on the large and easily-worked deposits that are characteristic of the OPEC countries.

All of the above suggests that the member countries of the OPEC must adapt themselves to the new and important challenges that will affect their future influence on the international petroleum scene.

PETROLEUM: THE BEGINNING OF THE END?

There are many indications that the era of petroleum is beginning to end. What is known as renewable energy, which encompasses the range of technologies based on self-sustainable energy sources, is the wave of the future. These include solar, wind and hydraulic energy and the use of the biomasses that derive from forestry and agricultural resources or industrial wastes. In one of the two scenarios for the near future found in the "forecasting" done by Shell International three years ago, there is a prediction that, by the middle of this century, up to fifty per cent of the world's energy needs might be satisfied by renewable sources. Into that category would fit photo-voltaic energy, wind-derived energy, biofuels, hydrogen, fuel cells, etc. Of all these new technologies, the ones which represent the biggest danger for the petroleum industry are those linked to transport fuels, since the industry depends more and more on sales to the transport sector.

If one thing has kept renewable energy in check up to now, it has been the greater profitability of hydrocarbons. This profitability has to do, in part, with the high initial cost of mounting the new technologies and also with the traditional calculations of the cost of hydrocarbons. Insofar as dependence on fossil fuels has turned out to be less expensive than a leap towards the new technologies, inertia has worked in favor of the former. The reasonable prices shown by hydrocarbons during most of the recent past have provided few incentives to incur in the large investments that will be needed to make renewable energy work as a commercial proposition. Beyond this, the traditional accounting used to determine the cost of hydrocarbons does not justify the change either, insofar as it does not or cannot quantify the so-called "hidden costs" of fossil fuels.

Where these "hidden costs" of petroleum – climate change or the effects of contamination on human health – *are* having an impact is in the political sphere. Such concerns are becoming a matter of priority in national and international agendas, thus detonating the political will that is needed to effect the change-over. It is in this sense that renewable energy-based technologies may become the biggest threat to the petroleum industry. The Kyoto Protocol, an international agreement which commits the industrialized countries to reduce their emissions of "greenhouse" gases, hangs over the petroleum industry like a gigantic sword of Damocles. In his last State of the Union address, then President Clinton not only urged the private sector to join with the government to solve the problem, he also proposed the creation of tax incentives to encourage the development of clean energy. In Western Europe and Japan, governments have been making a significant effort to promote renewable energy. Political factors seem to be the decisive factor behind the development of new energy technologies.

Are we facing the beginning of the end of petroleum? For those who are betting on the development of new energy technologies, the answer is "yes". Others, however, affirm that petroleum still has a long future before it, a future that will not, however, be exempt from strong upheavals. The latter position expresses itself as follows.

HOW LONG WILL THE PRE-EMINENCE OF PETROLEUM LAST?

As the magazine *The Economist* pointed out, energy is the world's leading industry. Not even telecommunications, information technology, the arms industry or the automotive sector approach the figures shown by that industry. They amount to between 1.7 - 2 trillion dollars per year. In the period that runs from 1990 to 2020, global investments in the energy field will total 30 trillion dollars, in terms of 1992 prices.[30]

When you talk about the energy industry, you are essentially referring to petroleum. According to the International Energy Agency, in 1997 petroleum represented 49% of the package of world energy consumption, gas 18%, electricity 17%, coal 11%, thermal energy 4% and renewable energy 1%. According to the same source, by the year 2020 world energy consumption will be distributed in the following way: petroleum 49%, gas 18%, electricity, 20%, coal 8%, thermal energy 3% and renewable

30. February 10-16, 2000

energy 2%. In other words, the division of world energy consumption will remain virtually identical in the second decade of this century and within this scheme, petroleum will continue to play the major role.

Judging by this criterion, the pre-eminence of petroleum would not seem to be threatened in the middle term. Furthermore, as a famous saying in the petroleum industry goes, cited by the above-mentioned issue of *The Economist*, "the best substitute for gasoline is gasoline". This being so, petroleum will only be replaced when an energy source appears which is equally cheap, easy to use and efficient and, in addition, less contaminating. Obviously, this does not look easy.

Notwithstanding the comfortable perspective that this version of things presents for petroleum, there are some dark clouds on the horizon and some of them may turn into storms. In essence, the three great threats to its predominance would be: the deregulation of the energy industry, the environmental movement and the volatility of prices. We are dealing, no doubt, with a dynamic equation of unpredictable consequences, which has as a common denominator the pressure towards technological innovation.

The deregulation of the energy markets is a process that began a number of years ago in countries like Great Britain, Australia, New Zealand and the Scandinavian nations. Today, not only have the rest of Western Europe and half the States of the United States set out on this path, many developing countries are following it as well. According to some analysts, the liberation of the markets will create the same pressures for change in the petroleum industry that were felt by the telecommunications and computer industry in the past two decades. The entrance of venture capital, which pushes for technological innovation and favors unorthodox management methods, may well unleash important changes in the energy world.

Most of the leaders of the world petroleum industry consider the environmental movement, referred to above, as the greatest prospective danger to the superiority of petroleum. Although the last summit, in November 2000, of the present or future signatories of the Kyoto Protocol ended in failure and the Bush administration refuses to support it, there is a virtual consensus within the industry that the restrictions foreseen by the Protocol will begin to felt in the middle term.

The volatility of prices is an another risk factor which might create a powerful economic incentive to search for petroleum substitutes. Despite the inertia that favors sticking to petroleum, if the political pressure from the environmentalists combines with factors of cost-efficiency, the results could be dramatic. A political crisis in Saudi Arabia in the aftermath of the September 11 terrorist events could easily drive prices into the stratosphere, thus setting off a situation where renewable energy becomes highly attractive.

REFLEXIONS ON THE GLOBALIZED SOCIETY

In the issues of the *Harvard Business Review* of November-December, 1996 and January-February, 1997, there appeared a couple of articles which are of the greatest importance for understanding the dynamics of the globalized society. Although some important aspects of the arguments which they presented did not agree, they shared a common denominator – a strong warning about the present trends of the phenomenon of globalization.

The first of these articles, written by Stephen S. Roach, chief economist and director of global economics for the Morgan Stanley & Co. investment bank, was entitled: "The sacred circle of productive awakening". In line with his argument, the strategy followed by the corporate world of the United States has become more and more centered upon reducing the size of companies ("downsizing") and lowering salaries. The results are companies that are less and less capable of maintaining, much less expanding, their share in global markets.

Roach makes a distinction between efficiency and productivity. In his view, reducing the size of companies (with all that it implies in terms of lay-offs) may be an expression of efficiency. To the extent that an emphasis is placed on a bigger return from capital, producing the maximum possible output with the minimum possible number of resources amounts to a rationalization of production. However, sustained productive growth has always been founded on knowing how to produce the maximum possible output from an expanded base of resources.

According to this author, by systematically reducing their productive capacities, U.S. companies are gravely affecting their possibilities of attaining an effective share in the world market. In other words, they are seriously jeopardizing their capacity of supply. What is more, insofar as they systematically reduce jobs and lower salaries, they wind up limiting demand in the U.S. market itself, thus hemming in the bases for growth in the domestic market. A lower participation in the global economy and a shrinking national market might be the inevitable results of the corporate strategy that is being applied in the United States.

In addition, states Roach, this strategy is likely to create strong reactions in the form of pressures exerted by public opinion. In his opinion, from a merely economic point of view, global competition gives employers a tremendous advantage over workers, who seem to be powerless. But from a political angle, the correlation of power is reversed and it is the corporations which might find themselves cornered by a critical public opinion. Political leaders, under the impact of an overwhelming economic anxiety, may come to impose their own remedies, by means of regulations that would seriously limit the competitive capacity of U.S. companies.

In this situation, Roach concludes, replacing long-term productive growth by short-term efficiency is a policy that is as short-sighted as it is dangerous.

The second of the two articles, written by Jeffrey E. Garten, Dean of Yale University's Business School, analyzes a book by the well-known U.S. economist William Greider, entitled *One World, Ready or Not: The Manic Logic of Global Capitalism*. The thesis of the book, which Garten describes as one of the most important of the decade, is that the risks of a global economy are out of control and it is heading towards a "cataclysm ".

Among the most dangerous tendencies shown by the global economy, there are three particularly significant ones. In the first place, the unrestrained increase of world productivity, the consequence of which is that the world will soon find itself flooded by a surplus production that it cannot assimilate. The multinational corporations, locked in a brutal competition, have expanded to all parts of the planet. While the workers of the emerging countries do not have the capacity to buy what they manufacture, consumers in the West cannot keep up with the mountains of new products. One example: the global surpluses of the automotive industry will soon be equal to the production potential of U.S. industry as a whole. What is going to happen when 2 billion non-Western workers join the global economy in the next decade, working for absurdly low salaries but at a rate of efficiency nearly as high as those of Western workers? Where is the purchasing power to absorb this production going to come from?

The second tendency under consideration is the constant and uncontrolled flow of money across borders. In 1983, the reserves of the central banks of the world's five richest countries greatly exceeded the value of transactions in the world's financial markets. Ten years later, the situation was reversed and the gap is growing wider all the time. In 1994 international financial transactions reached the trillion-dollar mark. To the irrational flow of money across frontiers must be added the exponential growth of funds which, by their very nature, are highly unstable. The excessive expansion of ever more exotic financial instruments has created an unmanageable level of risk.

The third tendency is the rapid industrialization shown in the emerging markets, which threatens the sustainability of ecosystems. If China, for example, which now has one car for every 680 inhabitants, reaches the level of ownership of the developed world, the resulting pollution would be gigantic.

According to Greider, it is essential that we begin to take a long-term view of things. Humanity should pause and reflect, without thinking about the next elections, the next quarterly earnings report or the next monthly paycheck. Otherwise, the world will be heading towards a precipice.

Both articles alert us to the need for long-term reflections rather than ones that merely highlight short-term gains.

THE SETTING OF THE RISING SUN?

The recession of the "land of the rising sun" goes back to the end of the eighties and had its origins in the bursting of the speculative bubble in its financial and real estate markets. Japan is as big as the State of California but its population is nearly half of that of the United States. This means that the Japanese are concentrated in densely-inhabited cities where the price of land reaches exorbitant levels. By the end of the nineteen-eighties building land in the city of Tokyo had come to attain a value, on paper, that was higher than the combined value of property of 48 States of the United States. According to Marvin Cetron and Owen Davies, the terrain of the Imperial Palace in Tokyo came to be worth more than all of the properties in the State of Florida.[31]

Although the value given to Japanese land was based on a belief shared by all of its citizens, there did not exist objective criteria to measure its real price. Insofar as the frugal Japanese accumulated massive savings and the banks gave housing loans at absurdly low interest rates, it was possible to finance this system of unreal valuation. The excessive paper value given to real estate was used, in turn, for all sorts of credit guarantees: ordinary loans, mortgages, the purchase of stocks on the installment plan, etc. On these foundations a gigantic house of cards was built, which collapsed at the very mo-

31. *Crystal Globe*, New York, St. Martin Press, 1991

ment that the Japanese lost their trust – a psychological factor in the end – in the nominal value given to each square meter of real estate. This sparked off a long and traumatic recession.

In 1996 the Japanese economy began to show the first signs of recuperation and everything seemed to indicate that the end of the crisis was around the corner. In order for the recuperation to become a reality, however, two things were needed: the reactivation of demand and the energizing of investment. The clumsy economic measures adapted by the Tokyo government in 1997 spiked any chance of this happening. In that year a polemical 3% increase in the consumption tax was approved and at the same time social welfare deductions were raised. As a result of all this, the process of reviving consumption was curbed. Furthermore, the rigorous budget policy carried out by the government, with the objective of reducing the fiscal deficit, which had reached 5.5% of the GDP that year, led to a strong contraction of public spending. The government of Hashimoto fell into the same error that George Soros had attributed to the European Union: trying to combat recession with stricter fiscal measures.

A short time later a factor that was external to Japan would make itself felt, puncturing all hope of recuperation: the Asian crisis. This came to affect the fundamental generator of Japanese economic growth, plunging a region that absorbed 40% of its exports into great difficulties. At the same time, the high loan-exposure of Japanese banks in the countries affected by the crisis tended to make their already dramatic financial situation more acute. According to a report made at the time, the average exposure of the main Japanese banks in such volatile markets as Thailand, Indonesia and South Korea, amounted to between 40-50% of their capitals. In some cases, like that of the Bank of Tokyo-Mitsubishi, loans to those three countries represented 90% of their capitals.

The above situation was worsened by a very special factor: the rupture of the harmony of Japan's productive apparatus and of its social contract. If one thing had characterized the Japanese economy, it had been, precisely, its elaborate system for achieving harmony. Through it, an interweaving of the big conglomerates, banks, suppliers, workers and the State ensured that decisions and responsibilities were shared by everyone. In addition, everyone respected, as though it were a dogma, the norm on life-time employment. This situation changed drastically. An interesting article published by *Business Week* throws a lot of light on this subject. The magazine showed how half of Japanese industrial production came from small and medium producers: 800,000 companies in which a good part of the work was still done by hand in small manufacturing units. These enterprises are the natural suppliers of Toyota, Sony and the other giants. This business sector has been mercilessly attacked on both flanks. On one side, by the big banks, which find it easier to recover their loans by demanding payments from the small and medium companies than from the big corporations. On the other, by the big corporations themselves, which require them to provide products with an ever-higher quality at a lower price, thus forcing them to compete with low-cost Chinese suppliers. Caught in this vise, the small and medium companies were hit by a chain of bankruptcies, which are becoming more and more pronounced.[32] In 2001 alone, 19,000 such companies went bust.[33]

At the same time, the great industrial conglomerates of Japan are increasingly turning their backs on the country's crisis. Thus, they see the solution to their problems, not in a reactivation of the Japanese economy, but in the massive purchase of undervalued properties in countries like South Korea, the Philippines and Thailand. *Business Week* reported on the way in which the big Japanese corporations launched a massive assault on the companies of the countries that were hit by the 1997 crisis. Of course, they had several motives: buy at a good price, take advantage of the depressed salaries of those nations and increase the volume of their exports on the basis of these platforms. The result of this process has been the closure of Japanese plants, which have higher productive costs.[34] One thing is clear: the throttling which the

32. February 19, 1998
33. *The Economist*, February 16-22, 2002
34. April 20, 1998

small and medium producers have suffered from and the massive export of productive capitals hardly serve as a support for the reactivation of the Japanese economy.

Slowly and inexorably, Japan is sliding down the slippery slope of deflation, without clear prospects of economic recovery. Not in vain did *The Economist* point out recently: "The only debate is about how long the recession will last and how profound it will be. Those who are charitable consider Japan to be irrelevant. Those who are less charitable consider it to be a burden. Those who are fearful consider it to be a danger".[35]

STRUCTURAL UNEMPLOYMENT

Nowadays the economic process revolves around private capital, whose maximum expressions are the financial markets and the transnational companies. Both have, as a common denominator, a personage who oils the gears of and sets the guidelines for the globalized economy: the nameless stockholder. For him there is only one valid consideration when he buys stocks or bonds: short-term profit. The need to respond to the short-sighted demands of a gigantic number of anonymous stockholders has become the fundamental reason for being of the economic process now in force.

35. *The Economist, Ibidem*

Within this context, the large corporations fiercely compete among themselves to win the attention of stock-holders, shedding themselves of everything that might weigh down their chances of attaining higher yields. The short-term maximization of profits is the essence of the new economic game. The case of Germany is a good proof of this. Despite an annual 1.8% increase in productivity since 1979, twice that of the U.S., return on capital in the German economy was only 7% between 1974 and 1993, compared to 9% in the United States. German society was forced to assume great sacrifices in order to deal with the "inefficiency" of its economy.

The search for a higher short-term yield on capital depends on two basic elements: technology and the reduction of the work force. Technological advances, joined to implacable massive lay-offs, have made productivity shoot up and increased the profit margins of industry. *Business Week* put the increase in corporate earnings at 34% since 1992, as a result of these two factors.[36]

For many years there was a wide-spread belief that earnings were converted into the creation of new jobs. In this sense we may quote the famous theorem of the former Prime Minister of Germany, Helmut Schmidt: "Today's profits are tomorrow's investments and the jobs of the day after tomorrow". Nevertheless, the symbiotic relation that existed between earnings and work in the past has now been

36. March 11, 1996

broken. Minimal differences in the price or the quality of a product or service may drive a producer out of the market. It is the inexorable logic of the globalized market, which encourages a fierce competition to produce the highest quality at the lowest possible cost. Obviously, the recipe which combines technology and lay-offs is ideal for reaching such objectives. It is for this reason that economists speak of "structural unemployment" today, contrasting it with the cyclical unemployment that is produced in times of economic crisis.

A few years ago, Jacques Chirac, President of France, pointed out that the countries which make up the European Union had 18 million people without jobs and 50 million citizens who were "threatened with social exclusion". The countries which belong to the OECD – the club of the industrialized nations – now have around 35 million unemployed people. Among the wealthy countries, it is only in the United States that the phenomenon of unemployment seems to be reversing itself. That, at least, is what the official statistics would lead one to believe.

Nevertheless, the promising figure that obtains for the United States may be nothing more than a mirage. The well-known *Business Week* columnist Robert Kuttner stated the following: "Officially, unemployment is only 5.6%. But the Bureau of Labor Statistics' new 'U-6' formula, which amplifies the measurement of unemployment and includes workers who are forced to work part-time, is 10.7%. Lester Thurow, for his part, puts 'real' unemployment at more than 14%."[37] This seems to confirm the suspicion that the figures on the growth of employment which have been published in the United States in recent years may be no more than statistics on hidden unemployment.

No matter whether the statistics are accurate or not, the one thing that is clearly proved is that the labor situation in the United States is changing its shape. Under the new structure, most people who lose their jobs usually find another one after a time. However, the new jobs are not only less stable, but they are also lower paid. A few years ago a book entitled *The Judas Economy: The Triumph of Capital and the Betrayal of Work* was published in the United States. It was written by William Wolman, chief economist at *Business Week,* and former *Business Week* staff writer Ann Colamosca. According to the book, a person who finds a new job after losing a previous one usually takes a salary cut of up to 60%.

This undeniable reality of structural unemployment is one of the most outstanding characteristics of the new world economy.

THE HEEL OF ACHILLES

Some years ago *Business Week* published an article that threw a great deal of light on the reality of employment in the United States. It explained that,

37. April 22, 1996

while corporate earnings had been increasing in a very significant way in those years, salaries and benefits had declined in a systematic manner. The article voiced a question which is frequently asked in U.S. society: If the corporations are doing so well, why have so many people been pushed aside?[38]

According to the magazine, the average salary in that moment was, after inflation adjustment, the lowest since 1973. Furthermore, the prevailing trend in employment was clear: an increase in part-time contracts, a wide spread of temporary employment and a steady reduction of permanent posts.

In the words of *Business Week*: "In the nineties, companies have continued their process of restructuring in order to control costs and although the economy grows, high levels of lay-offs have been maintained. The percentage of workers who lose their jobs after a year or more of employment has significantly risen to 15% of the total labor force during the three-year period that ended in 1995, according to the Bureau of Labor Statistics".

The magazine also noted that while contracted manpower declined, temporary employment had risen by 27% and the tactic of hiring workers as independent contractors, with minimum benefits and job guarantees, was becoming more and more common. *Business Week* summed up the situation with precision: "Nowadays labor costs are abnormally low in relation to the historical standards".

38. September 1, 1997

These conclusions continue to be valid up to the present time and mesh with the warnings formulated by a group of distinguished U.S. economists about the shortsightedness and lack of social conscience of that country's corporate world. Among the exponents of this line of thought we find the following: Lester Thurow, Stephen S. Roach, William Wolman, Ann Colamosca and Jeremy Rifkin.

Thurow, former Dean of the MIT Business School, has sounded an alert about the dangerous disorganization and social disintegration that may come in the wake of this breaking of the "social contract" in the United States. Robert Reich – former Secretary of Labor, Harvard Professor and current candidate for Governor of Massachusetts – has declared that the resentment of the masses towards the business elite may lead to the emergence of dangerous demagogues. Stephen Roach, of Morgan Stanley, believes that the U.S. corporate world's strategy of lay-offs will make it incapable of maintaining its share of global markets. Wolman and Colamosca, of *Business Week*, warn against a "Judas economy" in which the triumph of capital rests on the betrayal of labor. And so the argument grows.

As Thurow notes in his book *The Future of Capitalism,* it is not an accident that 40% of the total national wealth of the U.S. has become concentrated in the hands of less than 1% of the population at the same time that "the capitalists have declared a class war against manpower".

To resume, the United States is in a curious situation. While the percentage of national income represented by salaries has notoriously declined, the share of national income represented by corporate earnings has grown with particular vigor. This contradiction is the basis of the common man's rejection of the globalized economy, which he blames for all of his recent troubles. As long as this sentiment applies, it will be very difficult to advance towards effective free trade and economic integration. What is more, this contradiction bears within it the germ of a potent political reaction, capable of nourishing the ultra-nationalists of the United States.

SILICON VALLEY

The twentieth century history of the U.S. economy has witnessed the emergence of three mythical names: Wall Street, Detroit and Hollywood. From the first arose the world of high finance, from the second the automotive sector and from the third the film industry. In recent years, a fourth name has joined this pantheon of great economic successes: Silicon Valley. That area embodies the new post-industrial society and constitutes the most polished expression of the United States' ability to respond to the challenges of globalization. In strict economic terms its strength came to surpass that of Wall Street or Detroit or Hollywood. The market value of the group of companies located in Silicon Valley reached

452 billion dollars by the end of the nineties, whereas the financial corporations of Wall Street were valued at 405 billion, the car-makers of Detroit at 113 billion and the Hollywood studios at 56 billion.

By the end of the nineteen-eighties, the industrial strength of the Asian Pacific Rim countries made it likely that region would become the great center of the world economy in the twenty-first century. The United States, by contrast, looked like an economic power in decline, unable to stand up to the threat of the "slant-eyes". Nevertheless, the U.S. managed to take a great technological leap towards the post-industrial economy, while Japan proved itself incapable of following it in this adventure. Silicon Valley represents the paradigm of the U.S. capacity for response.

Silicon Valley is the home of 20 of the world's 100 biggest software and electronics companies. On the main avenue of this economic nerve center are found the headquarters of companies like Intel, Cisco Systems, 3Com, Sun Microsystems and Netscape Communications. In their best moment, these five companies came to have a market value of 257 billion dollars, much higher than the combined value of General Motors, Ford and Chrysler. However, more than 7,000 companies were located in Silicon Valley. In boom times, its portentous economic success led eleven new companies to join their ranks every week and every day saw the birth of 62 new millionaires in the stock markets. The significant thing about this emporium is that its power resides in the strength of intelligence, not manufacturing capacity.

Situated on the outskirts of Stanford University, Silicon Valley embraces communities like Menlo Park, Palo Alto, Santa Clara and San José. Its history goes back to the nineteen-forties, when the then Dean of the Engineering Faculty of that university, Frederick Terman, had the idea of creating an academic-technological community that would rival that of universities like Oxford and Bologna. Under the auspices of Terman, Hewlett-Packard became the first company to establish itself there. However, Silicon Valley owes its name to the founding, in 1957, of the Fairchild Semiconductor company, the first in the world to work exclusively with silicon. The essence of Silicon Valley is its peculiar combination of academic knowledge and managerial talent, which exactly fits in with the values of Stanford. Among the most memorable dates in its history are the founding of Intel in 1968, Atari in 1972, Apple in 1977, Sun Microsystems in 1982 and Netscape in 1994, each event representing a new and important stage of technological development.

Among the keys to its success there were three critical factors: the concentration of an immense mass of talent, the creation of a structure suitable for intelligence and the presence of an unconventional managerial culture. As regards the first, it benefited from the synergetic effect of combining 7,000 high-tech companies, with the consequent crossbreeding of creativity and intelligence that this process implies, which led to a permanent feedback of ideas. The second factor, a structure that rewarded intelligence, meant that a characteristic of Silicon Valley was its ability to convert a concept into a major company. Supported by an agile and sophisticated juridical and financial structure, any idea that was good enough could be rapidly turned into a company whose stocks would be quoted on the stock exchange.

The third factor was its culture of the anti-conventional. Among its outstanding traits were the acceptance of risk and the reward of failure. In other words, it was based on the notion that it was not possible to achieve true technological innovation without taking big risks. This mentality, in turn, enabled it to regard failure as an inevitable part of the process that finally made possible the technological leap. Within this ambient, investors were willing to support repeated failure in the expectation of final success. It is worth noting that this managerial conception turned out to be the opposite extreme to the Japanese view, where a single failure leads to discredit and a definitive ostracism.

Everything seems to indicate that the factors which were so important to the success of the Valley and the New Economy in general were largely responsible for its current crisis. The over-saturation of companies led them to compete among themselves to get hold of the available talent, raising salaries to stratospheric levels. The ease with which any good idea was translated into stocks sold on the financial market gave rise to what is called "venture capital", which introduced immense amounts of risk into the financial system. The deliberate acceptance of the idea that high levels of uncertainty are an essential part of the same game unleashed financial adventures that turned out to be unsustainable and resulted in calamitous losses.

HOW TO SURVIVE ASIAN COMPETITION?

In 1997, the constant accumulation of wealth which East Asia had taken for granted faced a crisis of great proportions. The change in the region's fortunes showed itself in different ways, from the silent heavy industry plants of South Korea to the shining but empty condominiums and shopping centers of Bangkok. There is no simple explanation for what occurred, since the crisis involved many variables. Nevertheless, a common denominator was present in every case: the impact of low-cost Chinese competition.

This fierce Chinese competition subjected the diverse economies of the region to strong stresses, making many of the weaknesses hidden within them come to the surface. These weaknesses, in turn, gave rise to a loss of confidence in the financial stability of the region and brought a wave of monetary devaluation and stock market falls.

When the currencies of these battered economies were depreciated, they began to find the path to recuperation. The reason for this was simple: a cheaper currency also means cheaper exports. This situation recalls the one that occurred in Mexico after the devaluation of its peso, when hundreds of U.S. companies rushed to install themselves south of the Río Grande in order to take advantage of a cheaper currency. By making their exports less expensive, the economies of East Asia found a second wind which enabled them to confront the low-cost competition from China.

For China, on the other hand, things do not look that easy. Its own economy, although very successful, also conceals immense weaknesses. As MIT economist Rudy Dornbusch explained in an interesting article a few years ago, more than 7 million industrial companies exist in that country. At the end of the nineties, they were arranged in the following way: 5.7 million companies of a private nature, running from small concerns to large-scale enterprises; 1.5 million community companies whose ownership is in the hands of a city or a town; and finally, 118,000 state-owned companies. The gigantic growth of the Chinese economy has been based on the first two kinds of companies, that is, private or municipal ones. Nevertheless, the state companies were responsible at that time for a third of installed industrial capacity, half of available assets, two-thirds of urban employment and 75% of investments. A large part of these state companies suffer heavy losses.[39]

39. *Business Week*, September 15, 1997

For the 110 million Chinese who work in state companies, they represent more than a simple source of employment. These companies provide them with a broad spectrum of social services, which include housing, health, education, pensions and funerals. Nevertheless, in order to face up to revived competition from the region's countries, China will inevitably have to sacrifice its state companies. They have become a heavy burden which will not allow China to keep up with the pace which she herself imposed on the race. It is evident that this frantic rhythm of competition will also force the rival countries to make incalculable sacrifices. The result of this will be ever lower prices.

How can the West survive this productive avalanche of the "slant-eyes"?

EAST ASIA: WHEN ECONOMIES CLASH

The productive process of East Asia was marked by a technological ladder. The highest rung was occupied by Japan, which had the highest degree of technological development. On the following rungs were perched the Asiatic tigers and the lowest ones were reserved for the new emerging economies of the region, like China, Indonesia, Thailand, etc. As the Japanese increased the level of complexity of their production – moving, for example, from textiles to domestic appliances and then to computers – the tigers were able to occupy the rungs which it had vacated. In turn, Indonesia, Thailand and the rest took over the spaces left by the tigers. This gave a highly complementary character to these economies.

In order for the above process to function, however, two conditions were necessary. First, that Japan would always continue to climb the technological ladder. And second, that a prudent technological distance between these three groups of nations would be maintained. These two conditions gradually disappeared. On the one hand, Japan touched the roof of its technological capacity and could not climb any higher. And, on the other, the technologies of the region's other players began to draw too near to each other. As a consequence, these economies lost the complementary character which had formerly characterized them and turned into competitors. Over-production and the resulting fall in prices came to affect all of them.

The reason why Japan reached the ceiling of its capacity to gain access to new technologies was determined by its own educational system. Theirs is a culture of conformity, more suitable for creating worker-bees than for producing the individual creative talent that characterizes the technological leap in the new fields of advanced technology. Japan stayed trapped in the mass production of computers, semiconductors and cars, without reaching the more ethereal sphere of producing "ideas", the vanguard of technology where "software", "online" services and biotechnology lie.

In addition, the technological distances that separated the different producers of the Asian Pacific Rim shrank. All of them wound up basing their productive processes on the same kinds of mass-production industries. Those who came up from behind assumed that Japan would abandon a whole set of industrial areas, leaving them, as was traditional, an empty place. But it did not turn out that way. The result was a traffic jam in which no one could advance and the cars began to bump into each other.

The Japan of the "keiretsu", that is, the mega-conglomerates, came up with a few basic solutions to this problem. On the one hand, they made the enormous mass of small and medium companies which form their traditional supply base compete with China and, on the other, they moved their production plants to other countries with lower production costs. Finally, they used robots.

In fact, Japan's mastery of robotics gives it a special advantage. Starting in the seventies, the land of the rising sun gradually entered this field, showing a firmness of purpose which the other industrialized nations lacked. By the middle of the nineties, Japan counted upon an army of half a million robots designed to reduce their production costs, which amounted to 70% of all the industrial robots which then existed in the world. The economic benefits of robotics are clear. As Paul Kennedy correctly points out: "If a robot replaces a worker on one shift per day it will pay for its costs in about four years. If a robot is used on two shifts, it will pay for itself in two years and if it used on all shifts, it will pay for itself after merely a year".[40]

Nevertheless, it was not only for economic reasons that Japan decided to follow this path. There were also demographic and racial considerations behind it. The structure of the Japanese population is like an inverted pyramid: the elderly are becoming more and more numerous than the young and its birth rate is much lower than the world average. Japan thus faces the specter of depopulation. Logically, that means a shortage of manpower to deal with the requirements of an industrialized economy. The obvious solution would be to open her doors to immigration, letting Philippine, Chinese or Pakistani workers fill the gap.

But the ancestral racial exclusiveness of Japan is opposed to it. The solution is robots.

The result of this whole process has been growing unemployment in a country which, since the end of the Second Wold War, proclaimed its faith in lifetime jobs. As *The Economist* noted, at the end of 2001 unemployment in Japan reached its highest post-war level, 5.6%, which was one percent higher than in the preceding year.[41]

40. *Op. cit.*, p.100
41. February 16-22, 2002

THE ECONOMY OF KNOWLEDGE

The information revolution began in the middle of the nineteen-seventies. Behind this process was the spectacular fall in the price of computer capacity or, what amounts to the same thing, the gigantic rise in that capacity. In real terms, the price of the processing capacity of computers fell at an average annual rate of 30% during the past two decades. In turn, the capacity to transmit information through the global network of computers, telephones and televisions rose a million times during the same period. Nowadays, a small portable computer, which may be purchased for a thousand dollars, has a greater capacity for processing information and functions ten times as quickly as one that cost five million dollars in the seventies.

This revolution has led to the creation of what have been called "knowledge-based economies", which are based on the production, distribution and use of information knowledge. They represent the maximum expression of the post-industrial economy. The most characteristic aspect of the information revolution is its presence in the most varied fields of the economy. In contrast with the technological waves which preceded it, like those of steam-power or electricity, information technologies may applied to a wide range of sectors: manufactures, administration, services, agriculture, etc. Internet alone has been transformed into the most formidable commercial medium that has ever been utilized. Its world scale would be sufficient to grant it an unprecedented potential. However, it also benefits from the rapid advances shown by the technology of multimedia, at a time when television and Internet are tending to merge more and more.

In 1996, the United States, the country which has learnt how to transform itself into the driving force of the knowledge economy, generated 33% of its GDP from the high-tech information industry.

There are many who affirm that, thanks to instantaneous communication and the magnitude of the information that derives from this knowledge-based economy, it will be possible to arrive at a nearly perfect free market. The curious thing about all this is that while the world economy as a whole becomes more and more dependent on this industry, this industry itself has become more and more dependent on one man and one company: Bill Gates and his all-powerful Microsoft.

Bill Gates obtained his control over this territory in diverse ways. In the first place, the sheer magnitude of his earnings and the capacity for generating new technology that derives from it. In second place, Bill Gates is devoted to the systematic purchase of all those companies which produce innovations which Microsoft itself has not been able to make. In merely two years it came to acquire 37 such companies. A typical case is that of WebTV, a Silicon Valley corporation that is a pioneer in the technology for accessing Internet through television, which Microsoft bought for 425 million dollars. At the beginning of

2002 it acquired the cable television company Cox Communications at a price of 500 million dollars. This acquisition rested on the premise that the kind of industry in which Cox is in the vanguard will play a very important role in broad-band Internet access.

In third place, Microsoft (that is, Gates) makes use of the conventional tactics of any monopolist. It pushes competitors out of the market, extending its monopoly over a critical area of the business to parallel activities and tying the use of products vital for the market to the purchase of its other products. Microsoft's attempt to dominate the Internet superhighways achieved world-wide celebrity. By offering its "Explorer" program free of charge and requiring the buyers of its omnipresent "Windows" program to simultaneously subscribe to "Explorer", Microsoft was on the point of driving its competitor Netscape, pioneer of Internet, out of the market.

In this situation, the supposed era of the perfect free market to which the knowledge-based economy would lead us is subject to the growing monopoly of a single company. A company which is spreading to new areas on a daily basis. From the direct sale of cars to the sale of airline tickets via Internet, there will be no place to which the tentacles of Microsoft do not reach. It is not by chance that the U.S. Department of Justice wanted to make the Microsoft case an example to others and devoted a disproportionate share of its anti-trust efforts to dividing up the company. The ambiguous result obtained after years of court fights is proof of the strength the company has reached and of the futility of going against the tide.

In fact, the story of Gates is not exceptional. In the world of multimedia as a whole we observe a marked trend towards the creation of mega-conglomerates that control everything.

From the AOL-Time Warner-CNN empire to the gigantic News Corporation Limited of the Australian Rupert Murdoch or Walt Disney-ABC, a few mega-corporations control an ever-larger dominion. Furthermore, the situation is not that different from what is seen in the world of high finance, where corporations like Fidelity Investments, the Vanguard Group, Capital Research & Management, Quantum Fund or China Trust and International Investments control the destinies of entire countries.

It is a curious paradox that the "era of the free market" has led us to monopolies and oligopolies that recall the era of "savage capitalism".

THE COMMON MAN
AND THE GLOBAL ECONOMY

The French sociologist Henri Mendras coined the term "counter-society" to describe all those members of a given society who cannot – or do not want to – follow the rhythm and demands which that society imposes. Its typical protagonist would be that individual who, for lack of possibility or wish, does not manage to adapt himself to the speed at which his social environment moves, thus becoming a pariah within that society. That is, a person who is maladapted, displaced or excluded. At the present time, we may rightly speak of a world counter-society, made up of all those who have not succeeded in assimilating the revolutionary rhythm of globalized society. The number of people who are maladapted, displaced or excluded as a result may now be counted in hundreds of millions. What is more, every day there are more and more people, in different parts of the planet, who are frightened and anguished by the prospect of seeing themselves left out of the ranks of productive beings. They are ordinary men and women who live under the permanent threat of social exclusion.

The figures on this counter-society are frequently mentioned: 30% of the active population of the United States – that is, 40 million persons – are poor or live in a precarious social situation, while 30% of the active population in the three great regions of the industrialized world may be described as "unemployed" or "marginalized". If this is true of the developed world, what can the situation be like in the developing countries! There, the conjuncture of an accelerated technological progress based on automatization and the generalized abandonment of norms that guarantee social protection is causing a daily increase in the number of people who are unemployed or underemployed. Brazil is a good example of a country which has known how to substantially increase its competitiveness and presence in the world economy at the cost of growing unemployment.

The logic of this process is simple. Under the impact of a competition without frontiers or limits, reducing costs becomes the prevailing consideration and social concerns are left aside. In the face of this reality countries have tended to transform themselves into a real Persian bazaar, in which they compete to offer the best bargain to big capital in the race to attract foreign investment and guarantee their own economic growth. The result has been the abandonment of the collective sense and the State's role as an arbiter of social justice. What else can the State do, considering that the State itself is unable to face up to the volume and dynamics of private capitals? Powerless, the State has had to adapt itself to the circumstances, allowing mankind to become a wolf that preys on its own species.

The decline of the State is paralleled by the emerging strength of private transnational capitals. Going beyond the limits of frontiers or sovereign governments, they rule the globalized economy, imposing laws at their own convenience and forcing countries to compete in order to advance their own interests. Nevertheless, the fundamental question we have to ask ourselves is: what is the logic behind this transnational capital? The answer may be reduced to a simple consideration: short-term profit. The need to respond to the short-term expectations of a gigantic group of anonymous stock-holders has become, in fact, the fundamental reason for being of the economic process now in course. Within this context, the large corporations fiercely compete among themselves to win the attention of stock-holders, shedding themselves of everything that might weigh down their chances of attaining higher yields.

This leads to another question: who is this nameless stock-holder upon which everything depends? He (or she) is none other than the "common man": the factory hand, office worker, middling executive, widow, housewife, etc. That is, the same "common man" who is threatened by the market forces which he nourishes. The same "common man" who lives with the anxiety of seeing himself forced to join the swelling ranks of the great counter-society of our day. Through his investments in and search for maximum yields from pension or mutual funds, or by means of his direct investment, however small, in the stock market, he has turned himself into the axis of the very economic process which frightens him and limits his life.

Thus, following a curious circular process, the "common man" has become his own enemy, fiercely and pitilessly preying upon himself.

MANIAS, PANICS AND EXPLOSIONS

In recent years the financial markets have gone through a succession of intense crises. On each of these occasions the world economy was faced with a snowball effect, which threatened to get out of control and smash everything in its path. This financial situation, Hitchcock-style, is one of the most outstanding traits of the globalization process.

This insecurity has its origin in the consolidation of vast reservoirs of investments that are managed by professional financiers who face an enormous competitive pressure to obtain short-term profits. Such competition imposes time limits that are too short to allow productive investments to mature. The solution has been to simply abandon productive investments in favor of those which have been called extractive investments, that is, formulas which allow one to create money without creating value. According to a book entitled *The Death of Money,* written by Joel Kurtzman, editor of the *Harvard Business Review,* for every dollar that circulates in the productive economy, there circulate 20 to 40 dollars in the purely financial economy. While the daily trade of goods and services absorbs an average of 20 to 25 billion dollars, more than a trillion dollars daily circulate in the international financial markets. We are talking about money which has no other function than to produce more money by means of financial speculation. In short, the essence of the system consists of indefinitely increasing the amount of money that circulates in the financial economy, independently of any increase in the production of real goods and services. It is not in vain that Nicholas Brady, Treasury Secretary under former President Bush, came to declare: "If the assets in question were gold or petroleum, this phenomenon would be called inflation. In the case of stocks, it is called the creation of wealth".

The financial markets, which are "inherently unstable", as George Soros admits, tend to become substantially more dangerous in the light of a recent set of factors. In the first place, there is the tendency to replace financial analysts with theoretical mathematicians who work with sophisticated tools of probability analysis and "chaos theory" to elaborate stock portfolios on the basis of mathematical equations. In second place and intimately linked to the first, there is the appearance of what are known as derivatives. These instruments may be acquired by laying out a minimum amount of money, since payment is made on the basis of the margin of potential profit. Today more than 18 trillion dollars worth of derivatives circulate, a gigantic mass of money which rests on the foundation of a minimum support in cash. In third place, there is the confusion between the world of financial analysis and the world of show business, as *Newsweek* noted in its April 3, 2000 edition. In other words, television has transformed financial analysis into a fashionable "show". In fourth place, there is the profusion of high technology stocks, which frequently represent no more than a mere "concept". Most of the time, such stocks, says *Newsweek* (April 24, 2000), are little more than a matter of "hopes, dreams, fashion and momentum", since there is no formula for determining their true value. And so it goes.

It was precisely the crisis in high-tech stocks, as quoted on the Nasdaq, which give rise to the most recent fall of the markets. If the August 1997 fall on the New York Stock Exchange amounted to a more than trillion dollar loss, that of the week of April 10-14, 2000 led to a loss of 2.1 trillion dollars. You have only to look at the fall in the fortunes of some of the world's biggest billionaires between the end of 1999 and the beginning of 2000. Bill Gates, who was worth 92 billion dollars on December 23, 1999, was worth 51 billions on May 5, 2000. The fortune of Michael Saylor fell from 13.8 billion dollars on March 10, 2000 to 960 millions on May 19, 2000. Likewise that of Azim Premji (35 billion to 7.8 billion dollars between February and May) and Yasumitsu Shigeta (39 billion to 1.9 billion dollars between February and May) [42]. It is not by chance that Fernando Henrique Cardoso pointed out, in the Summer 2000 edition of *Foreign Policy*, that the financial markets are subject to "manias, panics and explosions".

THE ROLLER COASTER OF PETROLEUM

In little more than three years petroleum prices have shown dramatic fluctuations. These roller coaster dynamics have been devastating for any country whose economy is tied to that productive item. At the beginning of 1999 prices had fallen below ten dollars per barrel, which led OPEC, in conjunction with some non-OPEC exporters, to reduce daily production by 500,000 barrels. By the end of 2000 the rising spiral of prices was breaking through the 28 dollar barrier, despite the fact that OPEC had agreed to successive increases of 3.3 million barrels in daily production. At the end of 2001 prices threatened to go below 18 dollars and OPEC agreed on a reduction of 1.5 million barrels daily, on the condition that non-OPEC producers would accompany them with an additional reduction of 500,000 barrels. On each of these occasions there were reasons which explained the oscillations.

The fall of prices in 1998 and the beginning of 1999 had been based on the following considerations: the Asian crisis had significantly reduced the demand for petroleum; some non-OPEC producers had increased their production more rapidly than had been expected; the Niño phenomenon had created a particularly benign northern winter; Iraq had begun to pump bigger amounts onto the market, as the result of a partial lifting of U.N. sanctions; several members of the OPEC had been exceeding their quota (Venezuela being the most notorious case); the OPEC had authorized an ill-timed increase of production, etc. This combination of factors created a surplus of petroleum on the market on the order of 2 million barrels per day, which, in turn, allowed the wealthy countries to accumulate reserves of more than 2 million barrels, the highest level in a decade.

The price rise that took place some months later could also be explained: speculation on rising futures markets, based on predictions of economic expansion; the fact that, following an initial price rise, U.S. refineries exhausted their inventories in the hope of price decline that never materialized; the saturation of refining capacity in the United States as a result of the low investment in this field and the bottlenecks in their refining capacity deriving from environmental regulations; and the high taxes on petroleum products in the consumer markets.

The current fall in prices may also be explained. Before the September 11 terrorist attacks preliminary estimates (later confirmed) suggested that the World Gross Product had contracted during the second quarter of the year, for the first time in two decades. Nevertheless, U.S. consumer-confidence in economic recovery had prevented the row of dominoes from falling. After September 11 this confidence collapsed and to this must be added the crisis in the aviation industry.

Alan Greenspan and other specialists and economic publications foresee a quick recuperation of the U.S. economy, the great driving force of the global economy.

Will petroleum prices rise again in the near future? Only one thing is certain: few sectors are as sensitive to the volatility of the world economy as petroleum. In the suspense-filled economy of our days, this hydrocarbon is a hostage to the fluctuating mood of the market. This, in addition to the oscillating temperature of the world's most unstable region: the Middle East.

2020: TWO SCENARIOS

Thirty years ago the Shell Group of Companies began making a triennial study of future trends. Every three years Shell publishes its analysis of the alternative scenarios which, in its opinion, will mark the course of the next decades. In January 2000, the possible scenarios for the next twenty years were presented to the public in the London headquarters of that corporation.[43]

The two scenarios Shell foresees were the following: the consolidation of a globalized economy, under the norms of the Washington Consensus and the strong leadership of the United States or, alternatively, the erosion of the globalized economy, the Washington Consensus and U.S. leadership on the basis of a much more multicultural world. The first scenario was called the "business class" or "executive class" one, in reference to the characteristics of a world led by an international elite with shared values. The second was called the "prism" scenario, alluding to a world which will be colored by cultural factors.

The first scenario reaffirms U.S. economic leadership, a fully-integrated global economy and the ho-

43. *People and Connections: Global Scenarios to 2020*, London, 2002

mogenization of values and cultures. It also implies an increasingly weak State, the victim of pressures on many different levels. Within this frame of reference, the balance of power will tilt in favor of the big corporations and the nation-states will compete among themselves to attract foreign investment. This rests, of course, on a strict subjection to the Washington Consensus. The corporations, however, will not have it all their own way, since their validity and survival in the midst of a race that has acquired maximum speed will become ever more difficult. Faced by the threat of being overrun at any time by those who advance more rapidly, companies must learn how to make their own products and services obsolete before the competition does it for them. Within this scenario, the volatility of financial markets will continue to be the norm and the markets will equally punish the guilty, the innocent and the vulnerable.

The "prism" scenario rests on the premise that the United States will not manage to overcome the crisis in its high-tech sector and, at the same time, will be confronted by terrorism. This will force it into a withdrawal from its international commitments, relying more on the Americas. While this scenario does not imply an abandonment of "modernity", it does foresee the emergence of a pluralist "modernity". That is, the possibility that in a world economic scenario increasingly divided into regions, each region may have its own response and way of doing things. Thus, the relation among the regional blocks will determine the essential shape of the world economic order, with international financial bodies and global multilateral agencies losing their influence. Within an ambit in which respect for cultural particularities is the order of the day, the nation-states will recover much of their lost influence. What is more, it is not the nation-states which will have to fight to make themselves attractive to the great multinational capitals. Instead, the corporations will have to compete against each other in order to better understand and attend to the host nations and communities. In fact, the success of the corporations will be measured by their capacity to adapt to this pluralist atmosphere.

Only time will tell.

THE BANQUET OF WEALTH (OR THE ABYSS OF POVERTY)

Every year the business magazine *Forbes* publishes a report on the world's billionaires. The latest appeared in February 2002 and reveals the following facts: there are 497 people in the world who are worth more than a billion dollars; their combined assets reach 1.54 trillion dollars and these assets fell by 11% or 190 billion dollars in the previous year.

The above figures allow us to reaffirm three conclusions: The past few years mark the period of the greatest creation of wealth in the history of mankind; despite this fact, never before in history have losses of such magnitude been seen; and finally, the gap between the haves and the have-nots has never been wider.

In its June 11-17, 2001 issue, *The Economist* confirmed that the period elapsed since 1990 has witnessed "the most exuberant creation of wealth in history". Private wealth, of course. The magnitude of this private wealth is shown by the statistics. The combined assets of the billionaires listed by *Forbes* equal the combined GDP's of Holland, Switzerland, Belgium, Sweden, Denmark, Norway, Austria and Poland. That is, countries that belong to the developed world and have a total population of around 100 million people.

In second place, the dimension of the losses shown had never been so large. According to *The Economist* (August 25-31, 2001), 10 trillion dollars in global financial assets vanished between January and August 2001. Many dotcom billionaires that appeared in the July 2000 edition of *Forbes* were not listed in the June 2001 one.

In third place, the breach between rich and poor has never been so great. According to the 1996 Report of the United Nations Development Program, of the 23 trillion dollars that made up the world GDP, only 5 trillion corresponded to the developing countries where 80% of mankind lives. The 358 billionaires of that time had combined assets higher than the GDP of countries which house 45% of the world population. Today, the number of billionaires has risen to nearly 500 and a good many of them are as worth as much as the GDP of countries like Malawi (6.3 billion dollars, 11,308,000 inhabitants), Zambia (7.4 billion dollars, 6,300,000 inhabitants), Swaziland (4 billion dollars, 925,000 inhabitants), Rwanda (7.3 billion dollars, 7,609,000 inhabitants) and Burundi (3.8 billion dollars, 6,356,000 inhabitants), to cite only a few.

CHANGE FOR THE SAKE OF CHANGE

"Everything has to change so that it remains the same" is a classic saying by Lampedusa. It is a sentiment that has symbolized the corporate mentality of the United States in recent years. What should remain the same is, of course, the competitive predominance of a company. For this to happen change is necessary. The leading exponent of this line of reasoning has been Jack Welch, who until his recent retirement had been the CEO of General Electric for twenty years and is considered the most successful managerial wizard of recent times.

Welch was the precursor and the staunchest defender of the thesis that only permanent change, even change for the sake of change, can ensure a company's competitiveness.

There is a precise explanation for this: if you undo mental prejudices you create the conditions that are needed to detect and take advantage of opportunities. From this perspective, subjection to a defined strategy produces a kind of selective view of things, conditioned by preconceptions. This being so, Welch seemed to have also reaffirmed, perhaps without being aware of it, the concept which Jung called "synchronism". That is, the logic of chance, as opposed to the logic of causality which has marked Western thought since the time of Aristotle. In other words, he who defines his pursuit in a highly rational way tends to ignore that accident or coincidence that is likely to give him the answer he is seeking.

Justification for Welch's thesis of permanent change goes back a long way and also finds echoes in Clausewitz and Sun Tzu, two of the greatest theoreticians of the art of war, whose reasoning supports the conceptual matrix of the corporate attitude promoted by Welch. For both of those strategists, any planning of a battle or a military campaign that is too rigid tends to lead to failure, because continuous changes in circumstances, the imperfect execution of schemes and the independent will of the enemy leave such plans without a foundation. It is not by accident that they insisted on keeping one's options open. Thus, it is no surprise to learn that the first thing that Jack Welch did when he became the head of GE was to dissolve that company's planning office.

Nevertheless, this kind of cultural revolution in the corporate world seems to have reached its ceiling. In the latest World Economic Forum (held for the first time, not in Davos, but New York), business leaders from all over the world referred to the problems caused by this absence of clear markers: their clients do not understand them, stock-holders are mistrustful of strategies that are not defined and workers and employees feel insecure. Nor is it a coincidence that in the previous meeting of the Forum, in 1999, one of the most frequent complaints voiced by top executives was about the continual stress they face and the health problems caused by it. In a certain way, the message would seem to be clear: a little more foresight and calm, please.

III

LATIN AMERICA
WHO ARE WE AND WERE ARE WE GOING?

THE LATIN AMERICANS: WHO ARE WE?

In his book *The Clash of Civilizations*, Samuel P. Huntington makes a distinction between "Latin American civilization" and "Western civilization" (which, in his judgement, is reduced to Europe, North America and some other countries of European settlement, such as Australia or New Zealand). Behind the courtesy of granting us our own civilization there undoubtedly lie ancestral prejudices. That aside, however, Huntington has touched a sore point in a debate which Latin Americans themselves have not managed to resolve: Who are we? Are we part of Western civilization or not?

In his book *Latin American Thought,* the Mexican Leopoldo Zea, speaks of two Americas: "the Iberian and the Western". Although he recognizes that both derive from Europe, he does not necessarily equate them. This, in turn, has to do with an additional debate which has been carried on from time immemorial in Europe and the Iberian world itself. In the opinion of many, the latter does not fully belong to the West, since the two movements which were responsible for the essential features of Western thought never reached it: the Renascence and the 18th century Enlightenment. It is not in vain that some people say, when speaking of Spain, that "Europe begins beyond the Pyrenees". Octavio Paz has confronted this dilemma by pointing out that the Hispanic world constitutes a peculiarity within Western civilization and that, like the Slav world, forms a sort of "eccentric" model with regard to the central patterns of that civilization, as exemplified by countries like England and France.

That being so, we find that the starting point for our cultural heritage is an "eccentric" model. But at the same time, any definition of Latin American civilization would have to take into account the strong process of cultural fusion of Iberian, indigenous and African elements. The result of all this is a sort of "eccentric" version within the very eccentric model. How can we not be surprised, then, by the existential doubt that weighs upon Latin Americans when they ponder their own identity?

Two great currents of thought have run through the history of Latin America as a response to this existential doubt. The first, which originates in Venezuela, insists on searching for the specificity of our condition as Ibero-Americans. The second tries to find the answers by absorbing cultural reference points that have to do with Europe and the United States. The first current starts with Simón Bolívar, with his attempt to achieve the solidarity and integration of our nations and his emphasis on giving a factual social and political framework to our institu-

tions, based on our realities and roots. These ideas
were shared by Simón Rodríguez, Bolívar's tutor,
with his insistence on our need to be "original",
and the Venezuelan philologist and jurisconsult,
Andrés Bello, with his concept of the "cultural autonomy" of Ibero-America. This same path was also
followed by the national hero of Cuba, Martí; the
Uruguayan writer Rodó; and the Mexican politician
and writer Vasconcelos. At the other extreme we
find the path chosen by one of the main leaders of
Colombian independence, Santander; the Argentine
statesman and writer, Sarmiento; the Argentine jurisconsult, Alberdi; and, in general, the positivists
of the second half of the nineteenth century, who
saw in the political and cultural patterns of Europe,
particularly the Anglo-Saxon world, a natural alternative that would serve to elevate us from our "barbarism" and our limitations as a people. Even today
those who worship the Anglo-Saxon economy
model nourish this old current of ideas, perhaps
without even realizing it.

In addition to these two schools of thought, another came into being in the 1860's, which revolved
around a debate about our being "Latin Americans".
The notion of "Latin America" was a French invention. The term was coined in 1861, at the time that
Napoleon III sought to give legitimacy to his conquest of Mexico. Intellectuals like the Chilean José
Victorino Lastarria would forcefully respond to what
he called "the absurdity of making us Latins", seeing
in this expression an unacceptably imperialist con-

notation. Curiously, the debate was resolved with the imposition of a concept invented by those who sought to "re-colonize us in order to civilize us". Despite its military failure, the France of Napoleon III bequeathed to the region the term by which it is still known. A paradox of this nature can only be explained in terms of our people's profound insecurity about their origins and identity.

Beyond all of the doubts, debates and paradoxes, however, reality imposes itself. Western civilization finds its precise starting point in the Emperors Constantine and Theodosius, who were responsible for the fusion of the Roman Empire and the Christian Church. A particular civilization, destined to implant itself in Europe, originated from this amalgam of Christianity and the classical tradition. It is from there that we inherit our fundamental cultural nutrients. As Arturo Uslar Pietri points out in his book, *The Phantoms of Two Worlds* : "Family, home, urbanization, social relations, the situation of women and children − all of it came down to us from the Roman heritage of law imposed by the Church and the Laws of the Indies, by way of the *Siete Partidas* (the code of law compiled by Alfonso the Wise, the 13th century King of Castille). Our concepts of law, the state, crime and punishment, and property follow a straight line from the Justinian Code.[1]

Our part of America forms, in fact, a Catholic-Roman culture that is Latin, scholastic and Thomist.

1. *Barcelona*, Editorial Seix Barral, S.A.,1979, p. 278.

Leaving aside all our doubt and insecurity, we are inescapably part of Western civilization. To be sure, a very particular part of it.

As Bolívar said, "we are a kind of small human gender"

WHY LATIN AMERICA?

There is no agreement about the origin of the concept of Latin America. For some analysts, like Arturo Ardao, author of the book *Genesis of the Idea and Name of America,* and Ignacio Hernando de Larramendi, who wrote *Utopia of the New America*, it was the Colombian José María Torres Caicedo who employed this concept for the first time, well into the nineteenth century. According to Leopoldo Zea, in his book *Latin America: Third World,* it was the French academic L.M. Tisserand who coined the term in an article published in 1861 in the *Revue des Races Latines*. For Fernando Del Paso, author of *News of the Empire*, the notion of Latin America was originated by Michel Chevalier, ideologue of the "Pan-Latin" theory of Napoleon III. Finally, the Chilean writer Miguel Rojas Mix declares that it was his fellow countryman Francisco Bilbao who was the first to utilize the expression "Latin America", in a lecture given in Paris in 1856.

When one tries to assemble this jigsaw puzzle it would appear that it was, in fact, Francisco Bilbao who used the concept for the first time. The idea was then taken up and disseminated by Torres Caicedo, a highly-influential figure in Ibero-American cultural circles in Paris. In accordance with the thought of both men, the term covered the group of countries of the meridional Americas colonized by Spain, Portugal and France.

Without their wishing it, this formulation of Bilbao and Torres Caicedo perfectly suited the imperialist ambitions towards that part of the world held by the court of Napoleon III. In fact, as Fernando del Paso points out, apart from the conquest of Mexico, Napoleonic France wanted to transform countries like Guatemala, Ecuador and Paraguay into monarchies that would depend on the Court of Les Tuilleries. In the final reckoning, it was the period in which the great capitals of Europe sought to extend their empires to the four cardinal points of the planet. Whereas Ibero-America had been closed off to European imperialistic ambitions ever since the declaration of the Monroe Doctrine, the United States was then in a weak position due to its Civil War and this had opened the doors of the region.

To establish some framework of legitimacy for its hegemonic aspirations towards Latin America, France needed to invent a common identity that could link that region to itself. The "Pan-Latin" thesis, whose ideologue was Michel Chevalier, was the obvious solution. Just as there would later appear the "Pan-American" thesis to structure the link between the United States and the countries south of the Río Grande, so there emerged the "Pan-Latin" one at that time. This idea amalgamated within a common identity the Latin countries situated on both shores of the Atlantic. In a famous letter written in June 1862, Napoleon III emphasized that France had a historic mission to restore the strength and prestige of the Latin race that lived on the other side of the Atlantic. It was left to Tisserand, an academic who was close to the Napoleonic court and a follower of the Chevalier thesis, to give an official status to the term Latin America by using it in a well-known article he wrote.

The U.S. War of Secession ended in 1865 with the victory of the North and the consolidation of the Union. From then on the ban on outside interference in that corner of the planet reestablished itself, ending any new imperialistic ambitions coming from Europe. The regime of Napoleon III, in turn, fell as a result of the war with Prussia in 1870. It is highly curious that the term Latin America survived these two events, becoming adopted as a new symbol of regional identity. It is true that some intellectuals of the period would oppose the emerging concept. Nevertheless, given its origins and imperialist connotations, the little resistance to and easy assimilation of the term turns out to be surprising. We can find the reason for it in a strong intellectual current that sought to deny everything that would identify us with the Hispanic past.

We should not forget, in fact, that from the very moment in which independence from Spain was obtained, aspirations towards modernization tended to affirm a contrast with the hereditary order of Spain, an idea that became rooted in the thought of the region. What is more, the end of the era of Napoleon III coincided with the emergence, all over our America, of a powerful Positivist movement. This movement sought a definitive break with Hispanic cultural and political matrixes, which were identified with anarchy and "barbarism", and wanted to replace them with notions of order and progress. It was the moment when our intellectuals, astonished by the example of the United States and the ideas that were current in London and Paris, sought to refound Ibero-America on new bases. A concept like that of Latin America, which established a direct parentage with the matrixes of Western civilization, skirting round Spain, necessarily found a warm welcome. So it was that we transformed ourselves into "Latin Americans", obviating the need for much more descriptive notions of our origin.

THE DIFFERENT LATIN AMERICAS

In essence, Latin America would be made up of those non-Anglo components of population formed in the common mould of the Catholic religion and the Latin heritage. Ibero-America and Haiti would naturally fit into this structure. However, if we were to take the argument to its logical conclusion, we would have to also include not only the province of Quebec but also France. The latter by virtue of its overseas territories in the region, which are not colonies but integral parts of the French state and enjoy the same rights as the metropolitan country. Nevertheless when we speak of Latin America we usually use the term in the more restricted sense of Ibero-America.

Iberian America has, as its starting point, the Treaty of Tordecillas, signed between Spain and Portugal in 1494, which divided the then recently-discovered southern America into two parts: the Castillian and the Portuguese. Both parts would have the same roots in Iberian civilization, the result of eight centuries of physical co-existence and the fusion of races and cultures among Christians, Moors and Jews. As the Brazilian intellectual Gilberto Freyre has well pointed out, they would also have a common Hispanic matrix. In this interpretation, Portugal has, in fact, the same right to be considered part of the Hispanic world as Galicia, Catalonia or Andalucia, the only distinction being its status as an independent state. An independent existence that began in the reigns of two Portuguese Kings of the tenth and eleventh centuries: Alfonso Henriques and Dinis.

Starting with the common matrix just described, the Spanish and Portuguese would have to go through the same process of racial mixture and transculturation when they reached the New World, thus giving rise to a new human gender. These similarities aside, however, there are many differences between Brazil and Spanish America. In the first place, because of the much milder, more pragmatic and conciliatory character of the Portuguese version, which is free of the excesses and rigidity characteristic of the Spanish one. We might even say that Sancho Panza exemplifies the Portuguese/Brazilian strain, in contrast to the Spanish/Hispano-American Don Quixote. In the second place, there are historical reasons. The history of Brazil displays a process of moderate evolution, devoid of epic deeds and sudden shocks. As Leopoldo Zea has correctly pointed out, the Brazilians fell asleep one night as a colony and woke up to find themselves an independent empire and, some time later, woke up again to find themselves a republic. The history of Hispanic America, on the other hand, is that of permanently beginning all over again.

Hispanic America, for its part, also shows many differences among its diverse components. We have much in common, particularly two factors. In the first place, a history of parallel events. That is, three hundred years of subjection to Spanish centralism and Catholic fundamentalism; a simultaneous awakening to the ideas of freedom and independence; an independence movement characterized by the cooperation between and overlapping of our founding fathers and armies; an emergence into an independent life marked by the overthrow of the established order and the rise of a regime of *caudillos* (strong men or political bosses); a parallel stage of confrontations and civil wars between those who aspired to a modernization of structures and those who clung to the vestiges of the order inherited from

Spain; and the simultaneous emergence of a positivist generation that sought a definitive break with Hispanic cultural and political moulds in order to impose order and progress on anarchy.

In the second place, we have a common language, preserved from fragmentation and corruption thanks to the monumental grammar "destined for the use of Americans" that was published by Andrés Bello in 1847. In other words, a language that is mestizo but cultured, transformed into an instrument of cultural homogeneity.

But beyond our similarities, we Hispano-Americans also show important differences. Two of them turn out to be fundamental. The first are those which derive from our variety of latitudes and climates, which range from the four seasons of the Southern Cone to the permanent summer of the tropics, with a multitude of hues and variables in between. All of this has been responsible for a variety of sub-regional attitudes and patterns of behavior.

In second place are the differences which emerge from the different racial mixtures or the very absence of such mixtures. There is a Latin America of strong indigenous roots which, running down from Mexico and Guatemala, extends along the length of the basin of the Andean Pacific. Another strain, essentially White, is centered in the Southern Cone. A third, with a strong African presence, starts in the Spanish isles of the Caribbean and extends towards Panama, the coasts of Colombia and a good part of Venezuela. In contrast with the continent-state of

Brazil, which was able to assimilate its racial variables, preserving a unitary sense of nationality, the different countries of Hispanic America give very different connotations to their racial components. This ranges from the respect for racial mixture that is observed in, for example, Mexico, Venezuela and Colombia, to the racial superiority shown by those of White European descent in Argentina, with, once again, many tinges and variations of sentiment in between.

Nevertheless, leaving aside the differences between the various Latin Americas, or, to be more precise, the different Ibero-Americas, there is a common destiny of integration and solidarity which is the product of our Bolivarian heritage. In the past four decades, our nations have rediscovered the importance of this ideal and have gradually assumed the challenge of constructing a great Latin American nation.

TWO AMERICAS

A lot has been written about the contrast between the two great flanks of the American world. On one side, there is the Anglo-Saxon Protestant influence, whose paradigm is the United States, and on the other, there is the Iberian Catholic one, characteristic of Latin America. The astonishing development attained by the Anglo-Saxon world of the North and the perennial underdevelopment of the Latin world of the South are presented as unquestionable testimonies to the great difference between the two cultures. On one side, there is the culture that pushes from behind, thrusting towards the heights and on the other, the one that seems like a heavy burden that crushes and holds back any attempt at an effective progress.

This dichotomatic vision of the continent does not take into account the diverse cultural variables that were present throughout its process of formation. For example, it ignores two of its secondary cultural components: the French and the Dutch, the former, of course, having had much more weight than the latter. At the same time, it also ignores the specificity of the African world of the Antilles, which was formed under Anglo-Saxon cultural patterns but is very distant from the North in terms of its accomplishments. What is more, it does not emphasize the important differences between the Lusitanian and Hispanic contributions within Latin America itself, nor between the culture of "honor" of the South and the culture of "work" of the North in the United States.

Thus, for example, one might speak of the great similarities that existed between the "seignorial" cultures of Iberian and French origin that were imposed on America. The concept of the "hidalgo" (nobleman), which was proper to Spain, was at odds with all forms of manual work, just like the French notion of "derogance", which implied the loss of social status as the result of such work. In the same way, one might point to the resemblance between the

the slave and seignorial societies of the southern United States and those of Latin America. It might also be worth mentioning the more pragmatic, down to earth attitude of the Portuguese "Sancho Panza", in contrast with the more grandiloquent and excessive one of the Spanish "Don Quixote". And so on and so forth.

Despite what has just been said, simplifications have a didactic value and for that reason are useful. In this sense, even though one recognizes the limitations of a dichotomatic vision of American history, one may recur to a comparative analysis between the Anglo-Saxon North and the Iberian South. It is an example of the eternal contrast between Ariel and Caliban that was mentioned by the Uruguayan Rodó at the beginning of the 20th century.

What features of the Anglo-Saxon cultural mould, transplanted to this side of the Atlantic, were responsible for the transformation of the United States into the greatest economic, military and technological power of all times? What happened with the Hispanic mould that condemned its peoples, in this part of the world, to what has come to be known as the "culture of poverty"? In this sense, it is well worth the trouble of examining the great differences that marked the respective colonial histories of the United States and Hispanic America.

In the first place, we should note that the Spanish colonial world was essentially urban and was composed of a highly stratified society. It was a world of cities and, at the same time, of great hierarchical differences. The British colonial world was much more rural than urban, and in its most successful expression, profoundly egalitarian. In second place, the Hispanic world transplanted to this side of the Atlantic had an essentially feudal vision of society. In some manner, Hispanic America was transformed into a replica of medieval Castille. In the Anglo-Saxon world, on the other hand, the road towards capitalism and liberalism was taken at a relatively early stage. In third place, Spain brought with it a heavy bureaucratic apparatus. This included not only a legion of officials and magistrates but also an endless number of norms and regulations. England, on the other hand, colonized within the context of independent settlement companies, which competed amongst themselves to attract colonists, each offering wider "liberties, franchises and immunities" than its rivals. In fourth place, Spanish America was marked by a symbiosis between State and Church, which meant that the latter was given the rigid role of the inquisitor. In the Anglo-Saxon America of the North the competition to attract colonists also meant that there was a broad spectrum of different religious beliefs. In fact, the very start of English colonization arose from the search for religious freedom. And so the differences became ever more profound.

We can definitively say that the different cultural matrixes inherited from the Anglo-Saxon and Iberian worlds produced diametrically opposite results. At a time when the cultural factor increasingly tends to be seen as a key to the explanation of the evolution of different nations, it is essential to take it into account as we face up to our new challenges. It is a subject that is becoming more and more relevant.

THE CHALLENGE OF HISPANICITY

Few concepts have met so much resistance as that of hispanicity. On the European continent the rejection of Spain and the Hispanic has been a constant for centuries. In Latin America itself, the history of the 19th century, when independence was achieved, was marked by a search for identity which would allow it to establish a link with the Western world that avoided its Spanish heritage. Even in present-day Spain the concept of hispanicity is being questioned. The Spain of autonomous regions has joined hands with European Spain, leaving aside pureblooded Spain, the womb of hispanicity.

Pejorative references to the Hispanic world have been commonplace for a long time. There are many instances of this, which run from the famous saying that "Europe begins beyond the Pyrenees" to the systematic attempt to place the Hispanic on the margin of Western civilization. In his masterly book *Civilization*, Kenneth Clark says, "If one asks what Spain has done to broaden the human mind and raise the level of civilization, the answer is not very clear. Don Quixote, the great saints, the Jesuits in South America? Beyond that there has simply been

Spain"[2]. In his *History of Art*, Elie Faure eliminates at a stroke any reference to the Hispanic contribution to Western art. According to his argument, while art constitutes a process of constructing symbols, the Hispanic culture is one of the anti-symbol. That is, a culture which reduces all that is graceful and elevated in human nature to its most elemental and basic level.

Why this rage against the Hispanic world ? Why have the Spanish and the Latin Americans themselves always felt so insecure about their roots? The most obvious answer may have to do with the fact that the Hispanic world is atypical within the context of the West. Just like the Slav world, it forms a distinct model within this framework of civilization. When did Spain become different? What made it so peculiar?

In the first place, we might say that, situated as it is on one of the extremities of the European continent, Spain was always a meeting point between Europe and Africa, the Atlantic and the Mediterranean, Europe and America. Throughout the centuries, the Iberian peninsula has been a nerve center at which the most diverse races and civilizations merged: Phoenicians, Greeks, Carthaginians, Romans, Goths, Gypsies, Jews and Arabs, all of them made Spain into their own land. Nevertheless, we may find some additional answers in the historical evolution of the country itself.

2. *New York, Harper & Row Publishers, Inc.*, p.XVII.

Above all, Spain is a country with an immense capacity to absorb alien cultural elements, a nation with an extraordinary capacity for cultural and human synthesis.

Hispania was the Roman province which best assimilated that Empire. In fact, it was from Hispania that there emerged three of its best emperors – Hadrian, Trajan and Theodosius – as well as one of its greatest philosophers, Seneca. With the arrival of the Barbarians, Spain turned into the country which most completely absorbed the symbols of identity of the Goth invaders, transforming itself into a perfect synthesis of the Roman and Germanic worlds. In some way, Spain symbolized at that time the epitome of the Western World. The arrival of the Arabs in 711 A. D. introduced, however, a great change. From then onwards, its very capacity of absorption and synthesis worked to distance it from the rest of Europe. Throughout the eight hundred years of the Moorish occupation, Spain fully integrated the three human groups that lived together there: Arabs, Jews and Christians, giving rise to a new national identity. The endless process of Christian Reconquest meant that Spain continued to keep her back to Europe for a long time and when, at last, the bases for her reinsertion in the continent were established in 1492, the discovery of America took place. From then on the basic energies of the country were channeled towards the American adventure. Many have commented upon how Spanish America is the result of a process of cultural fusion, but we should remember that Spain herself went through it under the influence of the New World.

We may definitively say that Spain is different from the rest of Europe because its historical development was considerably more complex than that of her European neighbors. The amalgam of dissimilar elements was much richer in Spain than in the "central" countries of the Western world, such as France or England. Spain is "complicated" because its sources are richer.

To ignore the significance of this heritage would be an immense waste. What is more, it would imply losing sight of the potential for a great strategic alliance. By the year 2000 the Hispanic world had reached a population of four hundred million human beings and Spanish is now on its way to becoming the second most-widely spoken language in the world. Nineteen countries, on both shores of the Atlantic, thus share a common civilizing root and will have the capacity to meet the challenges of the world scene with the same cultural elements. What is more, this Hispanic heritage will become more and more decisive within the United States, the epicenter of world power. Los Angeles is already the second-biggest Spanish-speaking city in the world, after Mexico City and ahead of Madrid and Barcelona. The Hispanic population of that country now amounts to 12% of its total population. By the year 2025 more people will speak Spanish in the United States than in Spain and by 2050 the Hispanics will represent 25% of the U.S. population.

IBERO-AMERICAN IDENTITY

Within the sphere of international relations identity has the same value that kinship has in interpersonal relations.

The stronger a country's or region's capacity to assert the different aspects of its identity, the greater will be its capacity to establish itself on the world scene. The formation of spaces and alliances of a political or economic kind is determined, to a large extent, by matters of common identity.

As Latin America seeks a bigger role in international affairs, exploring and developing the different expressions of its identity becomes a major priority.

The most obvious aspect of identity which the region will be able to exploit is its latinity. When all is said and done, we recognize ourselves to be Latin Americans. On this point, we should remember, as we have pointed out, that the term Latin America was coined at the very moment that Napoleon III undertook the conquest of Mexico: it was not, of course, a mere coincidence. Behind the term there lurked a whole political enterprise that sought to impose the leadership and aspirations of France on Hispanic America. Thus, it is highly curious that the term Latin America was accepted by our nations. However, latinity has important limitations as a tool to define such an identity. Its very amplitude tends to turn it into a concept that is too vague.

If latinity suffers from too loose a grasp, hispanicity, by contrast, is entirely concrete. It is not only easy to identify Hispanic America, but it is also natural to link it with the mother country. In addition, the idea makes a lot of political sense when we consider a further element: the 30 million United States citizens who form that country's largest minority and think of themselves as "Hispanos". At first sight, the main limitation of this argument would be that it excludes the Portuguese world. Shutting out 160 Brazilians who occupy a territory of 8 million square kilometers, half of the area of South America, would not, of course, seem like a good idea.

Gilberto Freyre, one of the most distinguished Brazilian intellectuals of the twentieth century, wrote a memorable book entitled *The Brazilian among other Hispanics*. In it, he argues that Portugal has as much right to be considered Hispanic as Galicia, Andalucia or Castille, since they all share common roots. He also points to those traits of identity characteristic of the Hispanics which not only served to agglutinate the inhabitants of the Iberian peninsula but also had a strong influence upon their descendants on the other side of the Atlantic. It is in this sense, Freyre argues, that the Brazilian is just another Hispanic. Despite Freyre's good intentions, it is highly unlikely that the Brazilians and the Portuguese would like to shelter under this cloak of Hispanic identity. Stranger still, the same concept awakens resentment in Spain as well. Since "hispanicity" was an emblem used and abused by the Franco regime, many present-day Spaniards do not like the idea very much.

Thus we arrive at term Ibero-America. In contrast with "Latin America", it is sufficiently precise in its origins and a more practical instrument of use. At the same time, unlike the term Hispano-America, it turns out to be more descriptive of the original matrix shared by Spanish- and Portuguese-speaking Americans and would not be opposed by the Portuguese world. By defining ourselves as Ibero-Americans, we clearly express the elements of kinship within a family that is universally known.

TOWARDS A NEW PAN-AMERICANISM?

The idea of Pan-Americanism arose in the United States, under the auspices of the First Pan-American Conference, held in Washington in 1889. However, it is a concept that was more characteristic of the twentieth than the nineteenth century. In the nineteenth century, the United States was too busy structuring its own territory to think in terms of America as a whole. It was only when its own process of national integration was concluded that the giant of the North began to extend its presence towards the rest of the hemisphere.

In etymological terms, Pan-Americanism means "a single unit for the whole of America". Through this notion the United States sought to fulfill its ambitions towards the immense region situated to the south of the Río Grande. In the same way that France, decades before, had coined the term Latin America to justify its attempt at hegemony over Iberian America, Washington now used this new term for its own purposes.

Pan-Americanism tried to find its roots in two factors. The first, of a geographical and the second, of a historical kind. The geographical was plainly apparent and responded to the reality of that immense continent, situated between two oceans, which had been discovered by Columbus. The historical reason, for its part, referred to the fact that both Anglo-Saxon America and Iberian America shared the condition of being civilizations that had been transplanted from the other side of the Atlantic, as well as the experience of having emancipated themselves from their respective mother countries.

Latin American intellectuals of that period – like the Uruguayan Rodó, the Cuban Martí, the Nicaraguan Rubén Darío, the Ecuadorian Juan Montalvo, the Argentineans Manuel Ugarte and José Ingenieros – were suspicious of the Pan-American idea. Nevertheless, this notion gathered strength as a conceptual justification for a political and commercial relationship that was becoming more and more dynamic. In 1910 Buenos Aires was the seat the Fourth Pan-American Conference. It was there that the term Pan-American Union emerged, which would later be formalized through the creation of a permanent body with headquarters in Washington.

In the nineteen-thirties the notion of Pan-Americanism began to lose ground, mutating into a new concept: Inter-Americanism. This change was subsequently given a juridical form through the creation of two international agreements: the Inter-American Treaty on Reciprocal Assistance of 1947 and the Charter of the Organization of the American States of 1948. The difference between the two ideas was subtle but important. Inter-Americanism did not refer to the notion of a "whole", but rather to the "relationship" among its diverse components.

Curiously, as we enter the twenty-first century, the Pan-American concept seems to be enjoying an unexpected rebirth. In fact, instead of a "relationship" among the diverse

parts of the broad American continent, current tendencies may be pointing towards the formation of a "whole". In the economic and commercial field there is an inexorable march towards hemispheric integration. Much more significant than that, however, is what seems to be the creation of a cultural interdependence between the two great currents of America.

In the economic ambit Latin America has become an ever more vital interlocutor for the United States. By the end of this decade Latin America will surpass Europe and Asia to become the main commercial outlet for the United States. Sooner than later, the Free Trade Area of the Americas will become an inescapable reality, giving rise to a great economic block.

Nevertheless it is in the cultural field that the inter-relation between the North and South will become more pronounced. The cultural penetration of Latin America by the United States has been going on for a long time and is getting stronger and stronger, leading to an authentic fusion of cultures in the region. But it is not a one-way road. Latin America, as well, has been carrying out a cultural invasion of the North. The United States is feeling the impact of "hispanicity" more and more, which means that the Hispanic cultural presence has a stronger role in the new identity of the United States.

Numerous studies now point to the growing hispanicization of the United States under the impact of population growth. That aside, however, there are several factors that explain the growing presence of the Hispanic cultural identity in that society. In the first place, the younger generations tend to identify themselves with their cultural roots in a much more open and natural way than their elders. In second place, U.S. society as a whole has turned out to be more much more permissive than one might expect about granting the "Hispanos" a cultural context of their own. This ranges from the terrain of the "politically correct" – that is, the need to respect minority groups for political reasons – to the growing economic power of such a big sector of the population. In third place, Hispanic idols are beginning to be fashionable within U.S. society as a whole. Ricky Martin, Jennifer López, Cristina Aguilera, Andy García, Cameron Díaz, Carolina Herrera, Oscar de la Renta

– these are only some of the idols of Hispanic descent who have been absorbed into the blood stream of the host society.

The appearance of this potential rise in Pan-Americanism would seem to be based on reciprocal dependence and inescapable integration. By very different routes and with very dissimilar historical experiences, the two worlds, the Anglo-Saxon North and the Latin South, are merging as they head towards a common destiny. It is not, however, a question of one part imposing itself on the other, with the consequent abandonment of values and life styles by the weaker one. It is just the opposite: the establishment of a point halfway between the two extremes, with the inevitable reciprocal concessions and the acceptance of the other's values. This would represent a fundamental change in the traditional U.S. attitude towards Latin America, which has been full of contempt and prejudice.

THE UNDERLYING REALITY

While the U.S. elite is profoundly Euro-centric, the average citizen is only concerned with immediate and local problems.

In neither case does Latin America represent a significant concern in U.S. thought. Nevertheless, when you look below the surface there is an underlying reality which, in a gradual and inexorable way, will transform Latin America into an essential priority for U.S. interests. There are two basic reasons for the existence of this underlying reality: commercial trends, on the one hand, and cultural penetration, on the other.

Latin America has become an essential trade partner for the United States, with a commercial exchange which, in goods alone, reached 300 billion dollars in 1999. During the period from 1990 to 1994, U.S. exports to the region grew by 79%. This figure is in marked contrast with the increase of U.S. exports towards other regions of the planet: 10% to Japan, 5% to the European Union and 38% to Canada. Significantly, U.S. exports to Latin America grew by an additional 30% between 1996 and 1998, despite the economic difficulties of the region in that period.

According to the figures published by the U.S. Department of Commerce and the U.S. International Trade Commission, of the 642 billion dollars of total U.S. exports of goods in 1999, 134 billion, equivalent to 21%, went to Latin America. In simple terms, this means that our region is treading on the heels of the two richest economic groupings of the world: the European Union and the fifteen countries classified as Asiatic by the Department of Commerce. Exports to the former were 142 billion dollars, or 22% of the total, while those to the latter were 159.4 billion, equivalent to 24.8 %. In accordance with the calculations of the Department of Commerce, at the end of this decade Latin America will surpass Europe and Asia, becoming the main commercial outlet for products which come from the United States.

What is more, also at the end of this decade exports towards our region will surpass the combined total for the European Union and Japan.

Even more than in commerce, it will be in the field of cultural penetration that Latin America will make its presence felt with increasing force. The rate of growth of the Hispanic population in the United states is 8.5% annually, compared with 1.5% for the rest of that society. The Hispanic population of the United States is now a bit more than twice its size in 1980. Since 1990, this community has grown by 38%, compared to 9% for the rest of the population. At the present time, the 31 million Hispanics who live in the United States represent 12% of its total population. By the year 2005 it will have become the largest minority in the United States and by 2050 it will represent 25% of the total population.

The growing hispanicization of the United States is evident on every level. It is not an exaggeration to say that U.S. society is becoming fully bilingual. What is more, the Latin American cultural component has put down such strong roots that it is turning into an inseparable part of the United States bloodstream.

It will not take long for the underlying reality to emerge on the surface, obliging that country to give priority attention to the region. By virtue of the inescapable strength of numbers, Latin America will impose itself as an essential interlocutor for the United States.

THE HISTORIC ALLIANCE

The U.S. political system is extraordinarily vulnerable to pressure groups of an ethnic character. Countries like Israel and Greece have always benefited from the immense influence which their ethnic communities have within the United States. Latin America has the capacity to follow these examples. Developing a historical alliance with the Hispanic community in the United States is a priority task, the importance of which has not been grasped by the governments of Latin America. With the exception of Mexico, which has made this strategy one of the main instruments for exerting pressure on Washington, little or nothing has been done about it in the region.

As we have said, the 31 million Hispanics in the United States are a force of considerable economic and cultural significance. However, it is in the political field that their power is beginning to be strongly felt. Their potential impact on U.S. politics goes far beyond the gross population figures we have cited, because 76% of the Hispanic community is located in a key group of states which are responsible for 72% of the country's electoral votes, that is, the votes which elect the President. The concentration of this population in states like California, Texas, New York, Florida and Illinois is a decisive factor. In terms of electoral weight, California is the most important state, followed by New York, Illinois and, in fifth and sixth place, respectively, Texas and Florida.

Up to a few years ago, the low voting level of the Hispanics made their concentration in politically-key states a matter of theoretical rather than real power. Recently, however, it has been established that, while the population as a whole shows a descending curve of electoral participation, that of the Hispanics has risen. Between 1994 and 1998 the Hispanic vote rose by 27% while overall voting fell by 13%. Along with this general rise in electoral participation, the fact that the Hispanic vote is no longer monopolized by the Democrats, but is becoming increasingly bipartisan, is highly significant. This has forced both of the major parties to make a bigger effort to court and grant concessions to the Hispanic electorate.

This community has not only gone through a rapid expansion, concentrating itself in key electoral states and showing a growing level of political involvement, it has also demonstrated something else: a precise cultural identity. This turns out to be important for a simple reason. So long as an ethnic minority stays self-absorbed, it is easy for politicians to mobilize it. When, on the other hand, its linking elements are absorbed into the mainstream of U.S. society, it is harder to influence it. The Hispanic community has reaffirmed its cultural traits in recent years.

If the countries of Latin America do not learn how to take advantage of the gigantic potential of their kinship with the Hispanics of the United States, they will make a historic mistake: both sides form a single people.

DOES LATIN AMERICA HAVE A FUTURE?

The fall of the Berlin Wall represented the triumph of capitalism over socialism. What won, however, was the capitalist model in general, a model with different variants, each claiming the right to be the best expression of it.

Among these different tendencies we found the American/Anglo-Saxon version, the various European ones (the Rhenish, Alpine, etc.) and finally, the Asiatic one which had shown such a great success in Japan and Southeast Asia. In essence, the big difference between the American model and the rest had to do with the fact that the latter placed a greater emphasis on consensus, stable employment and the safety net of the welfare state, while the former had a much more aggressive character, an emphasis on short-term gains and fewer guarantees of job security.

It soon became evident that the American version had no rivals. The Asian model has collapsed as an option in the wake of the prolonged crisis suffered by Japan since the nineteen-eighties and the cataclysm that hit the economies of Southeast Asia beginning in 1997. The European varieties, for their part, showed themselves to be incapable of finding a response to the globalization of the economy. While all this was going on, American capitalism regrouped itself around a number of strategic sectors. To begin with, there was a conjunction among information technologies, telecommunications and entertainment, resulting in products which blurred the traditional distinction between goods and services, while bio-technology was strengthened. In turn, this joint advance of the two main sectors of high technology upheld a rapid acceleration of the financial markets, which led to the emergence of a multitude of new products.

The extraordinary dynamism of American capitalism enabled its model to become the definitive basis of the globalized economy. Both the European and East Asian economies had to capitulate to this new reality. Although the human and social cost of this globalizing process may be immense and its consequences in terms of political stability are still unresolved, one thing clearly stands out: the economies of the developed world have grown at an unprecedented speed.

Several years ago, Alvin Toffler referred to the distinction between quick and slow nations. This breach, which has always existed, has now become supreme, in the face of the exponential velocity which the developed economies are showing. For Latin America, the consequences of this situation have been dramatic. Whereas the developed economies are turning more and more into what are known as "knowledge-based economies", the Latin American ones are still hindered by the same old limitations. What is more, the overall collapse of the safety net embodied in social welfare programs, which has occurred throughout the region as a result of globalization, has seriously affected Latin America's most fundamental tool for development: education.

A number of Brazilian economists have given their country the name of "Belindia", that is, a mixture of Belgium and India. While a small number of states in southeast Brazil have the economic power of Belgium, the rest of the nation is characterized by the poverty of India. Without reaching the prosperity of southeastern Brazil, most of the Latin American countries mirror this dualism: they have established a few competitive economic niches but these have to bear an immense burden of under-development and poverty. Globalization has only served to strengthen these dichotomies to an extreme degree, allowing a few dynamic niches to find a place in the international economy while erasing whole productive sectors from the map. If it follows this route, which will only intensify existing political instability and social tension, it will be difficult for Latin America to find a way out. Under this scheme, only small, homogenous countries which have a high educational level and understand how to insert themselves into internationally-competitive niches might be able to find a solution. A typical case might be Costa Rica. In fact, in a global economy which obliges nations to be quick-footed, only the small and agile animals will be able to survive. As these animals become bigger and heavier, their possibilities of adapting to a Darwinian environment are reduced. There is no doubt about it: globalization means that the future of Latin America is becoming more and more insecure.

STRATEGIES OF HEMISPHERIC INTEGRATION

The ratification of the NAFTA created a heartrending internal breach in the United States. The same thing occurred with the ratification of the GATT agreements in the autumn of 1994. In order to obtain congressional support for these agreements, President Clinton had to abandon his attempt to ask the Congress to renew the so-called "fast track" authority. This mechanism (now renamed the "trade promotion authority") allows the Executive to negotiate trade agreements on the understanding that the Congress may only approve or reject the package as a whole, without being allowed to amend it provision by provision. Without the "fast track" the extension of NAFTA towards the rest of Latin America was suspended. It thus became impossible to fulfill the original intention – that, beginning with Chile, the countries of Latin America would be incorporated, one by one, into the North American Free Trade Agreement.

The gap that resulted from the limitations placed on NAFTA's extension to the South was exploited by the main countries of the hemisphere in different ways. In one way or another, each of them designed its own strategy to deal with the situation. The two major countries of Latin America, Mexico and Brazil, each came up with a well-articulated response.

During this waiting period, Mexico saw an excellent opportunity to consolidate its position as a natural bridge between the United States and Latin America.

If NAFTA had continued to advance towards the south at a steady pace, Mexico would have seen a gradual decline in its importance, not only in relation to the United States but also to the rest of the region. The delay imposed by this legislative process allowed it to strengthen its position. The strategy it followed consisted of rapidly multiplying its bilateral free trade agreements with most of the region's countries. In this way, agreements were signed with Colombia and Venezuela for the establishment of the Group of Three, while it simultaneously negotiated accords with Chile, Costa Rica, Bolivia and the other countries of the Central American Common Market.

In accordance with this strategy it was essential for Mexico to present itself as the indirect gateway to NAFTA, for which reason all of the new treaties negotiated by Mexico bore the indelible seal of the rules established by the North American Free Trade Agreement. Mexico thus sought to strengthen its position, so that when the time came for the inevitable negotiation with the giant of the South, MERCOSUR, it would already have guaranteed a leading role for itself. If it failed to do this, it ran the risk of seeing a direct agreement between the United States and MERCOSUR.

Brazil's strategy followed a completely different route. As the keystone of MERCOSUR, Brazil wanted to exploit the waiting period to group South America within that mechanism of integration. Following this strategy, it advanced in the direction of a South

American Free Trade Association, signing accords with Chile and Bolivia, and later with the Andean Community itself.

Brazil's objective was clear: to form a South American block, led by MERCOSUR, which could negotiate on the best possible terms with the giant of the North. This implied, of course, entering into direct negotiations with the leading power, the United States, avoiding the mediation of Mexico. In a parallel manner, however, Brazil foresaw the negotiation of a free trade agreement between MERCOSUR and the European Union, not only as a healthy counterweight to the United States but also as a formula to strengthen the importance of MERCOSUR.

While the two major powers of Latin America worked out their strategies, the United States came up with one of its own. Since it was impossible for it to extend NAFTA towards the South in the short term, the White House sought an alternative route: it launched a proposal for establishing a Free Trade Area of the Americas by the year 2005. With this strategy it not only sent a clear message of hope to Latin America, it also expressed a sense of clear purpose at a time of uncertainty.

Nevertheless, the precision of the promise was in sharp contrast with the possibility of its being fulfilled in real life.

In fact, the White House had rarely found itself in such a difficult situation. It was not only burdened with its failure to win agreement on "fast track" and the "state of war" which the ratification of NAFTA had provoked in the Congress, but it was also faced with the recent damage suffered by its own party in the Congressional elections.

In fact, the overwhelming triumph of the Republicans in the legislative elections of November, 1994 saw the emergence of a new type of Republican, nationalistic and opposed to free trade. Whereas, before, the major opponents of NAFTA and free trade had been Democratic-linked organizations like the unions and the environmentalists, the opposition now included a new band of far-right Republicans. This lack of support for going forward with integration towards the South and the pressing problems that arose in other latitudes meant that the initiative to establish a hemispheric Free Trade Area soon declined into a matter of bureaucratic routine and formalistic pronouncements.

Now that Bush is in the White House and has strengthened his power as a result of the September 11 terrorist attacks, the proposal of a Free Trade Area of the Americas may become more of a viable possibility. It will be interesting to see the reactions of both the Latin American countries and the U.S. Congress.

THE CHALLENGES OF QUEBEC

The summit held in Quebec in April, 2001 established the bases for the setting into motion of a Free Trade Area of the Americas by the year 2005. While heads of states and governments met there, thirty thousand demonstrators made it clear that a lot of people are angrily opposed to globalization, without possibly grasping that the worst enemy of globalization is, precisely, a world divided into regional blocks. In any case, the most professionally-run mass protest movement of the past decades made itself felt and got across the essence of its message: that it was wrong to let the multinationals exploit cheap manpower and harm the environment all over the world. Behind the efficient organization of the protests and the idealism of the demonstrators there was the money of U.S. unions, which have an interest in blocking any initiative that represents a threat to jobs in that country.

Among the many challenges that arise from the establishment of a Free Trade Area of the Americas, there are three that have a singular importance: achieving "fast track" in the United States, future negotiations about labor and environmental standards and the diversity of approaches towards free trade. The first has to do with recovering the ground lost in 1994, when then President Clinton lost his fast track authorization to negotiate trade agreements without legislative interference. This power is fundamental for the successful negotiation of such a complex and wide-ranging free trade agreement. The White House has promised to obtain it, but it is not easy at the present time, when the recession is sinking its claws into the U.S. economy.

The second of the challenges has to do with the pending negotiations on labor and environmental standards. All products made in the industrialized economies carry the burden of the costs imposed by their domestic regulations in these fields. Such regulations are the result of pressures exerted by their trades unions and environmental groups. Insofar as the developing countries are not subjected to such stringent regulations, their manufactures enjoy advantages that those of the developed countries do not have. It is for these reasons that the industrialized nations have been insisting that the developing ones impose the former's standards in these fields. However, any attempt to "level up" the standards of the poor countries to those of the rich ones only results in driving out of the market all those countries which are unable to adjust themselves to highly demanding norms. The danger that many see is that, under pressure from its unions, environmental groups and the growing horde of anti-globalizers, the United States will try to impose its labor and environmental standards on the hemispheric negotiations. Fortunately, Bush is not friendly to such standards.

Finally, we face the problem of the many different approaches towards free trade. The U.S. government believes that the important thing is a rapid advance towards free trade. If global negotiations on the level of the World Trade Organization are going slowly, then priority should be given to negotiations on a hemispheric level and if these, in turn, become stuck, then priority should be given to incorporating into NAFTA those countries of Latin America which are ready to join it. In Latin America, on the other hand, there are a variety of positions. They range from the attitude of countries like Chile or Argentina, which want to join NAFTA without having to bother about the agreement on a Free Trade Area of the Americas, to that of others, like Venezuela and Brazil, which have profound reservations about the Free Trade Area. Within this scenario, there is the possibility that a few countries will wind up in NAFTA, while the hemispheric Free Trade Area will be shelved.

LATIN AMERICA'S FIRST LINE OF DEFENSE

The natural aspiration of every state is to gain the widest possible international recognition. This will not only strengthen its voice in international affairs but it will also help it to put its policies into practice. By the same token and for the same reasons, every region wishes to reach the widest possible level of international recognition. Such recognition is a synonym for credibility and credibility, we must not forget, depends to a large extent on image.

A central feature of the relations between Latin America and the United States has to do with this matter of image. Respect for an interlocutor begins with one's perception of him. In 1926, the President of the United States, Calvin Coolidge, made the following statement: "It would seem that revolutions and natural disasters are the main products of Latin America". In 1950, George Kennan, artificer of the containment policy and intellectual father of U.S. foreign policy on Latin America, wrote the following lapidary phrase: "It would be difficult to imagine another region of the earth where nature and human behavior have combined to produce a more hopeless and unhappy ambient for human life than that which is found in Latin America". Political instability and natural disasters: for a long time those were the stereotypes which dominated the vision which the citizens of the United States had of Latin America. To this combination was added, more recently, a third element: narcotics-trafficking.

In the face of such precedents, how can we stop this contempt for the region and its inhabitants from coloring the image that many in the United States have of Latin America?

The well-known U.S. political scientist Howard Wiarda is among those who have analyzed this question. In an important work on the subject he expressed the following thought: "Americans tend to think that Latin Americans are unstable, backward and undeveloped beings, plagued by incompetence. It is not surprising that Americans tend to assume that they can solve the problems of Latin America in their own way and that the history and customs of the region may be ignored in the process. Americans tend to regard Latin American leadership in the same way: unstable, not very competent and almost infantile, like children who need to be guided".

Analyzing the fundamental reasons for this perception, Wiarda declares: "These attitudes of condescending superiority have deep roots. They derive, in part, from historical prejudices held by Protestant and Anglo-Saxon civilization towards the essence of a Catholic, Latin and even inquisitorial culture. In part, they also derive from the belief, widely-held in the United States, that Latin America and its leaders have low marks for talent and accomplishment".[3]

In other words, we find, on the one hand, ancestral prejudices. That which Carlos Fuentes, in his book *The Buried Mirror,* labeled an "alliance between modernity and Protestantism, founded on a secular opposition to Spain and all Spanish things". But we find, on the other hand, other kinds of prejudices. Those which derive from racial contempt towards a mestizo region which, despite being situated in its own hemispheric ambit, did not successfully meet the challenge of development.

Existing prejudices have always been nourished by the very nature of the information which is available about Latin America. Historically, the U.S. press has tended to concentrate on a small number of highly problematical topics which have a direct or indirect influence on their own country: civil war in Central America, narcotics-trafficking, the collapse of the Mexican or Argentine economy, etc. Inevitably, contact with the region is based on news about its most negative aspects.

To the above we must add a characteristic which has become more and more acute in recent years.

3. *Foreign Policy,* Spring, 1987.

This is the tendency to oversimplify the information. The habit of reducing complex political, economic or other kinds of processes to black and white pictures. A manifest intellectual laziness, characteristic of contemporary journalism, which is unwilling to make the effort that is needed to get to the heart of the problems. The result of all this is a gallery of heroes and villains, which leaves little room for a more balanced interpretation.

Obviously, the place for heroes is reserved for all of those administrations or countries which are in harmony with the conventional wisdom prevailing in the United States. The lack of intellectual sophistication in the predominant journalism and the ingenuousness which characterizes all conventional wisdom combines with a suffocating international order which reduces the credibility given to nations to the level of sheep that follow the herd.

Things being as they are, the perception that others have of us winds up becoming an accumulation of reductionisms.

Prejudices are intensified by a process of selection that only reports the most negative news and are further worsened by oversimplification, ingenuousness and the workings of an international order that, both on the economic and the political fronts, requires submission to a certain set of rules.

Is there way out of this apparent dead end? How can we achieve a suitable image in the face of criteria of this kind? How can we improve our image without losing our dignity in the process? How can we avoid having to behave like sheep in order to escape from the gallery of villains?

It is clear that if you do not have a good image you will not be respected either and where there is no respect there will never be fairness. The positive image of a state or region constitutes – there is no doubt about it – its first line of defense. A bad image is the first stage of a path that is full of risks. Unfortunately, there is no easy answer to the problem of Latin America's image in the United States. It is a spiny subject which we will always have to handle with extreme care. It is highly probable that the solution will result from the growing influence of the Latino population in the United States and the imperatives of trade. As that country continues to go through the profound process of cultural fusion generated by the growth of its Hispanic community it will become more open, sensitive and permeable to the realities and values of the nations which lie to the south of the Río Grande. To that will be added the pragmatic demands of the rapid growth of hemispheric trade.

ECONOMIC INDIVIDUALISM VERSUS THE COLLECTIVE IDEAL

During the 45 years that marked the existence of the Cold War, the world lived through an intense confrontation between two great value systems. Washington, the maximum expression of the West-

ern empire, embodied the ideals of an individualism rooted in liberalism. Moscow, the head of the
communist world, represented Marxist collectivism.
The origins of liberal individualism reached back to
a concept in which the social body was based on a
single category: the citizen. A concept in which the
State was obliged to limit itself to guaranteeing the
minimal conditions under which individual initiative, the "invisible hand" of the market, would be
enabled to create collective wealth. Marxist collectivism, for its part, went back to the Communist
Manifesto of 1848 and to the vision of a unitary society whose own social coherence would come to
make the State superfluous.

Nevertheless, on both sides of the fence, the weight
of new realities wound up disfiguring the original
conceptual roots. In the communist camp, the State
came to be an omnipotent presence and the single
party the factor that governed social solidarity. In
the Western one, a sense of the collective tended to
play an ever more important role, while in the same
way the State was transformed into a driving force
for the economy.

In fact, under the influence of the Depression that
began in 1929, the ideas of Keynes and the principles of the Welfare State gradually laid the foundations for the new interventionist role given to the
State in U.S. society. Franklin D. Roosevelt's New
Deal started the process through which the State
assumed this guiding role, which reached its full
expression with the "Great Society" of Lyndon

Johnson. Meanwhile, the end of the Second World War marked the emergence of the Social Democratic and Christian Democratic ideologies (the former's origins go back to Marxism), which extended the ideals of social solidarity to continental Europe and emphasized the regulatory and promotional role of the State.

Nevertheless, in the years which saw the collapse of communism, the Western world's commitment to social and collective ideals became weaker, as did the principle of the interventionist State. In fact, the West had already spent several years in an attempt to go back to the original roots of liberal individualism. To a large extent, the Reagan-Thatcher coalition reinserted the Anglo-Saxon world into the old liberal moulds. What is more, thanks to Washington's strong influence over the international financial agencies, many nations around the world felt the effects of the ideology that was current in that capital. All of this led to a notorious reverse for the ideas of social orientation which had prevailed in continental Europe and Latin America before then.

In this state of affairs, the fall of communism meant, at the same time, that individualistic ideals prevailed over collective ones. By the end of the twentieth century the Western world revolved around an individualistic tradition with liberal roots. It is worth asking ourselves, however, if this individualism, based on the primacy of the "homo economicus", is valid on all levels and for all societies. As the French economist Francis Perroux rightly points out: "Every capitalist society owes its smooth functioning to sectors which are not impregnated with nor moved by the spirit of profit and gain. When the top official, the soldier, the magistrate, the priest, the artist and the wise man are dominated by that spirit, society collapses and every kind of economy is threatened... A spirit which precedes and is alien to capitalism upholds the framework in which the capitalist economy functions".[4]

By the same token, there are societies which cannot do without the unifying ideal of the collective. This is the case, precisely, with Latin America. Ours is a multicultural region, full of profound inequality, which needs social ideals to unite and mobilize its creative forces. To offer, as the only ideal for the future, the prospect of the slogan which symbolized the France of Louis-Philippe d'Orléans – "enrich yourself" – may make sense for societies like that of the United States. But in no way does it respond to the realities of nations submerged in poverty, endemic disease and educational deficiencies.

The individualistic vision of someone like Mario Vargas Llosa, who even rejects the sense of national identity as an alienating factor, may be fashionable in the intellectual centers of the industrialized world, but there is no room for it in the Latin American ambit. Those kinds of perceptions only serve to widen the breach which has always existed between the elite and the common people and the duality of

4. *Le Capitalisme*, Paris, Presses Universitaires de France, 1962, p.20.

societies in which our versions of Wall Street and
Madison Avenue co-exist with the most primitive
features of the Third World.

The creation of a civic culture, the longing for
material and ethical progress and the sense of responsibility towards the collectivity can only be fulfilled by mobilizing the spiritual fibers of a nation
towards a higher ideal. The absence of a sense of
purpose which goes beyond the individual and the
pecuniary is the best prescription for ensuring the
continuing prosperity in Latin America of the drugs
barons and every other kind of corrupt person. Leaving aside the failures of populism and the obvious
excesses of statism, the ideal of the collective continues to be fundamental if we wish to imbue our
peoples with a sense of destiny.

THE AMAZON: THE MOST VULNERABLE REGION IN THE WORLD

The new trends in international law point to a looser
notion of sovereignty. Under this concept, few regions of the world have become more vulnerable than
the Amazon. In fact, as these ideas of international
law emerge, we hear talk of establishing an international guardianship there, limiting national sovereignties, creating the right of intervention or even
establishing supra-national authorities to protect defenseless ethnic groups and natural reserves in the
name of mankind. Thus it is that the more than 7

million square kilometers that comprise a jungle region that is shared by Venezuela, Brazil, Colombia, Ecuador, Peru, Bolivia, Guyana, Surinam and even French Guyana runs the risk of being removed from the full sovereignty of its respective states and handed over to a supra-national guardianship.

In light of this situation, while the industrialized countries have devastated their forests, are responsible for 75% of the carbon dioxide that gives rise to the greenhouse gas effect and use more than 80% of the chemical substances which erode the ozone layer, attention focuses on the Amazon when the time comes to pay these environmental costs. Seen as the great vegetal lungs of the world, this rain forest should, the argument goes, be frozen in time and space in order to safeguard the wasteful habits of production and consumption of the wealthy countries. Numerous non-governmental organizations are heading in the same direction as the great powers: all of them wish to immobilize the region and turn it into a combination of human zoo and botanical garden, protected from any human contact that is not indigenous.

For their part, a wide variety of multinationals share the same point of view about the Amazon. We could cite, in the first place, a number of important multinational mining companies. Geological surveys of the region speak of the nearly 2 trillion dollars worth of mineral resources buried in its entrails, and this is on the basis of a still-incomplete exploration. If the gold, cassiterite, lignite, diamonds and other mineral treasures of that region were to be offered for sale in international markets, the price of these resources would plunge, affecting gigantic investments in other parts of the world. The best way of keeping prices up and not jeopardizing such investments is to block mineral exploitation in the Amazon. It is not in vain that the interests of some of the main transnational mining companies converge with those of non-governmental environmental groups in their support for a prohibition of mining in that region.

The other kind of multinational companies who have their eyes on the region belong to the biotechnology industry. For them, the immense wealth of biodiversity that exists in the region represents an unequalled reserve of genetic codes that are capable of being pillaged. As Paul Kennedy correctly states: " 'The genetic revolution' will probably involve the extraction of the genetic resources of the underdeveloped countries, incorporating those resources into commercial varieties produced in the laboratories of multinational companies and later reselling them at a considerable profit to the underdeveloped countries in the form of improved varieties. There are now heated accusations that the genetic resources of the developing countries are being stolen through the 'biological imperialism' of the big corporations".[5]

That is, there are allegations that the genetic codes of numerous medicinal species that form part of the biodiversity of the Amazon have been patented by the great transnational biotech companies. This would

5. *Op. Cit.,* p.91.

lead us into the dramatic situation of finding ourselves unable to make a commercial use of the immense wealth of medicinal resources which derive from the region's plants, since the patents that provide a monopoly over their use would be in the hands of a few multinationals. In other words, we would be deprived of one of the great economic resources of the twenty-first century.

Another type of transnational is also looking at the Amazon, in this case an illegal kind which represents, unfortunately, a unique example of how Latin American creativity is able to develop a highly competitive business enterprise: we are talking, of course, about the powerful narcotics industry. It has turned the dense Amazon rainforest into its natural center of operations, spreading its tentacles throughout the region. Beneath the shade of its great trees, the drugs barons have mounted a sophisticated infrastructure that includes plantations of narcotic plants, clandestine drugs laboratories, airstrips, etc.

There is yet another kind of multinational that is interested in the region: that which organizes the illegal extraction and contraband sale of gold and precious stones. Taking advantage of the virtual slave labor provided by an army of poor, illegal miners, the mafias which run this trade funnel these minerals towards international markets. This criminal enterprise has caused irreparable damage to jungle ecosystems and is a veritable plague in the sub-region.

It is clear that we should safeguard the full right to sovereignty over the Amazon of the countries in whose territories it lies. To achieve this, those nations should be wary of subscribing to the juridical, political and economic ideas about the protection of the Amazon that are so fashionable today, understanding, instead, that they may not correspond to our own interests. At the same time, however, they must understand that their governments will have to show a stronger and more watchful presence in the jungles of the Amazon. Such a vigilance not only has to do with sending in the armed forces and mounting systems of electronic surveillance to make sure that narcotics-trafficking and other illegal enterprises do not flourish. It also means designing and implementing public policies to guarantee a rational and sustainable development of the region's natural resources. In short, they must deal with the vacuum of power which has resulted from the weak exercise of their sovereignty over the Amazon.

The principle of sustainable development is the key to everything. The different nations, through the full exercise of their sovereignty, are responsible for preserving the harmony that must exist between the demands of development and a complete respect for ecosystems. Any initiative that tries to deny this principle should be rejected at once.

THE UNITED STATES AND MEXICO: THE HOT FRONTIER

By the end of the nineteen-nineties the frontier strip between the United States and Mexico had become one of the most booming manufacturing zones in the world. This strip, which is 210 kilometers wide and 3,380 kilometers long, houses hundreds of "maquiladoras", which are the source of hundreds of thousands of jobs. It has a population of more than 10 million and the wealth it represents, around 150 billion dollars, gives it an economy that is bigger than Poland's and nearly the size of Thailand's. During the nineties its population grew by 30% and its Gross Domestic Product showed an annual growth rate of 5-7%.

Along this strip, which runs from the Pacific to the Atlantic, there is a group of U.S. and Mexican border cities which are becoming rapidly integrated to form genuinely bi-national metropolises. Such is the case of San Diego and Tijuana, El Paso and Ciudad Juárez, Laredo and Nueva Laredo, and Brownsville and Matamoros. Of course, the maquiladoras are on the Mexican side of the border and the administrative offices proliferate on the U.S. side. According to an article in *Business Week*, the Mexican side of this hot frontier zone is becoming, after China, the favorite site for global investments. Up to now, however, most of the maquiladoras located there belong to U.S. corporations.[6]

The strong U.S. presence in this strip does not only respond to basic geographical factors but also to the existence of the Free Trade Zone that unites the two countries. What is more, the devaluation of

6. May 12, 1997.

the Mexican peso that took place in December, 1994 led to a substantial fall in Mexican salaries, which acted as an incentive for a wave of new investments from the North. With the total cost of wages, electricity and real estate at a quarter of their value in the United States, nothing could be more natural than this massive transfer of jobs to the zones. *The Economist* points out that a worker on the U.S. side of the border earns a salary that is three to four times higher than that of his Mexican counterpart and in certain cases he may earn up to twelve times as much.

This immense industrial zone of Mexico offers multiple advantages to the United States.[7] At a time when the U.S. manufacturing industry is beset by the lower production costs of the emerging economies of East Asia, it has been able to find the solution in this frontier ambit. For the rest, the zone has turned into a kind of a plug to block holes in the containing wall erected against the migrant workers of Mexico, who, if the zone did not exist, would illegally cross the frontier. This is in line with the thesis set forth some years ago by the French intellectual Jean Christophe Ruffin in his book *The Empire and the New Barbarians*. According to Ruffin, the only way that the industrialized countries may be able to defend themselves from the migratory masses of the "barbarian world" is to create, as the Romans did, "soft" frontiers or buffer zones that will absorb and at the same time contain those masses.

7. July 7-13, 2001.

There is no doubt, however, that this strategy also threatens to create grave problems for the United States. At a time when the economic worries of the average American have become a dominant political note, this massive transfer of jobs to Mexico is a controversial political subject. This not only means that NAFTA is disliked and distrusted by a lot of voters, but it also has an important effect on the possibilities of U.S. support for the Free Trade Area of the Americas.

For Mexico, on the other hand, this thriving frontier industrial zone not only represents an important solution to its problems of unemployment, but it has also enabled it to achieve a significant level of economic growth and increase the volume of its exports. Nevertheless, Mexico has not been exempt from problems either. In the first place, the economic prosperity of this industrial zone has been achieved at the cost of depressing social conditions. That is, such low production costs only exist because of the over-abundance of cheap manpower, living in an urban environment of poverty.

As *Business Week* points out in the article we have cited, the workers in these maquiladoras compete, in terms of salaries, with the cheapest manpower of the Asian economies. In most of these factories the work force is largely made up of women with a minimum level of education. All of this takes place in the midst of an urban environment marked by marginal living conditions. It is estimated that it would be necessary to invest 8 billion dollars to supply these productive urban centers with basic utilities like drinking water, water treatment plants, rubbish collection services, etc. This apart, the very overcrowding and poverty that characterize the zone have turned it into a breeding ground of crime and drugs-trafficking.

Beyond this, while U.S. industry has become the main beneficiary of this emporium of maquiladoras, the U.S. government has felt the effects of the trade surplus that Mexico has earned as a consequence. The renewal of U.S. competitiveness that has resulted from taking advantage of the opportunities offered by the Mexican frontier strip favors the interests of U.S. manufacturers, but it has inevitably had a negative effect on the trade balance of the U.S. economy as a whole. At the end of the nineteen-nineties, the U.S. showed a trade deficit of 15.9 billion dollars with Mexico. One consequence of this has been an increasing demand from Washington that Mexico buy more U.S. products.

Within the logic of globalization the great productive centers of the world have sought to protect themselves by finding pools of cheap manpower. The European Union recurs to the former communist countries of eastern Europe. Japan and the Asiatic tigers rely on Indonesia, Malaysia, the Philippines and Thailand. The United States, for its part, has found this pool a few meters beyond its southern frontier.

THE FOURTH CAPITAL

The fall of the Berlin Wall brought about the consecration of the free market. A natural expression of this was the belief in the universal validity of the "homo economicus", characterized by his utilitarian aggressiveness and search for economic gain. Curiously, while the ideals of the free market and the "homo economicus" apparently represent the spirit of our time, the subject to which more published pages have been dedicated in the past decade has been that of culture and cultural identity. Among the authors who have explored this subject we find Samuel Huntington, Lawrence Harrison, Thomas Sowell and Benjamin Barber.

Within this school of cultural analysis there is a current which emphasizes the role of the degree of interpersonal trust that exists within each society as a fundamental element of economic development. Among the leading exponents of this idea are Francis Fukuyama (who is going back on his former glorification of the free market), Alain Peyrefitte and even a wide variety of writers of management books, who argue that internal loyalty and trust are important factors in the success of large corporations (Frederick Reichheld, Thomas Teal, Jeffrey Pfeffer, etc.). Within the current which regards trust as a primordial economic factor, there has appeared a school of thought with distinctive traits. Its members share a belief in the principle of "social capital" and its leading exponents include Robert Putnam and James Coleman.

In accordance with the followers of the "social capital" school, economic development (a "sustainable" one, that is) has traditionally focussed on three elements: natural capital (raw materials), physical capital (manufactures) and human capital (knowledge). They argue that there is a fourth element, which unites the others and is critical for development: social capital. This may be defined in a double sense. In the first, it is the organic interweaving of institutions and associations which sustains a society. In the second, it is the set of values and rules which determine the framework for interpersonal relations within that society, among which the sense of trust and civic responsibility stands out. The closer a society comes to this ideal of structured institutions which allow for the growth of interpersonal trust and civic culture, the greater will be its "social" capital. Even the World Bank has adopted the idea, which is now included among the parameters which guide its granting of loans.

For most countries in Latin America, the ideas formulated by the school of social capital can only lead to somber reflections. If we accept that the fundamental bases of development are raw materials, manufactures, knowledge and institutions that reflect a civic culture, then it becomes clear that Latin America is at a great disadvantage, since most of its nations only shine with respect to natural capital. The region thus has to place an emphasis on creating the three other types of capital. The attainment of physical capital requires the creation of varied set of conditions which encourage economic diversification, the expansion of our industrial base and the incorporation of aggregate value in our exports. Human capital must be based on the sustained growth of education, science and technology. And social capital must rest on the restructuring of our institutions and the strengthening of civic culture. Of all of these, however, it is the fourth kind of capital which must be given priority. As history has repeatedly shown, even societies which are short of raw materials may achieve a true development and with this, industrial growth and knowledge, when they have sound institutions and a genuine civic culture.

THE CULT OF ANXIETY

One of the most interesting battles in the world of the big corporations of the United States was the one which took place between Microsoft and Netscape a few years ago. It had to do with control of the Internet information superhighways. Netscape had achieved a comfortable lead in the early days of Internet, thanks to its "Navigator" program. Nevertheless, the giant Microsoft suddenly appeared on the scene with its "Explorer" program, trying to wipe Netscape off the map and control the Internet superhighways in the same way that it had done with the strategic markets of information technology.

Why did Microsoft – that is, Bill Gates, the world's richest man – think it was necessary to crush

Netscape? The answer is simple. If he had not done it, he would have run the risk of seeing Netscape launch its own programs for personal computers through the Net, thus threatening the Microsoft empire. That was something which Bill Gates, of all people, could not allow, considering that his own success had been based on smashing all of his rivals who had shown themselves to be vulnerable or technologically-backward. That is, those which had left some loose end which prevented them from keeping up with the last word in high technology. Among his victims were corporations like Intel, which been, for a time, the leader in microprocessors, and WordPerfect, which first put word processors on the market.

This situation highlights the prevailing reality in the field of advanced technology. He who nods off is overrun by he who approaches from behind. As Andy Grove, the president of Intel, one of the companies that was a victim of Microsoft, correctly points out: "in this world only the paranoid survives". A few years ago, Nathan Myhrvold, who has a Ph.D. in physics and is one of Gates's closest deputies, said that it did not matter how good your own product might be, because you were only 18 months short of failure. According to many analysts, this period has now been reduced to six months and is becoming ever shorter. This is, in fact, the very peculiar world of high technology, where one always lives in suspense and runs the risk of being pushed aside at the least oversight.

Although this situation is especially notable in the world of Gates and Groves, it applies, to a large extent, to the U.S. corporate world as a whole. The competitive pressure faced by the companies of that country is such that their continuance and survival depend on their ability to constantly renovate their goods and services. In an atmosphere in which razor-thin margins of profits and prices are capable of influencing the decisions of stock-holders and consumers, the anxiety of the captains of industry reaches the highest level. It is not an accident that one of the conclusions found in the published summary of the deliberations of the 1999 World Economic Forum at Davos, Switzerland was the following: "The executive presidents of corporations are showing increasing signs of stress, insomnia, cardiovascular problems, loneliness, marital failures and depression, among other problems".[8]

On the level of states as well, global competition presents new challenges that are not always overcome. Consider the case of Japan and Germany, which embodied the two great economic miracles of the post-War period. Like the phoenix, both countries rose from the ashes to become the second and third economies of the world, respectively. By the nineteen-eighties Japan had grown so strong that some analysts, like George Friedman and Meredith Lebard, in their work *The Coming War with Japan,*

8. Cited by Shell International, *People and Connections*: Global Scenarios to 2020. Public Summary, London, 2002.

predicted that an armed conflict with the United States would be the inevitable result of their economic rivalry. In fact, after reaching second-place in the world economy in the nineteen-seventies, Japan was able to incorporate into its economy, during the eighties, an aggregate production capacity that equaled that of France. What is more, in the nineties it was able to build up the equivalent of a second France, through a network of factories established in other countries. Germany, for its part, became the driving force behind the economic integration of western Europe – the mainstay of the Common Market which eventually led to the creation of the European Union. In the case of both Japan and Germany, technology was the fundamental reason for success.

Their respective economic models became so admired that they were considered to be valid alternatives to the Anglo-Saxon market economy. In contrast with the latter, however, their norms were thought to be more rational and socially responsible. Compared with the economy characterized by Wall Street, with its short-term vision and dictatorship of stockholders who only think about quarterly earnings, those of Japan and Germany seemed to justify the wisdom of long-term planning. The link between their industries and banks and the social consensus among the diverse productive forces created an atmosphere that was more structured and much less predatory. In addition, it was recognized that the safety nets of their welfare programs was an essential part of their systems.

However, the rapid acceleration of capitalism that resulted from globalization shook the foundations of both models. At the same time, their educational systems, which were based on the primacy of the group over the individual, proved to be incapable of facing the challenge of technological change. Today Japan and Germany look beaten and are sunk in recession. Japan is sliding down the slippery slope of economic deflation and its unemployment rate has risen to 5.6%. Germany has a fiscal deficit that threatens to get out of control and has merited a formal reprimand from the European Commission, and at the same time shows a 10.4% unemployment rate. According to *The Economist*: "Those who are charitable consider Japan to be irrelevant. Those who are less charitable consider it to be a burden. Those who are fearful consider it to be a danger".[9] *Newsweek* recently quoted the following words of Gerhard Fels, President of the German Business Institute : "We are no longer the locomotive of Europe, but the brake at the end of the train".[10]

Well then, if Bill Gates is worried about being displaced by some new competitor and the health of the executive presidents of the major corporations of the U.S. is being ruined by competitive anguish and Japan and Germany have not risen to the challenges of the present world economy, what can the poor countries of Latin America do in the midst of

9. February 11-16, 2002.
10. February 11, 2002.

this ferocious global competition? When you hear so many Latin American business and political leaders speak with such enthusiasm about the virtues of globalization, you have to ask yourself if they really understand the consequences of the system they praise. Haven't they ever heard of the "structural unemployment" which the global economy is creating or the growing gap between "winners" and "losers" in this Darwinian struggle for survival, or how the great multinationals are gobbling up the traditional companies of the region? Adapting ourselves to the globalized economy may turn out to be a necessity. In the final account it is a model which still shows an overwhelming strength. But it is one thing to accept the inevitable and quite another to celebrate a state of things that forces us into an ascending spiral of anxiety and uncertainty.

In its projections for future scenarios that appeared in the year 2002, the Shell Group of Companies foresees, between two possible routes to 2020, a world in which globalization will have adapted itself to a plural and multicultural reality. A world in which the different regions of the planet would each have a very important role to play. The events following the terrorist attack of September 11 might well point in this direction. For the rest, this vision is in harmony with the position adopted by the developing countries during the latest meeting of the World Trade Organization in Doha, Qatar. Under the leadership of India, Brazil and South Africa, these nations demanded an equitable treatment, singling out the need for those who are well ahead in the race to dominate the global economy to take their needs and limitations into account. This is the only way in which Latin America will reach an effective viability.

Let us hope that those who celebrate anxiety so much will cultivate the best contribution ever made by the Anglo-Saxon world and that is not, of course, the market economy, but common sense.